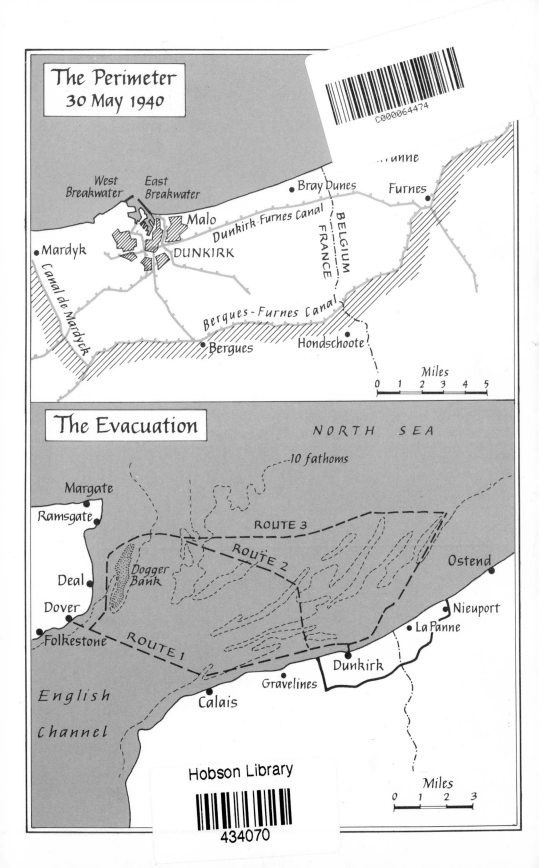

The Perimeter
30 May 1940

West Breakwater
East Breakwater
Bray Dunes
Furnes
...unne
Malo
Dunkirk-Furnes Canal
BELGIUM
FRANCE
DUNKIRK
Mardyk
Canal de Mardyck
Berques-Furnes Canal
Bergues
Hondschoote

Miles
0 1 2 3 4 5

The Evacuation

NORTH SEA
10 fathoms

Margate
Ramsgate
ROUTE 3
ROUTE 2
Dogger Bank
Ostend
Deal
Dover
Nieuport
La Panne
Folkestone
ROUTE 1
Dunkirk
Gravelines
English
Channel
Calais

Miles
0 1 2 3

# Dunkirk: The Incredible Escape

*Also by Norman Gelb*

The Berlin Wall
Scramble
Less Than Glory
The British
The Irresistible Impulse
Enemy in the Shadows

# Dunkirk: The Incredible Escape

### NORMAN GELB

MICHAEL JOSEPH

LONDON

MICHAEL JOSEPH

Published by the Penguin Group
27 Wrights Lane, London W8 5TZ, England
Viking Penguin Inc., 40 West 23rd Street, New York, New York 10010, USA
Penguin Books Australia Ltd, Ringwood, Victoria, Australia
Penguin Books Canada Ltd, 2801 John Street, Markham, Ontario, Canada L3R 1B4
Penguin Books (NZ) Ltd, 182–190 Wairau Road, Auckland 10, New Zealand

Penguin Books Ltd, Registered Offices: Harmondsworth, Middlesex, England

First published 1990

Copyright © Norman Gelb 1990

Typeset in 11/12pt Electra by Goodfellow & Egan Ltd, Cambridge

Printed and bound in Great Britain by Richard Clay Ltd, Bungay

A CIP catalogue record for this book is available from the British Library

ISBN 0 7181 3203 3

*For Amos,*
*my son and friend*

War reveals dimensions of human nature both above and below the acceptable standards of humanity.

– J. Glenn Gray, *The Warriors – Reflections on Men in Battle*

# Contents

# List of Illustrations

1. Prime Minister Churchill and Foreign Secretary Lord Halifax. (*Imperial War Museum*)
2. Chief of the Imperial General Staff Sir John Dill, Secretary of War Anthony Eden and BEF commander Lord Gort. (*Imperial War Museum*)
3. Vice Admiral Bertram Ramsey, Flag Officer Commanding Dover.
4. Crowds of troops wait on the beaches. (*Imperial War Museum*)
5. Queues of men waiting for rescue boats. (*Imperial War Museum*)
6. Troops sprawled over the sand dunes behind the beaches. (*Dunkirk Veterans Association*)
7. Troops wading out to ships. (*Camera Press*)
8. Troops wading up to their necks. (*William Kershaw*)
9. Troops in a dinghy rowing out from the beach. (*William Kershaw*)
10. The eastern breakwater at Dunkirk harbour. (*William Kershaw*)
11. Troops waiting in the sand dunes. (*Imperial War Museum*)
12. Black smoke from blazing oil storage tanks. (*William Kershaw*)
13. Troops wading out to a rescue ship. (*Imperial War Museum*)
14. A pier of trucks built out into the sea. (*National Archives, Washington*)
15. An improvised beach pier. (*National Archives, Washington*)
16. Queues of men snake across the Dunkirk sands. (*Hulton Deutsch Collection*)
17. Troops aboard ship. (*Imperial War Museum*)
18. Survivors of the rescue ship *Mona's Queen*. (*Imperial War Museum*)
19. French and British troops aboard a vessel. (*Camera Press*)
20. Evacuated troops watch smoke rise from bombed oil storage tanks. (*Camera Press*)
21. A row of destroyed British army trucks. (*National Archives, Washington*)
22. Abandoned vehicles on the beach. (*National Archives, Washington*)
23. Sunken and beached vessels. (*Dunkirk Veterans Association*)

# PART ONE

*Chapter 1*

# Dunkirk

A T DAWN ON May 10th, 1940, the armies of Nazi Germany burst through the borders of their country to begin a march of conquest across Western Europe. Spearheaded by a formidable armada of tanks and closely supported by the most powerful fleet of attack aircraft ever assembled, they set out to accomplish what German armies had failed to achieve in the First World War a generation earlier – to crush France and humble Britain.

Though braced for the attack, Allied defences – outmatched, outmanoeuvred and overwhelmed – quickly crumbled under the onslaught. In less than three weeks, Adolf Hitler achieved the most extraordinary military triumph of modern times. Not only was the French army, previously deemed the most indomitable fighting machine in the world, on the verge of collapse but the British Expeditionary Force, which had been sent across the English Channel to help stop the Germans, was trapped against the sea at Dunkirk on the north-west coast of France.

Disaster loomed for the forces resisting the Nazi advance. Hitler's conquests had been relentless. Austria, Czechoslovakia, Poland, Denmark, Holland, and Luxembourg had already fallen to him. Most of Belgium had been overrun and its surrender was imminent. Norway was about to succumb as well and even the proud French were heading for a humiliating capitulation.

In London, senior government officials and top military officers were astounded by the rapidity and magnitude of the German rampage across northern France and by the peril suddenly and without warning facing the British Expeditionary Force. The BEF comprised almost all of Britain's combat-ready troops, cadres and experienced officers. The realization that it was trapped with its back to the sea, and had little hope of breaking out, was staggering. The war had just begun but Britain was about to be left without an army.

It was grimly accepted that virtually all of the army's heavy equipment, which had accompanied the BEF to France, was irretrievably lost. But plans were hastily patched together to try to save some of the troops. Ships and boats were assembled to shuttle across the English Channel to bring as many as possible back to England from Dunkirk. But German bombers had been blasting the town's port facilities for days, rendering them well-nigh useless. And onrushing German ground forces were just a few miles from the town. Not even the most optimistic of British leaders believed the evacuation could be successful. At best, it was thought, a comparatively small number of men – maybe thirty thousand out of ten times that number – could be lifted off before the German trap snapped closed. Some senior British officers were convinced that practically none of the men would get away.

A National Day of Prayer for the troops across the Channel was ordained in Britain, prompting some of them who learned of it to conclude that they were already written off as doomed. Government aides advised that the British public, which had been shielded from the details by censorship, should be apprised of the situation so that when the worst finally occurred it would not come as too devastating a shock.

A German invasion of Britain was believed to be in the making and those who already knew of the BEF's plight feared that the country might be left without the means to repel it. Winston Churchill, newly named Prime Minister and scorned by a number of senior figures in London as a political dilettante, the wrong man for the job, warned the House of Commons to brace itself for 'hard and heavy tidings'.

Some thought those tidings would be too hard and heavy to bear. Junior government minister Harold Nicolson and his wife, writer Vita Sackville-West, contemplated suicide. Though not normally given to morbid sentiments, senior Foreign Office official Sir Alexander Cadogan was disheartened enough to confide to his diary, 'I should count it a privilege to be dead if Hitler rules England.' As fears mounted for the fate of the British army at Dunkirk, a senior cabinet minister, exasperated by Churchill's determination to fight on, no matter what the cost, urged that efforts be made to secure 'honourable' peace terms from the German dictator, leaving him to consolidate his European gains before resuming his conquests.

What was happening was having a profound impact well beyond the countries and armies immediately involved. Much more was to be decided at Dunkirk than would be immediately realized. The two nations which would ultimately determine the outcome of the war were greatly affected by the consequences. The American government was led to believe that Britain was in such deep trouble that a government submissive to Hitler might conceivably take charge in London. Pressure was building up in Washington for the United States to reconcile itself to unchallenged Nazi domination of Europe if the

British, without an army, were in fact forced to their knees. Instead of rushing badly needed war supplies to the struggling Western democracies, preparations were made to dispatch great numbers of US troops to Latin America where Hitler was believed to be planning to follow up his European triumphs with incursions in the Western Hemisphere. At the same time, the United States government seriously considered annexing the British West Indies for American national security purposes.

In Moscow, Soviet officials also watched developments with growing anxiety. The Soviet army had been crippled by the execution or imprisonment of most of its officer corps on trumped up treason charges during purges orchestrated by Soviet ruler Joseph Stalin. Despite the non-aggression treaty Stalin had signed with Hitler in August 1939, the German Führer had repeatedly insisted that the destruction of Soviet communism and the conquest of Russia were among his priority objectives. With France on the verge of collapse, if Britain were also humbled, no adversary would remain to distract Hitler from turning his ferocious attentions eastward.

The story of Dunkirk is therefore one of many dimensions. At its core, it is the tale of the great escape, of the transformation of a massive defeat for the British army into what would ultimately prove a disaster for the German forces which had driven it into a seemingly terminal trap. It is an account of how a monumental maritime rescue operation was pieced together in short order with limited understanding of what was involved and with practically no chance of success – and how it succeeded. On a personal level, it is a tale of contrasts – of clarity and confusion, true grit and deep despair, prodigious ingenuity and dazzling incompetence, selfless camaraderie and blind panic – all ingredients of one of the most extraordinary exercises in survival ever undertaken.

What follows in these pages is also an account of how it all came to pass. It is about lessons unlearnt, warnings ignored, and mistakes repeated. It is about governments and generals fumbling and blundering their way towards what was about to become the greatest conflagration the human race has ever known, a war which might have turned into an even greater calamity had the ten days of Dunkirk not occurred or if they had ended differently.

# Prelude

IN THE YEARS before, the countries of Europe, still recovering from the ravages and grief of the First World War, had once more been drawn towards catastrophe. In Germany, at the heart of the continent, ominous perpetrations and pronouncements signalled the approaching crisis.

Germany had been battered into abject submission by the United States, Britain and France in the earlier 'Great War'. As a nation, it had been ruined. As a military power, it had been emasculated. That its forces would in the not too distant future be capable of routing armies of their conquerors and trapping them against the sea in the pandemonium of Dunkirk was unimaginable. Nevertheless, even before the post-First World War generation had grown to maturity, Germany had recovered and, under Nazi rule, had become an armed, swaggering colossus. More than that, it had become a bully and a menace, a threat to other nations in Europe and, it seemed, to the United States as well. A malignant mood, underscored by police state terror, convulsed the land which had given the world the wonders of Beethoven, Goethe and Albert Einstein.

German factories and shipyards churned out vast quantities of the instruments and materials of war and Adolf Hitler loudly proclaimed his determination to use them if necessary to get what he wanted. He began his march of conquest in March 1936 with a comparatively modest exploit. He dispatched troops into the German Rhineland which had been demilitarized by the terms of the Versailles Treaty at the end of the First World War, and followed that by annexing Austria. Next on Hitler's agenda for expansion of the German Reich was Czechoslovakia's Sudetenland province which bordered Germany. Having reacted timidly to his earlier territorial transgressions, Britain and France now sternly warned the German Führer to desist or risk plunging Europe into war again. But when he persisted with his demands and threats, they consulted among themselves, backed down, and ended in September 1938 by in effect offering him the disputed Czechoslovak province as a gift.

A chronicler of the period vividly caricatured the performance at the time of the leaders of the Western democracies as they struggled to salvage their dignity while submitting to being ignominiously browbeaten:

> Like frightened householders who hear a burglar below, the British and French governments discussed what preventative measures they should take, picked up a poker and then put it down again, shouted downstairs that if the burglar did not make off, they would fall upon him, or at least call the police; even considered parleying with him, perhaps proposing that if he left the fish knives, they saw no objection to his taking other cutlery in reason; at last, fell back on deriving what comfort they might from the thought that at any rate he did not know the formula for opening the safe.

Hitler did, however, know the theory, practice and effect of terror, unlike his generals. They had counselled him against the remilitarization of the Rhineland, warning that the forces of neighbouring France had the capability and legal justification to blow 'us to bits'. Similarly, senior German military men had been strongly opposed to the move against Czechoslovakia, believing it would lead to a major war in which Germany would again be defeated. Some of them – including Army Chief of Staff General Franz Halder, Chief of Military Intelligence Wilhelm Canaris, and commanders of the Berlin military region – had even devised a plot (which was never attempted) to overthrow Hitler before it could happen. But the German leader had judged that the Western democracies would at worst confine themselves to protests.

He was right. The British and French were terrified by the prospect of another major armed conflict. Recalling the slaughter of the First World War, in which a generation of young men had been decimated and vast national resources had been squandered, many in both countries were convinced that no development, no cause, no provocation could justify another resort to arms. Some felt that Germany had been so harshly treated by its conquerors by the peace terms imposed at Versailles that it was natural for it to strive to retain self-respect and perhaps even some lost territory. Some feared that if Germany were slapped down and humiliated again, the Soviet Union, with its loudly proclaimed threat to prevailing Western values, would come to dominate much of Europe (which is how things eventually turned out).

Besides, who would do the slapping down? By the time the Hitlerian menace became unmistakable, British armed forces were outmatched in size and technology by the Germans. Economic factors loomed large as well. It was calculated that if required to finance another major war, Britain would soon be bankrupt, unable to afford essential food products and raw materials imported from overseas.

Though bordering Germany and therefore more concerned about Hitler's expansionist aspirations, France also showed few signs of wanting to challenge the German leader. It boasted a formidable army. But recollection of its horrific losses in the First World War when one in every ten Frenchmen in uniform – almost 1,500,000 – had been killed and another million had been maimed led to the formulation of an exclusively sit-and-wait defensive strategy designed to bar the enemy from intruding upon French soil.

Thus was spawned the infamous Maginot Line along the Franco-German border. That chain of fortifications, which contained 'every resource of material and design known to military science', was considered as formidable as a line of battleships at anchor. It would hold back the Germans should they dare to try to invade. But there was no similar barrier on France's northern border with Belgium, and General Maurice Gamelin, the sixty-seven-year-old commander-in-chief of the French army, had little idea what the next war might involve. Dismissing the two instruments that were to seal France's fate, Gamelin was convinced, 'Aircraft do not decide the outcome of a battle' and 'Armoured divisions are too heavy and cumbersome; they may penetrate our lines, but the lips of the gash will close behind them and we shall crush them with our reserves'.

The Soviet Union had more reason than most to fear Nazi Germany. Hitler had repeatedly declared his determination to obliterate bolshevism and he made no secret of his belief that Slavs were sub-human creatures. As the German leader's march of conquest progressed, the Soviets sought to enlist Britain and France in an anti-Nazi defensive alliance. But loathing of communism and distrust of the Soviet Union, which had only recently been promoting the violent overthrow of Western bourgeois government, were too deeply implanted in the West for Moscow's turnabout and its calls for unity to arouse much sympathy there. In addition, the Soviet army, its officer corps emasculated by political purges, was not believed capable of adding significant military might to any alliance. Prime Minister Neville Chamberlain had 'no belief whatever in [the Soviet Union's] ability to maintain an effective offensive, even if she wanted to'.

As for the United States, Chamberlain believed, 'He would be a rash man who based his calculations on help from that quarter.' Isolationist sentiment prevailed in America and Americans, if they thought about the British Empire at all, generally considered it a tyrannical institution, unworthy of support. Even later, when Britain felt it was left with no alternative but to go to war with Germany, Chamberlain confided, 'Heaven knows I don't want the Americans to fight for us. We should have to pay too dearly for that if they had a right to be in on the peace terms.'

For the most part, the United States was at the time spared Europe's sense of once more being drawn towards murderous armed conflict. Americans had enough of their own worries not to want to take on those of Europe as well. The economic depression which had set in with the Wall Street Crash of 1929 had settled deep into the mood and pulse of the nation. The richest country in the world was pockmarked with joblessness, poverty and despair. Millions of Americans were in trouble. Breadlines in the cities and forlorn migrants drifting along the country's highways in search of hope badly shook America's traditional 'can do' confidence. It was evident that there were things that America could *not* do.

One thing most Americans, regardless of political persuasion, wanted not to do was get embroiled again in foreign squabbles. Those on the left wanted the United States to stay clear because any involvement – even confined to lending material support from afar – would mean diverting resources from programmes designed by President Franklin Roosevelt and his New Deal to lift the country out of the depression. Those on the right maintained that involvement would shift America's limited military resources away from their prime function of guarding the security of the United States. Even many who felt strongly about European developments believed it was wrong and rarely effective to try to sort out other people's problems.

It was argued that America's First World War experiences demonstrated that the United States was right to remain aloof. The earlier conflict was dismissed as having been a pointless brawl in which American lives and money had been squandered on behalf of European ingrates and incompetents for nothing more than a chance to do the same a few years down the road. Best-selling books and magazine articles and a high-powered Senate investigating committee blamed the greed and unscrupulousness of arms merchants for America having been drawn into the earlier European conflict. So strong and pervasive was isolationist sentiment that Congress passed neutrality legislation decreeing that when war broke out again anywhere, Americans would be banned from selling munitions to any of the belligerents.

President Roosevelt, and American political leaders generally, abominated Hitler and were disgusted by Nazi attitudes and perpetrations. William Dodd, the American ambassador in Berlin in the early years of Hitler's rule, had 'a sense of horror when I look at the man'. But a greater sense of horror was induced by the image of war and the possibility that America might again be bamboozled by Europeans into taking part in one. Though suspected by many isolationists of deliberately leading the country in that direction, Roosevelt was no less appalled by the prospect. He had, however, come to believe that the United States would ultimately have to meet the challenge of Nazi Germany. Aside from a possible military threat to the United States, as Germany began digesting parts of Europe the President was told by trusted advisers that America's economic recovery and well-being was at stake:

> Germany does not have to conquer us in a military sense. By enslaving her own labor and that of the conquered countries, she can place in the markets of the world products at a price with which we could not compete. This will destroy our standards of living and shake to its depths our moral and physical fiber, already strained to breaking point.

However, Roosevelt was inhibited by prevailing popular sentiment from publicly suggesting that the United States might take sides as Europe tumbled towards war. A storm of protest was unleashed when an American bomber crashed during a test flight in California and it was discovered that among those killed in the crash was an official of the French War Ministry.

Those Americans who believed that Hitler had to be stopped and that the United States would have to help in that task were disillusioned by the performance of the European democracies as war clouds gathered overseas. William Allan White, a Kansas newspaper editor who was soon to be the guiding spirit of a nationwide anti-Nazi lobbying organization, was scathing:

> What an avalanche of blunders Great Britain has let loose upon the democracies of the world! The old British lion looks mangy, sore-eyed. He needs worming and should have a lot of dental work. He can't even roar.

William Bullitt, the American ambassador in Paris, informed Roosevelt that in their secret feverish consultations on how to appease Hitler without appearing to do so, British and French leaders were acting 'like little boys doing dirty things behind the barn . . . The prospects for Europe are so foul that the further we keep out of the mess the better.'

The efforts of Britain and France also to keep out of 'the mess' by letting Hitler do as he liked could not be long sustained. A turning point was reached when, in March 1939, after having annexed the Sudetenland province with the acquiescence of Britain and France, Hitler seized what was left of Czechoslovakia. It was finally undeniable that each time one of Hitler's demands was granted, another would be made, a realization confirmed when the German leader pinpointed Poland as his next major target for conquest. Britain and France ordered partial mobilization of their armed forces. Rearmament was accelerated. Trenches were dug in London parks. Anti-aircraft guns were shifted into position. Gas masks were distributed to the public. Britain and France issued assurances that they would honour their treaty obligations to come to Poland's aid if it were attacked. The prospect of imminent war came to shroud Europe like a peasoup fog.

On August 23rd, 1939, the Soviets, convinced that the Western democracies were determined to direct the Nazi threat their way, signed a non-aggression pact with Germany, assuring Hitler that he had nothing to fear from them. At dawn nine days later, German forces invaded Poland. Three days after that, on September 3rd, Britain and France declared war on Germany.

What followed was a monumental blunder by the Western democracies. The bulk of the German army and virtually all of the German air force was committed to the conquest of Poland. Although not yet fully prepared for combat, French forces at the front far outnumbered German defenders on the Siegfried Line. In some places, German defences didn't exist at all. RAF Bomber Command was restricted mostly to dropping propaganda leaflets over Germany, 'to arouse the Germans to a higher morality', Winston Churchill later noted dryly. No serious effort was made to benefit from the huge military advantage the Western Allies momentarily enjoyed. Action which might at that stage have had a great impact on the course of the war was limited to consultations between Paris and London on what to do.

While these consultations were in progress, a start was made, however, in dispatching a British Expeditionary Force to France. Infantry and support units were shipped across – two divisions during the first days of September, to be built up to ten divisions during the autumn and winter. Some Territorials who had gone off to camp for their annual training sessions in August were sent over directly, without having a chance to return home to organize their affairs and take leave of their families. Many would never return.

Rumours of an imminent German offensive circulated with increasingly tiresome frequency in the months following the fall of Poland. From late September onwards, Allied troops were repeatedly put on the alert and just as often stood down again. However, Lord Gort, commander of the British Expeditionary Force, was certain the Germans would not launch their attack before the spring. Unfavourable ground and cloud conditions during the autumn and winter would hamper the operations of their tanks and aircraft.

Lord Gort (John Standish Surtees Prendergast Vereker before he succeeded to his father's title) had been appointed to command the BEF the day war was declared. There was much grumbling about the appointment. His personal valour in combat during the First World War, when he had won the Victoria Cross for leading his men in battle after being seriously wounded, was unquestioned. But several senior figures doubted his leadership abilities. His appointment over the heads of a number of generals senior to him in rank and experience, sparked considerable resentment. General Sir Edmund Ironside, the senior officer on active service, a dynamic, vastly experienced but aging soldier, had expected to get the BEF command and was disappointed when made to settle instead for becoming Gort's successor as Chief of the Imperial General Staff, which he considered little more than a glorified desk job. Ironside was convinced that Gort didn't 'even begin to know how to run the bigger things'.

General Alan Brooke, named to be one of Gort's three BEF corps commanders, was deeply jealous of Gort and 'had no confidence in his leadership'. Brooke did not consider him capable of exercising sufficient independent initiative. The question of independent initiative was to prove a matter of critical importance despite the fact that Gort and the BEF had, to Brooke's horror, been put under French command because of the comparatively small British ground force contribution to the Allied cause – one-tenth the size of that of France. The BEF commander was to take his orders from General Gaston Billotte, commander of the French First Army Group, who was in turn subordinate to General Alphonse Georges, commander of Allied forces in north-east France, who was himself subordinate to the supreme Allied commander, General Gamelin.

With Maginot Line fortifications blocking the Germans off from direct access to France, it was Gamelin's firm belief that the attack on his country would come by way of Belgium, along substantially the same route Kaiser Wilhelm's armies had taken in the First World War. He would foil this assault by swivelling the forces he had poised along the Franco-Belgian border – including the BEF – into Belgium when the Germans launched their offensive. They would be stopped cold there before they could reach French soil.

As soon as his victory over Poland had been assured in mid-September

1939, Hitler had begun shunting troops and equipment to the Western Front to prepare for his offensive there. It was to be launched without delay as soon as preparations were completed. His generals were thrown into despair. An autumn attack, they maintained, would be folly. The days were too short. The weather was unpredictable. Fog would inhibit the use of attack aircraft. Ground conditions would be unsuitable for panzer operations. An early onset of winter was possible, to make conditions even worse.

General Halder recorded in his diary that none of the 'higher headquarters' believed the westward offensive had 'any prospect of success'. Even Hitler's trusted crony, *Luftwaffe* commander Hermann Goering, favoured delay. But Hitler was intoxicated by his triumph in the east. Enraged by the timidity of his generals, some of whom again plotted to depose him and again failed to execute that plot, the German leader insisted that the attack westward be launched as soon as possible.

The offensive was accordingly scheduled for November 12th and necessary preparations were made. But forecasts of inclement weather forced a cancellation. Refusing to be intimidated by the elements, Hitler ordered that his forces remain on stand by, ready 'to exploit favourable weather conditions' at the earliest possible moment. But the weather remained bad and the offensive had to be postponed repeatedly right through the autumn and early winter.

Exasperated, anxious, suspicious of advice to the contrary, fed up with delays, Hitler decided early in January that he would wait no longer. He commanded that the planned combined land and air attack on the Allies be launched through Belgium and Holland on January 17th, 1940. Detailed preparations having already been made, the attack would have taken place, and possibly resulted in disaster for the German army and Hitler, if an accident had not forced another postponement.

On January 10th, as the forces which were to invade the Low Countries were about to move into attack position, a German military plane on a domestic flight lost its way in the clouds and made a forced landing across the border in Belgium. The pilot, Major Erich Hoenmanns, a reserve *Luftwaffe* officer on active duty, had been trying to find an excuse to fly to Cologne to see his wife there. His passenger, Major Helmut Reinberger, a staff officer of the German 7th Airborne Division, gave him that excuse. Reinberger was bound for Cologne on urgent duty but rail traffic congestion had kept him from getting there by surface transport. Documents he was carrying included top secret *Luftwaffe* operational instructions for the coming invasion.

Stepping from the plane and realizing it had touched down in Belgium rather than across the border in Germany, Reinberger immediately tried to set fire to those documents. Belgian soldiers who rushed to the plane when it landed quickly extinguished the blaze. When the two Germans were escorted to the local military headquarters for interrogation, Reinberger seized the charred documents which had been put on a table and thrust them into a stove. Again he was foiled, this time by a quick acting Belgian officer who, despite burns to his hand, managed to salvage enough of the papers to reveal that they were plans, replete with maps, for the German assault on Belgium and Holland. They were immediately passed on to senior Belgian officers.

The Belgians were at the time so fearful of being drawn into the war that their initial conclusion was that it was a set-up, a plant, possibly to trick them into inviting Allied forces into Belgium and thereby provide Hitler with an excuse to launch an invasion of their country. However, the documents seemed to confirm intelligence reports from other sources, including well placed anti-Nazi military officers in Berlin, which told of an imminent German attack. Besides, a close examination of both the circumstances and the way the captured Germans behaved seemed to indicate that this was no attempted deception. The two officers appeared genuinely troubled by the situation in which they found themselves, with good reason. Hoenmanns had been making an unauthorized flight at a critical time and Reinberger knew that he should not have been carrying those secret documents on such a trip.

The German air attaché in Brussels was anxious to speak to the two men as soon as he could gain permission from the Belgian authorities. When he did, in a room that was bugged by the Belgians, the first question he asked was whether the documents had been destroyed. Reinberger, fearing for his military career and probably his life, assured him that they had.

The German High Command was, however, not convinced this was true. Sudden Belgian troop movements led them to conclude that the plans Reinberger had been carrying had been recovered intact and that they had very likely been passed on to the British and French. Although Goering consulted a fortune teller who assured him that this had not happened, Hitler was furious and reluctantly accepted that there was no alternative but to delay further the planned assault on the West so that strategy for the operation could be reviewed. (Reinberger and Hoenmanns were fortunate not to be handed back to Germany. They were soon to be sent to Canada as prisoners of war and stayed there for the duration.)

The Belgians had indeed passed details of the captured documents on to Allied senior commanders who immediately put their forces on the alert. The Allied troops deployed in France to meet the expected German attack were organized in three army groups. Elements of the French Second and Third Army Groups were positioned to guard the Franco-German border, with some of the most elite French forces deployed in or behind the Maginot Line where, because of the fortifications, they were least needed. Still barred from taking up defensive positions in Belgium by the Belgian authorities, who remained hopeful that their country could sit out the war, the French First Army Group, to which nine divisions of the British Expeditionary Force had been attached (one of the BEF's divisions was shifted south to help man French defences near the German border), was deployed along the 'Little Maginot Line'. That extended two hundred miles from the top end of the Maginot fortifications along the Franco-Belgian border to the sea. Most of these troops were braced to swivel swiftly into Belgium to meet and block a German breakthrough once Hitler had launched his main attack there.

With the approach of spring, all concerned realized that the quiet months of watchful waiting would soon come to an explosive conclusion. As the German general staff prepared for their long delayed Western offensive, Allied attention focused on Scandinavia and particularly on Swedish iron ore shipments to Germany. These went by rail from the mines at Gallivare in Sweden to the port of Narvik in Norway and then by ship through Norwegian territorial waters to north German ports. Without that ore, the German war effort would collapse. Winston Churchill, who had been brought into the War Cabinet as First Lord of the Admiralty when war had been declared, had been pressing Chamberlain to let the Royal Navy mine Norwegian waters to block the passage of German ore freighters.

On April 8th, 1940, Chamberlain finally agreed. It was expected that the Germans would respond by trying to seize key Norwegian ports, a move the British and French intended to pre-empt by dispatching forces of their own to occupy those ports before the Germans could get there. But Hitler moved first and Allied forces which were belatedly landed in Norway suffered a series of decisive setbacks. They would soon have to be evacuated, leaving Norway to endure Nazi occupation till the end of the war.

The miscarriage of the Norway operation aroused anger and resentment in London. Men and ships had been lost. Chamberlain's government was held responsible. Criticism of the Prime Minister quickly extended beyond that costly setback. So recently acclaimed for having saved peace with honour by appeasing Hitler, Chamberlain was now resoundingly denounced for Britain's failure to prepare adequately for the German Führer's onslaught in Europe, for the gloom and foreboding which had come to envelop Britain, and for the inability of his government to provide dynamic leadership at a time when the German western front offensive was believed imminent.

The Prime Minister's position became untenable. Despite the solid majority enjoyed by his Tory Party in the House of Commons, he could no longer rally enough support there to control the situation. He recognized as much and prepared to resign. Churchill was a strong candidate to succeed him. From the moment he had joined Chamberlain's cabinet, he had been its most assertive and dynamic member. He repeatedly pressed for greater effort in the prosecution of the war. He sparkled with ideas, proposals and schemes for beating the Germans. To the irritation of some of his cabinet colleagues, he did not confine his attentions to his official realm at the Admiralty but explored all areas of possible military and diplomatic advantage in the war. What was more, he appeared to be the only member of the cabinet capable of delivering a truly fighting speech.

But many senior figures in the Tory Party took serious exception to Churchill's past performance as a maverick who had switched political parties to suit the moment. They also objected to the flamboyant manner in which he now upstaged Chamberlain and other War Cabinet members. Presented with the suggestion that Churchill might become prime minister, a prominent Tory went so far as to pray 'that such a catastrophe will be averted'. Hearing one of his inspiring radio orations, a junior member of Chamberlain's staff was led to conclude that Churchill would indeed become prime minister before the war was over, but he feared that, 'judging from his record of untrustworthiness and instability, he may in that case lead us into the most dangerous paths'.

Lord Halifax, Chamberlain's Foreign Secretary, rather than Churchill, was thought by many to be the Prime Minister's natural successor in this time of crisis. A much respected figure with a reputation for considerable intellect, firmness of spirit, and wide experience in international affairs, Halifax had strong support among the Tories in Parliament. Several leading figures in the opposition Labour Party also preferred Halifax to Churchill. As Chamberlain prepared to step down, it was not clear which of the two would take over from him to lead the country in the perilous days ahead.

While the British parliamentary crisis was coming to the boil, France was also undergoing political convulsion. On May 9th, ignoring still another intelligence report of an imminent German attack, Premier Paul Reynaud had delivered an angry diatribe against the military

High Command of his country. He had long believed that the French army needed a more forceful, more astute commander-in-chief than General Gamelin. Reynaud had earlier decided to put Gamelin out to pasture. Now he demanded the general's immediate removal, citing partial French responsibility for the Allied fiasco in Norway as last-straw justification. The premier declared that if France continued to be subjected to the kind of military leadership Gamelin had provided, Hitler was certain to win the war.

This vilification of the French commander was immediately challenged by Minister of War Édouard Daladier who had long been a personal and political rival of Reynaud. Daladier, who had been replaced as premier by Reynaud just a few months earlier, asserted that Gamelin was an excellent military chief and denounced Reynaud for giving the general no opportunity to defend himself against the abuse to which he was being subjected.

Unable to gain sufficient support for his position from other members of his cabinet, Reynaud dissolved the government to make way for the appointment of a new cabinet over which he would be able to exercise greater control. Gamelin did not intend to wait for that to happen and for himself to be formally dismissed and disgraced. He immediately composed an anguished letter of resignation. It was impossible for him to serve any longer under a head of government who thought so little of him.

As the commander of Allied forces in France wallowed in an agony of resentment and humiliation and as the premier of France retreated into seclusion convinced that he had his political enemies in Paris on the run, German commanders on the Western Front prepared to make their squabbles look very petty indeed within a matter of hours.

# Onslaught

ON THE MORNING of May 10th, 1940, Belgian troops manning Fort Eben Emael near the Belgian-German border, were braced for trouble. Intelligence reports the night before had alerted their officers to an imminent German assault. They were confident they could deal with it.

The huge fort, towering over the Albert Canal near its confluence with the Meuse River, was the most up-to-date fixed fortification in the world. Measuring 770 by 900 yards and completed only five years earlier, it bristled with modern defence refinements. Constructed of steel and concrete, it was manned by a battalion of specially trained troops and turreted for artillery, anti-tank guns, light cannon and machine guns. It was equipped with electrical generators that made it independent of external power supply. It housed vast ammunition storage compartments, elevators to deliver ammunition to gun positions, a communications centre, and a hospital. The doors to its various compartments and sections could be quickly bolted with steel beams to prevent them being forced. Its walls were encircled by barbed wire and, where it did not front on the Albert Canal, by anti-tank obstacles and minefields as well.

So formidably constructed and powerfully armed, Eben Emael – named after a nearby village – was believed by all who had inspected its features to be capable of keeping an enemy at bay no matter how fierce his attack. What was more, the fort's commander was confident he could retain command of the adjoining border area too; his guns could knock out nearby bridges if they were in danger of being seized by the enemy. It seemed as though all possible contingencies had been taken into account. What was not expected was the unique form the assault on the fort would take and the direction from which it would come.

As dawn broke, troop-carrying gliders which had been lifted off from an airfield at Ostheim across the border in Germany silently swept out of the sky and with amazing precision, nine of them landed right on top of the fort. The seventy-eight German shock troops they carried were led by Sergeant Helmut Wenzel; the glider carrying Lieutenant Rudolf Witzig, commanding the operation, had broken its tow rope and landed elsewhere. The airborne invaders leapt from their gliders and immediately proceeded with the exercise for which they had been in rigorous training for more than six months in Germany and on previously seized Czechoslovak fortifications. Confounding the defenders within the fort by their surprise arrival, using flame throwers and newly developed powerful hollow charge explosives, they effectively immobilized Eben Emael in less than an hour. It was a bold, imaginative exploit carried out with great resourcefulness and daring. Belgian troops deployed nearby rushed to dislodge this comparative handful of invaders but were foiled first by Stuka dive-bombing attacks and then by the arrival of German paratroop reinforcements.

Meantime, other German troop-filled gliders also came to ground as planned in Belgium west of the Albert Canal. The troops they disgorged weren't quick enough to prevent Belgian guards from blowing up a bridge across the Canal. But they seized two others spanning the waterway and quickly went about making good their control of the border region. The incapacitated, beleaguered defenders of Eben Emael formally surrendered on the morning of May 11th. Within thirty-six hours, the German invaders were able to overcome border obstructions that had been expected to hold them back for at least a week until Allied reinforcements could dig in at strong defensive positions further back.

While Belgium's border defences were being overrun, Holland, which had also attempted to preserve its neutrality, was reeling from a German assault as well. In an operation timed to synchronize with the invasion of Belgium, Hitler's bombers launched surprise attacks on installations at the three major Dutch airfields – sparing the runways so that they might be put to immediate use by the *Luftwaffe* after capture. Airborne troops were then quickly glided or parachuted down to take control of those airfields and seize other strategic points in the country. The intention was to leapfrog defensive positions at the canals which crisscrossed Holland, the natural barriers which could obstruct the advance of an invading force. Fighter planes were dispatched to strafe the streets of The Hague to demonstrate to Dutch leaders that Hitler was determined to have his way.

French and British installations in northern France had come under aerial attack as well. Awakened at dawn by the crump of falling bombs, troops for whom the war till then had seemed a charade hurriedly crammed themselves into their uniforms and rushed to seek shelter. At installations which were spared initial bombing, troops were roused early as well as soon as word of the bombing spread. They were quickly formed up to await orders. The variously named long wait – the Phoney War, Bore War, *drôle de guerre, sitzkrieg* – was over. Almost as if he believed the play acting might have gone on forever, a British officer stationed near Lille just south of the Belgian border noted in his journal, 'So there's to be a real war after all.' It would prove more agonizingly real than he or anyone else imagined.

This, finally, was the dreaded commencement of the replay, magnified a dozen times over, of the Great War, the memory of which remained alive in the hearts and memories of countless people across Europe and elsewhere. That morning's orchestrated German onslaught was the overture to a struggle that would convulse virtually all of Europe for the next five years, devastate other parts of the world as well, claim tens of millions of lives, leave hundreds of millions grieving, and end European world dominance by bringing new superpowers centre stage in global affairs.

'The battle which begins today', Hitler proclaimed on the morning of his westward march of conquest, 'will decide the fate of the German nation for the next thousand years.' As the first heady reports of the day's operations came in, the German Führer, though jittery as always, had reason to believe the Nazi millennium he had forecast had in fact begun. His armed forces reported no initial setbacks, no serious bungling, no resistance that had not been overcome. They appeared well on their way to achieving their immediate objectives. They had not yet engaged in any major clashes with the mighty French or the British but, added to Hitler's unbroken chain of previous triumphs, first impressions of how the battle was going fortified German troop morale and confidence. In a quick note to his wife the next day, General Erwin Rommel, commander of the 7th Armoured Division, was able to boast, 'Everything wonderful so far.' General Halder, the German army's chief of staff and former anti-Hitler conspirator, noted in his diary that 'reports on the whole corroborate satisfactory picture developing . . .'

Meantime, the Allies were no longer barred from deploying their forces on Belgian territory. Having been thrust unwillingly into Allied ranks and aware of how feeble were its own military resources, Belgium had been calling desperately since dawn of May 10th for help from France and Britain. The Allied High Command had been receiving word of ominous German troop movements right through the previous night and, despite the succession of earlier false alarms, was able to respond quickly. At six o'clock in the morning, the First Army Group – composed of three French armies and the British Expeditionary Force – received orders to swivel into Belgium from the positions they had held along the Franco-Belgian border. These forces were to deploy as planned along the Dyle-Meuse River Line in Belgium to stop the main enemy thrust dead in its tracks, wear the Germans down and then drive them back. It was sound textbook soldiering.

During the first day of the German offensive, and for several days afterwards, the full significance of what was transpiring on the battlefield was not fully grasped in either London or Paris. Close attention was of course paid to reports from the front as they came in. But despite the extreme perils of the moment, attention in both Britain and France was not undivided. Leaders and officials in both countries were distracted by the political crises paralyzing their senior commands. Until those were resolved, neither government could concentrate fully on dealing with the German onslaught.

In London that morning, Prime Minister Chamberlain, having previously reluctantly agreed that he would have to resign, changed his mind. With the war escalating dangerously, he decided that as a matter of honour it would be wrong for him to leave his post. The emergency, he thought, would neutralize the clamour for his resignation. He was wrong. The latest developments made it important to guarantee national unity by forming a government that would include senior representatives of the opposition parties, and that was something Chamberlain could not do. The Labour Party wanted no part of him and told him so. To his surprise and humiliation, several prominent Tories also made it plain that because of the German offensive, it was essential that he resign quickly and without fuss. Abandoned and repudiated by people whose support he needed, he was left with no choice but to have his car summoned and to make the journey up Whitehall and along The Mall to Buckingham Palace to inform King George VI that he was stepping down.

Halifax and Churchill remained the favoured, indeed the only prime ministerial candidates. But Halifax had strong doubts about taking the job. He believed that, though not impossible, it would be difficult for him to perform the duties of prime minister from his perch in the House of Lords. He would have to function in the Commons through ministerial subordinates. He felt that he would 'speedily become more or less honorary Prime Minister, living just outside the things that really mattered'.

Halifax might nevertheless have considered the job if there had been some way to keep the grandiloquent, opinionated Churchill, the irrepressible gadfly with a million ideas and proposals, the most energetic symbol of British defiance, out of his cabinet where he might overshadow the prime minister and complicate his control of the situation. According to Maurice Cowling, a Cambridge University chronicler of the period, 'It was only the realization that Churchill would make a great deal of trouble if he [became prime minister] that made [Halifax] insist on Churchill grasping the nettle.'

Though he had his dedicated supporters, Churchill remained an object of suspicion and even dislike to many Tories in the House of Commons. Nevertheless, he was the preferred choice of several senior parliamentary figures. He had been a government minister during the First World War and people with wartime ministerial experience were in short supply. When, to Chamberlain's regret, Halifax disqualified himself as a candidate, Churchill became the only one likely to command the support of a majority in Parliament and therefore the only possible choice to take over as prime minister.

Chamberlain informed King George as much. The King was not pleased. Nevertheless, Churchill was duly summoned to the Palace to receive the King's commission. The following day the King wrote in his diary, 'I cannot yet think of Winston as PM . . . I met Halifax in the garden [of Buckingham Palace] & I told him I was sorry not to have him as PM.'

Had it not happened the way it did, had Halifax agreed to become prime minister, the course the war was to take and the fate of Britain, Europe and the world might have been very different, as will be seen. As it was, when congratulated on his appointment by his bodyguard, Detective W. H. Thompson, while returning from the Palace, Churchill replied, 'I hope it is not too late. I am very much afraid that it is.'

The pressures Churchill came under in taking command of his country at one of the most perilous moments in its history were compounded by the undisguised resentment he faced from those in his own Conservative Party who considered him a mischievous adventurer, incapable of responsible leadership. Lord Davidson wrote to former Prime Minister Stanley Baldwin, 'the Tories don't trust Winston . . . After the first clash of war is over it may well be that a sounder Government may emerge.'

Suspicions about Churchill's abilities and staying power were shared by many holding government and military office. Sir Alexander Cadogan, Permanent Undersecretary at the Foreign Office, described him as 'useless' in his diary. General Ironside believed Churchill 'has not got the stability necessary for guiding the others'. Ian Jacob, military assistant secretary to the War Cabinet, said, 'We had known of Churchill . . . above all as a cantankerous, headstrong, and redoubtable controversialist . . . We worried how this difficult and seemingly erratic character would get on as leader of a team in a situation of such grave urgency.' John Colville, then a junior member of the prime ministerial staff and later also a devoted, valued Churchill aide, observed:

> . . . the mere thought of Churchill as Prime Minister sent a cold chill down the spines of the staff at 10 Downing Street . . . Churchill's impetuosity had, we thought, contributed to the Norwegian fiasco, and General Ismay [secretary of the Committee of Imperial Defence] had told us in despairing tones of the confusion caused by his enthusiastic irruptions into the peaceful and orderly deliberations of the Military Coordination Committee and the Chiefs of Staff. His verbosity and restlessness made unnecessary work, prevented real planning and caused friction . . . Our feelings . . . were widely shared in the Cabinet offices, the Treasury and throughout Whitehall.

With Churchill in office, many in Whitehall and in the Conservative Party were convinced that, 'the country had fallen into the hands of an adventurer, brilliant no doubt and an inspiring orator, but a man whose friends and supporters were unfit to be trusted with the conduct of affairs in a state of supreme emergency'.

Some Conservatives made little effort to conceal their feelings about the new British leader. In the days that followed Churchill's appointment, Chamberlain, who was kept on in the cabinet by him as Lord President of the Council, raised cheers from the Conservative benches of the House of Commons when he entered the chamber while Churchill was often received in silence, a deliberate snub.

Despite the strong support and best wishes expressed by his friends and admirers, Churchill must have felt humiliated. But he gave no sign of recognizing the awkwardness of a situation in which the opposition members of the Commons appeared to be offering him more enthusiastic backing than a good portion of his own side of the House. He knew the importance of appearances and wasted no time in launching a campaign to dispel the feeling in Britain that the country was inadequately led or impotent in the face of the German onslaught. His defiant public statements and speeches were masterpieces of rhetoric. 'You ask,' he told Parliament, 'what is our aim? I can answer in one word: Victory – victory at all costs, victory in spite of all terror, victory, however long and hard the road may be . . .'

Some Tories remained little impressed with his stirring oratory. Nor were all of his chief associates happy with his practice of holding cabinet meetings which began late at night – he was a strong believer in long midday naps – and which sometimes continued into the early morning hours. When one such session did not begin until 10.30 p.m., Lord Halifax, whom Churchill had asked to stay on in the

cabinet as Foreign Secretary, thought it was 'Quite intolerable . . .
One must acquiesce during these two or three days. After that I shall
tell him that if he wants midnight meetings, he can have them without
me.' Colville was moved to note in his diary, 'There seems to be some
inclination in Whitehall to believe that Winston will be a complete
failure and that Neville [Chamberlain] will return.'

As for the French, their political crisis on the day the German
onslaught began was not only badly timed; it was grotesque. It was the
kind of spring day – warm, bright and sunny – people in ordinary times
wrote songs about. Parisians strolled through the Bois de Boulogne,
lounged over coffee and croissants at outdoor cafés on the Boulevard St
Michel, and watched street artists at work in Montparnasse. But these
engaging scenes were no more than a charming façade. The grim
reality was that, despite the signs of normalcy in the streets of Paris,
France was once more in grave danger and its leadership was in
disarray. When Hitler's forces began blasting their way westward in the
early hours of May 10th, the country was without a government and its
political and military command was a steaming cauldron of distrust,
resentment and hatred.

Realizing the dangerous absurdity of such turmoil at the top when
the nation was under threat, Reynaud immediately withdrew his
resignation as premier and cancelled his plans to appoint a new
government. Fearing that confusion might result from a change in the
military High Command at that critical moment, he also felt he had
no choice but to keep Gamelin on as military commander and to patch
things up with him. 'The battle is joined,' he wrote to the general.
'The only thing that matters is to win it. We shall work together to do
so.' The army commander replied in a similar spirit. Privately
Reynaud indicated to Paul Baudouin, secretary to the government's
War Council, that this exchange did not make him any more
confident of the general's talents or abilities. 'We shall see,' he said,
'what Gamelin is worth.'

Whatever the premier's persisting doubts about him, the French
army commander displayed no lack of self-assurance. Though normally undemonstrative, he strode up and down the corridor at his
Vincennes fortress headquarters outside Paris that morning, humming
contentedly to himself. It may have been that he believed the German
attack had finally handed him the battlefield opportunity for which he
had been preparing for years. But the enemy had just rescued him
from forced retirement and disgrace. That may also have contributed
to this uncharacteristic public display of satisfaction.

*       *       *

As the Allies went about sorting out their political predicaments and military dispositions, the Germans relentlessly proceeded with their offensive. By mid-morning of May 11th, their lightning tactics had effectively shattered the Belgian Army's first line of resistance which had been expected to bog them down for a few days at least and their forces were preparing to press confidently forward across the country to confront the Allied troops moving into back-up positions on the Dyle-Meuse Line in Belgium.

The Dutch were taking a beating as well but were proving far more stubborn than the Germans had anticipated. Where they had not yet been completely overwhelmed, they fought back vigorously. But their forces had been too fully stretched guarding a frontier more than two hundred miles long to be able to concentrate defences adequately at key vulnerable locations. The Dutch air force, small and obsolete, had been virtually demolished by the enemy at the very start of the attack. Their venerable tanks, comparatively few in number, could not long cope with German attackers battle hardened in Poland.

Once German airborne troops had successfully landed behind Dutch lines to seize strategically located canal spanning bridges, Holland was effectively beaten. However, the Dutch obstinately refused to submit. At five in the morning on May 13th, three days after the launching of the German assault, King George was awakened in London by a phone call from Queen Wilhelmina of Holland who pleaded with him to dispatch military aid for her beleaguered troops. The King passed word along to the competent military authorities and noted in his diary, 'It is not often one is rung up at that hour, and especially by a Queen.'

In fact, the British had already sent a battalion of troops to help the Dutch but in the prevailing confused circumstances, it failed to make contact with the enemy and, as Holland appeared doomed to defeat, it was hastily withdrawn. Acting in accordance with previously arranged plans, the French 7th Army had rushed into Holland to bolster Dutch defences but also did not stay long. Under concentrated German dive-bombing attack, running short of ammunition and aware of the imminence of the Dutch collapse, it also withdrew. In advancing, it had performed with immaculate precision but had neglected to take account of a key factor – the capabilities of the enemy.

Such were those capabilities and so ruthless were the terror tactics of the invaders, whose bombs flattened the heart of the city of Rotterdam to show the Dutch how futile was their resistance, that a mere five days after the invasion was launched, Holland was forced to surrender.

The Allied High Command had not at first been discouraged by developments. War was war and some setbacks were to be expected when the enemy was permitted to choose the time and place to strike. The true impact of the invasion was yet to be felt. Reducing the situation to what he then thought were its basics, Churchill observed on the morning the offensive was launched, ' . . . the German hordes are pouring into the Low Countries, but the British and French armies are advancing to meet them, and in a day or two there will be a head-on collision.' Reports that the Germans may have used a secret weapon to make short work of Belgian resistance at Fort Eben Emael triggered rumours that they had developed nerve gas or some such terrifying instrument of conquest. Extensive German use of tracer bullets led to reports from inexperienced troops that the enemy was shooting balls of fire at them, another frightening innovation. But British and French commanders refused to be panicked. It was the kind of thing they left to civilians who had no idea what war was about. Gort's chief of staff, Lieutenant-General Henry Pownall, wrote in his diary, 'So far so good.'

They were much encouraged by how smoothly their forces were swivelling into their assigned positions along the Dyle-Meuse Line – the French 9th Army from Namur to Mézières, the French 1st Army between Wavre and Namur and the British Expeditionary Force between Louvain and Wavre. Belgian forces would cover the remaining gap between Antwerp and Louvain. This unbroken defence line, assigned the task of absorbing the German thrust and throwing it back, was well on its way to being set firmly in place. It was a complicated operation but had been meticulously planned and, with a few minor hitches, was completed in less than forty-eight hours.

As they moved into position, welcomed by the cheering, waving, flower-throwing Belgian civilians through whose towns and villages they rolled, the Allied forces came under surprisingly light enemy air attack although their commanders had risked deployment by daylight because of the emergency. Some astute observers wondered where the much touted *Luftwaffe* was and whether the Germans, who were bombing and strafing helter-skelter elsewhere, were deliberately refraining from air attacks. Colonel Marie-Joseph-Victor de Villelume, Reynaud's military adviser, perspicaciously wondered, 'Are they letting us walk into a trap?'

But a British defence expert, Lieutenant Colonel T. A. Lowe, wrote reassuringly in the *Daily Mail*, 'An offensive on the scale the Germans have launched is an alarming thing in the beginning. The weight is such that it is bound to succeed at first . . . But . . . we are ready for whatever may come and we have the means ready to counter it. Our fighters will swarm against the German bombers; our anti-aircraft guns will keep them high . . . On land, tank will meet tank.' It was an illusion.

Taking up their new positions in Belgium, the British and French were appalled to find little evidence of the defensive fortifications the Belgians were supposed to have erected along the line they were to hold. At the strategic Gembloux Gap, high ground which his troops were supposed to defend, a French commander found 'no defence works [though this was] one of the key-points in the defence line, no decent trenches, no barbed wire . . . practically nothing at all'. Having no previous familiarity with the terrain, the British were painfully surprised to find that the River Dyle, along which they were to make a stand, was in places an easily forded narrow stream rather than the substantial natural barrier they had assumed it to be. In one place British forces advancing to their assigned positions were fired upon not by the enemy but by jittery Belgian troops who believed they were German paratroopers. Units of Major-General Bernard Montgomery's 3rd Division ran into trouble on the Franco-Belgian border when a customs official, having received no special instructions, refused to let them pass because they had no 'permit' to enter the country. When argument failed, a heavy truck driven at speed through the border barrier proved to be permit enough.

There were other confusions, complications and muddles and some friction between Allied officers as to who was to be where, a difficulty inevitable because there had been no earlier consultations between Allied staff officers and the previously neutral Belgians. But for the most part the movement into Belgium proceeded promisingly. British Chief of Staff Lord Ironside was convinced that once in place, the Allies would block the main route to the west that he, like Gamelin, had no doubt the Germans intended to take, and that it would be a war of attrition in which the Germans would finally exhaust themselves battering against solid Allied defences. He noted in his diary, 'A long battle is going to ensue . . . On the whole the advantage is with us.'

It was a total misreading of the situation. As the Allies would soon discover, their shift into Belgium, so masterfully executed, fitted so neatly into German plans that it might have been programmed by Hitler himself. The fact was that when the assaults on Belgium and Holland were launched on May 10th, the biggest, most important component of the German operation was shaping up elsewhere. The much respected military correspondent of *The Times*, who confidently asserted, 'This time at least there has been no strategic surprise', was about to be proven profoundly mistaken.

Though he had been anxious to launch the offensive much sooner, and though infuriated by the repeated delays, Hitler had agreed that attack strategy would have to be reviewed after the crash-landed plane incident in January which gave the Belgians details of his invasion plans. It meant further delay but it gave Lieutenant-General Erich von Manstein an opportunity to outline a comprehensive alternative strategy to the Führer. Manstein proposed that the drive into Belgium, originally conceived as the main thrust against the Allies, be downgraded to the status of merely a diversion in strength. It would be powerful enough to tie down the repositioned Allied armies, the shift of which from northern France into Belgium was obvious and expected, and prevent them from disengaging to challenge the primary German thrust further south. That was where Manstein proposed that the armoured divisions spearheading the German offensive should strike, plunging through the Ardennes Forest and into France.

Most of Hitler's generals at first pooh-poohed the idea, for the same reason the French did. They believed an armoured romp through the Ardennes would be doomed to failure. They said the forest was totally unsuitable tank terrain. They said it would take many days, perhaps as long as two weeks, for the armoured divisions to negotiate a passage in strength through such countryside, by which time the element of surprise on which the manoeuvre depended would long have been forfeited. Arguments raged as to whether this was true or not and the generals were finally persuaded that the drive through the Ardennes need not actually take so long. More important, Hitler who had been growing disenchanted with the thrust-through-Belgium plan and who had also been wondering about the possibility of a drive through the Ardennes instead, was won over. Modified in a number of details, it became official German strategy and the formula for one of the most remarkable military routs in history.

Army Group B, under the command of Colonel-General Feodor von Bock, which was to invade Belgium and Holland in accordance with the original plan, was downgraded from thirty-seven to twenty-eight divisions, including three rather than eight armoured divisions, while Army Group A, under the command of Colonel General Gerd von Rundstedt, which was to rush through the Ardennes, was upgraded from twenty-seven to forty-four divisions, including seven rather than one armoured division.

By May 9th, von Rundstedt's forces, spearheaded by the most concentrated array of armour ever assembled, a vast throng of tanks and armoured vehicles, more than 1,200 of them, had been drawn up in three columns stretching a hundred miles back into Germany from the border of Luxembourg. By nightfall they had begun moving off and by dawn, with nary a challenge, had crossed the border of tiny Luxembourg – population 300,000; army five hundred men strong – and plunged into the 'impenetrable' Ardennes. The panzers were accompanied by motorized infantry and self-propelled artillery and escorted by an aerial cover of Messerschmitt 109 fighters. Their mission was to roll through Luxembourg and the knob of southern Belgium that protruded into the forest and then blast through into France.

The region was a bucolic wonderland, much of it an undulating countryside of thickly wooded landscape punctuated with forest villages and laced with narrow, sometimes steep winding roads. Though some of it was unobstructed pastureland, for the most part the Ardennes seemed as unlikely a route for an army of tanks as could be imagined. Accordingly, the weakest of France's armies, the 2nd and the 9th, had been assigned the task of guarding access to France from the forest.

More than half of the 9th Army consisted of reserve divisions. It was poorly equipped and officered largely by inadequately trained men with no combat experience. Its commanding general was André-Georges Corap who not only had no experience whatever of mechanized warfare but was so fat and physically out of shape that he had trouble getting into his car. It was expected that the forces under Corap's command would be required to do little more than fend off minor enemy probes. The same was true of the 2nd Army under the command of General Charles Huntziger who had never held an operational command before, having spent most of his army career in staff or diplomatic posts. His divisions were also partly manned by ill-prepared, under-equipped reserves who, despite intelligence warnings that an enemy assault was imminent, were in the process of being redeployed. Several of its most senior officers and thousands of its junior officers and men were on leave. These were the forces positioned just past the furthest reach of the Maginot Line fortification, on the hinge on which the Allied armies were swivelling into Belgium to stop the diversionary enemy advance there.

Though the French command had not expected anything like the long columns of enemy armour rumbling through the Ardennes, they had been immediately alerted to the advance of the German forces through the forest. A clash was both inevitable and imminent. Huntziger called on the mayor of the Ardennes resort town of Bouillon to ask that one of the town's hotels be turned into a field hospital. The mayor turned him down, explaining, 'Bouillon is a summer resort; our hotels are reserved for tourists'.

But the tourists wouldn't be coming that summer. Elements of General Heinz Guderian's 19th Armoured Corps showed up in Bouillon a day later but they weren't staying long enough to do justice to the town's amenities. They rolled relentlessly on towards France. As they advanced through the forest, the armoured columns were extremely vulnerable. Unable to spread out over open territory, they could not travel at maximum speed. Bunched up, they rumbled one behind the other along the narrow forest roads. Any breakdown or damage could halt an entire column and keep it halted until the stricken machine was repaired or shoved aside. Those that did break down or stall were immediately pushed off the road. Snarls and tie-ups did occur but were quickly remedied.

Attacks from the air could have blocked the roads with wrecks of steel and brought all three columns to a halt. But Allied aircraft sent out against the tanks as they ploughed through the forest were at first instructed to restrict their operations to reconnaissance and then ordered to 'avoid bombing built-up areas' which meant that, though their accuracy in targeting left much to be desired, they were prohibited from attacking the German columns when they made the clearest targets – while passing through the villages and towns which dotted that densely wooded region.

The consequences of that restraint were soon realized and the prohibition was withdrawn. It made little difference. Allied bombers which attacked the armoured columns did not fare well. German developments in anti-aircraft weaponry and fighter-plane technology had made most of the bombers available to the Allied command at the Ardennes front obsolescent even before the war began. Of thirty-two RAF Fairey Battle light bombers sent to attack the panzer columns on May 10th, thirteen were shot down and all the rest were damaged before they could inflict much punishment on the invaders.

With most of their troops either hunkered down behind the Maginot Line further south or shifting north into the pre-arranged defensive positions in Belgium, the French had few forces available to confront the attackers while they were still east of the Meuse River. Defenders, some on horseback, sent to tangle with the advancing German columns put up a spirited display but were easily outmatched and quickly forced to pull back. Some withdrew across the River Meuse so quickly that now it was the turn of the Germans to wonder whether they were being lured into a trap.

Nevertheless, they rolled on through Luxembourg, across the southern tip of Belgium, into France and towards the Meuse, the main natural obstacle between them and the English Channel. The German vanguard reached the east bank of the river on the evening of May 12th – and the Allied command still had no firm idea what was happening. In London, Undersecretary of State at the Foreign Office Sir Alexander Cadogan believed that, though news from the continent was unclear, the 'main thing is our and French troops seem to be getting on to their positions [in Belgium] without much loss'. However, in Paris that evening, French War Council Secretary Paul Baudouin noted in his diary that three attempts had been made that day 'to get accurate information from GHQ, but in vain. We know nothing, or rather all we know is that the Dutch and Belgian resistance is crumbling'.

The day did not end as triumphantly for the Germans as they might have hoped. The French had succeeded in destroying the bridges across the Meuse before their advance guard reached the river. One of General Erwin Rommel's motorcycle battalions found a weir which had not been blown up and scampered across to establish a foothold on the other side. But at this stage, they were unable to exploit those incursions to any serious advantage. The tanks were the key to German plans and hopes and they were stranded east of the river.

At that point, the main thrust of the German offensive was in danger of collapsing even before it had gathered momentum. With no viable vehicle crossings, the columns of panzers were backed up for tens of miles practically track to track. But communications difficulties, failure to assimilate intelligence reports and administrative confusion prevented the dispatch of enough Allied aircraft to cause the Germans serious problems. This massive clog of armour was, however, an inviting target for French artillery on the west bank of the Meuse and, indeed, some of the panzers were put out of action by artillery fire. But secure in their belief that the Germans would not be able to get their tanks across, French commanders restricted the firing of their guns to economize on ammunition – enormous quantities of which were later to be captured by advancing German units.

The Germans were not so sparing with their ammunition. On May 13th, the *Luftwaffe* was called up to begin a massive assault on the French positions west of the river. 'Almost the whole of the German air force will support this operation,' the 1st Panzer Division, stopped in its tracks on the east bank, was assured. 'By means of uninterrupted attacks lasting for eight hours the French defences along the Meuse will be smashed.'

Most effective were wave after wave of Stukas – up to forty of them in each wave, each plane carrying two 500 pound bombs – which swooped down on the guns and on the concrete pillboxes in which troops took shelter. For men who had neither experience nor expectation of such awesome and sustained assaults, and particularly for civilians past the usual age of military service who had been rushed into uniform, the effect of these *Sturzkampfflugzeuge* was devastating. Men who were not killed, wounded, concussed or thrown into shock by the bomb explosions were terrified by the high-pitched screech of the sirens built into the plane to produce that effect. They threw themselves to the ground even when the bombs exploded well away from them. According to General Edmond Ruby, the air attacks were petrifying:

> The gunners stopped firing and went to ground. The infantry cowered in their trenches, dazed by the crash of bombs and the shriek of the dive bombers; they had not developed the instinctive reaction of running to their anti-aircraft guns and firing back. Their only concern was to keep their heads well down. Five hours of this torture was enough to shatter their nerves.

Requests for fighter planes to drive off the enemy aircraft turned into desperate pleas for aerial cover, to no avail. At a time when his troops were being bombed, bombarded, battered and dispersed, General Huntziger, incapable of understanding what was happening, replied, 'If I am obliged to engage [my fighters] every time some threat arises they will be rapidly used up.'

Artillery took over when the bombing attacks let up. The Germans had brought their cannon, anti-tank and anti-aircraft guns, and medium tanks right up to the Meuse barrier. Firing almost point blank, they unleashed sustained fusillades against the defenders. French troops still sheltering in riverside bunkers which had survived the Stuka attacks were little more secure than those out in the open; protective armour for those bunkers had not been yet installed and they shattered when hit.

Under cover of such a bombardment, German infantry lowered inflated rubber dinghies into the river – more than two hundred feet wide along most of this stretch – and began their crossing. They came under heavy fire from defenders who had not been put out of action or driven off in panic. But those on the attack were élite combat troops not easily repelled. The ones who were not cut down before completing the crossing scrambled ashore, rushed to overwhelm defending positions, and quickly began digging in. Within a few hours, the Germans had established a series of footholds at several points on the west bank of the Meuse. But German armour was still stuck on the far side of the river and despite the horrifying bombardments to which they had been exposed and for which they had been totally unprepared, some French troops had stood their ground and succeeded in driving off several German attempts to convert those footholds into major bridgeheads.

The Germans were still dangerously exposed. French forces which had been driven from the river by the bombing and shelling were still largely intact, as were reserve units further back. If properly led, they had the capacity to obliterate the enemy footholds before they could be exploited to get the panzers across the river. But for counterattacks to succeed, they had to be launched immediately, before the Germans could consolidate those footholds. However, such action required coordination and French communications at the front, not overly reliable to begin with, had been virtually obliterated in the onslaught.

Not only were French officers unable to learn anything about German strengths and positions, they were left with limited knowledge of the condition and positions of their own forces. The most ambitious plan was for a concerted drive to be launched on the morning of May 14th to push the Germans back across the river. But by midnight of May 13th, German engineer troops were well on their way to patching up the destroyed bridge across the Meuse at Sedan so that it would be capable once more of carrying the weight of heavy armour. At first light, tanks rumbled across.

Army Group Commander General Billotte issued an urgent call for the bridge to be bombed. It 'means victory or defeat for us', he declared. Right through the day, British and French bombers – 170 in all – soared in through thick barrages of anti-aircraft fire to knock the span out once more. They did not succeed and eighty-five Allied planes were shot down. By mid-morning of May 14th, the belated French counterblow on the ground had been beaten off. By midday, German engineer troops had thrown other bridges across the Meuse and German armour was pouring across the river in three places. France had been penetrated in force by the enemy. The much trumpeted strategy for saving the country from ever again experiencing such a catastrophe was proved to have been built on dreams.

For French commanders who had believed such things simply could not happen, the situation was agonizingly incredible. Their 'impregnable' borders had been cracked in less than four days. Their famous Maginot Line, upon which enormous expense, energy and hope had been expended, had turned out to be irrelevant and a mocking waste of all three. When the news of what was happening at the Meuse was reported to General Georges, the commander of Allied troops in the north-east was devastated. An officer present at Georges' headquarters at the time said, 'The atmosphere was that of a family in which there had just been a death. Georges . . . was terribly pale. "Our front has been broken at Sedan. There has been a collapse." He flung himself into a chair and burst into tears.'

Word reaching senior Allied commanders elsewhere left them in ignorance. It told of some sort of unspecified trouble at Sedan. Gamelin and Ironside were totally unaware how serious a setback the

Allies had suffered. Both remained blissfully convinced that the main German assault was building up, as expected, in Belgium.

Superior German airpower was proving decisive. Senior French commanders subsequently did not appear to know exactly how many planes had been at their disposal when the Germans attacked. Though more planes were continually rolling out of France's aircraft factories, comparatively few of the available French fighters – little more than five hundred – were committed to close cover for ground forces once the battle began. When later pressed for an answer why so many had been held in reserve when the need for them at the front was so great, Gamelin replied, 'I confess . . . that I don't know.'

The commander of the French air force, General Joseph Vuillemin, conceded that despite losses, France ended up at the time of its capitulation a month later with more planes than it had at the beginning of the war. Nevertheless, General d'Astier de la Vigerie, commander of the French air force in the battle zone, later voiced frustration at the failure to use them when they were needed:

> Almost every evening I had to lift up my telephone and take the initiative to inform the commanders of the army and of the group of armies that I had, for the following day, a certain number of formations without missions, adding, 'Have you any to give them?' Their reply was invariably the same: 'We thank you very much but we do not have use for them'.

Of Britain's 1,873 RAF combat aircraft, 416 were based in France when the German offensive was launched. They were divided into two distinct units with different roles to play. The job of the Advanced Air Striking Force, composed of ten squadrons of bombers – Fairey Battles and Blenheims – was to inflict as much damage as possible on the German forces. They faced two major problems: though communications left much to be desired, their operations were at times effectively controlled from either England or French command headquarters, and they were suited only to daylight raiding which made them extremely vulnerable to German fighters and highly developed German anti-aircraft defences.

The Air Component of the British Expeditionary Force operated as a separate entity. The task of its four squadrons of Hurricane fighters, soon increased to ten squadrons, was to provide aerial cover for the troops and escort British bombers on their missions. The Air Component's four squadrons of Blenheims and five squadrons of Lysanders were meant for reconnaissance. But, as one Hurricane pilot recalled, for the RAF the air war over France and Belgium was a shambles.

'There was no intelligence. Communications were poor. Everything appeared to be *ad hoc*.'

Air commanders often didn't know where their Hurricanes should be sent to tangle with the enemy. The speed of the German advance meant that when specific instructions were given, bombers often arrived at designated target areas to find that the enemy had already moved on. Sometimes fighters sent to rendezvous with bombers they were assigned to escort arrived too soon or too late; sometimes they or the bombers didn't arrive at all. And the fighters, so badly needed for other purposes, had to squander some of their energies patrolling their own bases to guard against possible German bombing raids there.

There had been aerial encounters with the Germans, losses and wins, during the Phoney War. But the hopeless position of the Allied air forces in France did not become fully apparent until the start of the German offensive. Five of six Blenheim fighter bombers sent to attack a German position in Holland were shot down. German Dornier bombers swept in low over the airfield at Condé-Vraux in northern France, caught the squadron of Blenheims based there neatly lined up on the ground, destroyed six of them, and rendered all the others unserviceable. By the end of four days of the German offensive, the RAF had lost almost half of its 135 combat ready bombers in France.

British fighters going up in sections of three kept running into dozens of German planes, and sometimes formations of more than a hundred, the enemy bombers almost invariably escorted by great numbers of fighters. The Hurricanes took a heavy toll of German aircraft but were so vastly outnumbered that their own losses, in planes and pilots, also rapidly mounted. Replacements for both came and those were soon lost as well. Squadrons were soon so decimated that RAF pilots assigned merely to ferry replacement Hurricanes to France and then return to their bases in England were ordered by squadron leaders to whom they reported at French air bases to stay on and join the battle, some never to return. British airmen based in France agonizingly realized their limitations. Flight Lieutenant Sir Archibald Hope was sent aloft alone to guard his airfield when all the other planes in the squadron turned out to be unserviceable. He patrolled the base for two hours. 'One aircraft!' he later recalled. 'What could one aircraft have possibly done if there had been a raid?'

From the very start, 'kill' claims by pilots were highly inflated, making it difficult to appreciate fully what was happening in the air war. In the heat of battle, it was impossible for a pilot to know whether a plane he had attacked was shot down, only damaged, or merely deliberately emitting a trail of smoke for evasive purposes, a ploy German pilots had mastered. On May 11th, the BBC announced that the Germans had lost more than two hundred aircraft in two days of fighting, 'ten times more than Britain'. RAF fighter pilots in France were reported to be satisfied with nothing less than 'ten [kills] before breakfast'. If those reports had been accurate, the *Luftwaffe* would by then have been on its way to being knocked out of the war, which it patently was not.

Knowing how the war in the air over France was actually developing, Air Chief Marshal Sir Cyril Newall, chief of the Air Staff, realized, ' . . . we cannot continue indefinitely at this rate of intensity . . . If we expend all our efforts in the early stages of the battle we shall not be able to operate effectively when the really critical phase comes.' But when the French pleaded for RAF assaults on German pontoon bridges across the Meuse to keep the Germans from breaking through into the French heartland, planes of the Advanced Air Striking Force had to be dispatched to do the job. Of seventy-one Blenheims and Battles sent aloft to knock out those bridges, forty were shot down, and still those bridges stood.

French troops reeling under German bombing attacks cursed the failure of their leaders to provide them with aerial cover. The French government repeatedly requested British aerial reinforcements. BEF commander Gort also asked that additional fighter squadrons be urgently sent, as did Air Marshal Arthur Barratt who commanded British air forces in France. In London, Chief of Staff Ironside moaned that 'these calls . . . will continue until we have little left, but this battle may be decisive of the whole war . . .'

By May 15th, the seriousness of the RAF''s losses in France was seen in London to be taking on an additional alarming aspect. Advising against the dispatch of additional fighter planes to France, Newall expressed concern that Britain's home defences could be jeopardized by their loss and that airfields the Germans had captured in Holland and might still capture in Belgium were likely to be used by the *Luftwaffe* for short hop raids against British cities and military installations. Air Chief Marshal Sir Hugh Dowding, commander-in-chief of Fighter Command, pressed the point with great insistence. Dowding warned that Fighter Command could be 'bled white and in no condition to withstand the bombing attack which will inevitably be made on this country as soon as our powers of resistance fall below a level to which we are already perilously close'.

Earlier calculations lent credence to such forebodings. It had previously been estimated that the RAF needed sixty fighter squadrons to defend the country adequately, and that had assumed that the *Luftwaffe* would be operating from airfields in Germany. But now that the Germans had access to fields in Holland, which were much closer to targets in Britain, Fighter Command was down to a mere thirty-nine squadrons, and losing planes every day. Even before the extent and significance of the French setback on the Meuse was understood in London, a sense of foreboding was beginning to incubate there.

Foreign correspondents based in Berlin were assured by German government spokesmen that the German onslaught was purely defensive, that it had been launched to head-off aggression by Britain and France. But not even isolationists in the United States, to which the Allies continued to look for help, were prepared to believe that. Instead, the German offensive swelled the ranks of Americans who insisted that German expansionism could imperil the security of the United States. Roosevelt declared that his government would act 'to defend by every means . . . our culture, our American freedom and our civilization'. Secretary of State Cordell Hull declared that the world was threatened with 'an orgy of destruction not only of life and property, but of religion, of morality, of the basis of civilized society'. The *New Republic* magazine warned that the United States must be prepared for an Allied disaster in Europe.

Expressions of support for the Allies and sympathy for victims of the Germans reverberated across America. The government froze the American assets of Belgium, Holland and Luxembourg so that the Nazis would not be able to take possession of them through puppet governments. Growing numbers of Americans came to believe that the security of the United States itself was now under threat and agreed that the country's defences should be strengthened. But they thought in terms of a stronger navy and enhanced air power to warn off any potential threat from abroad. The idea of mobilizing a large army that might be sent to fight in Europe and once more plunge the nation into a foreign quagmire remained anathema to most Americans.

Whenever pressed, Roosevelt felt obliged by prevailing public opinion to repeat that he saw no reason to revise his belief that the United States could stay out of the war. Nevertheless, the President paid close attention to what was happening at the front. He called for continual updates from the War and State Departments on how the battle was proceeding and how the British and French governments were dealing with their troubles.

Reynaud pleaded for rush shipments of American arms. Churchill did the same:

> The voice and force of the United States may count for nothing if they are withheld too long. You may have a completely subjugated, Nazified Europe established with astonishing swiftness . . . All I ask now is that

you should proclaim non-belligerency, which would mean that you would help us with everything short of actually engaging armed forces. Immediate needs are, first of all, the loan of forty or fifty of your older destroyers . . . Secondly, we want several hundred of the latest types of aircraft . . . Thirdly, anti-aircraft equipment and ammunition . . .

Roosevelt replied sympathetically but explained that Congress would have to agree. The President did what he could to persuade Congress to bend America's neutrality status so that arms and munitions could be supplied to Britain and France to save them from defeat. But congressional resistance was formidable. California Republican Senator Hiram Johnson warned that any attempt to repeal or modify the neutrality act would be 'vigorously contested'. Most Americans appeared to agree that no matter which side deserved sympathy in the European war, it was really none of America's business.

Despite the intimate tone of Roosevelt's direct communications with Churchill, and though the President was relieved that a dynamic prime minister was now in charge in Britain, he wasn't absolutely certain that Churchill had the leadership qualities the pressures of the moment required. Having once served as Assistant Secretary of the United States Navy, he knew well the value of naval power and considered the British fleet to be America's first line of defence against ambitions Hitler might harbour in the Western Hemisphere. But the President was not impressed with the way, under Churchill's stewardship, the Royal Navy had mishandled the Norway episode. He felt that 'if things kept up the way they were going, the English were going to get licked'.

Presidential advisers also entertained doubts about Churchill's abilities. William Bullitt, the American ambassador in Paris, who kept pressing for stronger United States support for the Allies and whose views were much respected in the White House, thought as little of Churchill as he had of Chamberlain. He believed, 'There are no real leaders . . . in all of England in this time of grave crisis', a sentiment which he said was shared by Reynaud and other leading Frenchmen.

It was to be expected that Joseph Kennedy, the US ambassador in London, whose coterie of well placed contacts tended to be Chamberlain cronies and partisans, would be critical of Churchill too. It was no surprise in Washington when Kennedy urged that, despite Churchill's calls for help, the United States should take care not to find itself 'holding the bag for a war in which the Allies expected to be beaten'.

But Kennedy's influence in the White House had begun to dwindle during the Phoney War period when he had urged Roosevelt to intercede to work for a peace settlement that the President feared 'would blow up in our faces in a year or two'. The ambassador's pro-appeasement inclinations conflicted with Roosevelt's abomination of the Nazis. The President had told Henry Morganthau, his Secretary of the Treasury, 'Joe always has been an appeaser and always will be an appeaser. If Germany . . . [made] a good peace offer tomorrow, Joe would start working on the King and his friend, the Queen, and from there on down, to get everybody to accept. He's just a pain in the neck to me.'

Now Roosevelt was annoyed when Kennedy took it upon himself to advise Americans living in Britain – about eight thousand at the time – to make for home as soon as possible. The advice having been offered with all the authority of the American government's official representative in the country, the State Department felt obliged to help make the necessary arrangements. The British liner *Athenia*, bound for Canada with three hundred Americans among her 1,400 passengers, had been torpedoed by a German submarine the day after the war broke out. Twelve Americans had been among the dead or missing. In view of the continuing danger of German submarine attack, it was decided to send a clearly marked vessel across the Atlantic for those who wished to return to the United States from Britain and, as a further precaution, to inform both the British and German governments that it was doing so.

During the early months of 1940, the most important political question in Washington was whether Roosevelt would seek a third term in the White House. If he did so, he would break the tradition of a two-term limit for the presidency. Roosevelt was under strong pressure from the liberal wing of the Democratic Party to run again and frustrate the hopes of conservatives, including those among his own Democrats, to capture the presidency and repudiate or dilute his New Deal social policies. But tiring of office, Roosevelt had been thinking of a tranquil post-presidential career. He thought of retiring to his home at Hyde Park in upstate New York's rural Hudson Valley where he would take on the role of an elder statesman. He could gather his presidential papers for posterity and write about his time in office and about current events. After eight years in the White House, the prospect of a change of circumstances and scenery was attractive. As an invalid who had contracted polio many years before and who was confined to a wheelchair during most of his waking hours, relief from the immense physical pressures of the presidency was also a tempting prospect.

Developments across the Atlantic now became a factor in

Roosevelt's ponderings about whether to run again. The desire to educate the American people to the dangers they faced because of the war in Europe inspired Roosevelt to a new dedication and a renewed sense of his own importance. But it still did not provide a conclusive answer to whether he would agree to be a candidate for re-election. He told intimates that he did not intend to run 'unless . . . things got very, very much worse in Europe'. However, as he must have known, if things did get much worse, it was likely that Congress and the American public would be even more reluctant to get involved overseas. It would lumber Roosevelt – more than ever convinced that Hitler had to be stopped – with an even more difficult task than he had already undertaken. A presidential intimate believed, 'The question of whether Roosevelt would run is being settled somewhere on the banks of the Meuse River.'

The decision was a matter of crucial importance to the Allies. Any candidate hoping to be elected would have to promise never to tie America's future to the fate of any of the European combatants in any way. And he would have far greater difficulty than Roosevelt, who was a masterful political tactician and who was already working on ways to circumvent the congressional ban on sending arms to the Allies, in wiggling out of that promise. If he decided to step down America was more likely to keep its distance from Europe's turmoil, with incalculable consequences.

# Rampage

MUDDLE AND DISARRAY was the French response to the German onslaught which had taken Hitler's panzers through the Ardennes Forest and across the River Meuse barrier in the four days between May 10th and May 14th. But the moment had not yet passed when counterattacks could demolish the enemy bridgeheads across the river. General Corap established a containment line from which such efforts could be mounted. But the failure of communications and the collapse of morale, both shattered by air attack, unhinged the French response where it was not paralyzed altogether.

While most of the German panzers were still lined up front to rear on the far side of the Meuse, waiting their turn to cross, a French tank unit moved into position behind French lines to participate in a planned counterattack. Word of its identity and mission not having got through, it was mistaken for German. Local commanders thought enemy armour had zoomed forward in an encircling manoeuvre and whole units fled, believing they were about to be surrounded.

After rushing forward, the élite French 1st Armoured Division was a mere twenty-five miles from where General Rommel was consolidating his bridgehead but didn't know it. It just sat there waiting for instructions which didn't come.

Out of touch with who was where, some French units fired on each other. Other units disintegrated, the men making pell-mell for what they hoped would be safety. Reinforcements rushed in to bolster defence lines found that bridges over waterways they had to cross had been destroyed and no one available to explain why or who had given the order.

Unfounded rumours of German advances reached command headquarters where, for want of more accurate intelligence, they were believed, further confounding commanders who from the moment the battle had started had only limited information on what was happening and where. With few coherent orders being issued, the fall back gathered momentum. Men many miles back from the Meuse found themselves descended upon by swarms of troops who had bolted from the front, allegedly under orders of their commanders.

French units which did put up fierce resistance were undermined by the panic of those which did not. Their flanks endangered, they were forced to join in the retreat. Many men threw away their rifles and tore off their stripes or insignias of rank thereby signifying they were personally finished with the army and the war. Platoons, companies, whole battalions ceased to exist. Fearing attack from the air, some men abandoned their military vehicles in their retreat and took to the road. Many French tanks rolling unhesitatingly into battle ran out of fuel and had to be put out of action by their anguished crews who then had no alternative but to join the humiliating ragtag race to the rear. Many troops went into hiding in villages, farms or woods, waiting for the moment when they might safely surrender to the Germans.

At his Vincennes headquarters, General Gamelin was trying to function as overall Allied commander without a radio – without even a carrier pigeon, one of his staff officers moaned – and with unreliable civilian telephone links. He only belatedly grasped the extent of the setback on the Meuse. To receive information and issue instructions, the commander-in-chief relied on motorcycle riders who careered back and forth with reports and dispatches over roads jammed with vehicles and hordes of refugees. Some dispatch riders were killed or seriously injured in accidents, with no one at either end aware that, regardless of urgency, whatever messages they carried would never be delivered.

Commanders lower down the line of command were similarly cut off from contact with the forces they believed were at their disposal. Some had no idea where their units were, or indeed where the shifting front line was. Nevertheless, late on May 14th, with the French defences around Sedan on the verge of disintegration, General Georges, overall commander of Allied forces in the north-east, reported, 'The German advance appears to be blocked.' He had no idea of the actual state of affairs.

Attempts were made to reestablish control. 'When the destiny of France is in balance,' General Corap warned his troops, 'no weakness will be tolerated. At all levels, leaders have the duty to set the example, and if necessary force obedience. Pitiless sanctions will fall upon any leaders who fail.' It was futile. Battered and dispersed, Corap's 9th Army was on its way to extinction. The entry in its official diary on the morning of May 15th – Corap would be relieved of his command before the day was out – was a whimper of hopelessness: 'No information – communications cut – liaison unworkable – back areas blocked with convoys and wrecked columns – petrol trains in flames – wholesale chaos.' The rout was well underway.

Even if the French High Command had grasped what was happening, it would have required greater military skills than it possessed to do something about it. Many of the best Allied fighting troops were deeply committed in Belgium and well before the Germans had been expected to get past forward Belgian defences they had begun battering hard against points along the newly established Allied Dyle-Meuse defence line further back. General Blanchard's 1st Army, guarding the right flank of that line and best positioned to rush back south to reinforce General Corap's disintegrating 9th Army, was locked in battle. Its disengagement was beyond the capabilities or imagination of Blanchard under pressure.

Too much was happening too fast to be assimilated, understood and responded to with sound judgment. A French officer recalled seeing General Blanchard trying to absorb the information which had reached him.

> I spent more than an hour in the same room as the general . . . He sat in tragic immobility, saying nothing, doing nothing, but just gazing at the map spread on the table between us, as though hoping to find in it the decision which he was incapable of taking.

Blanchard's superior, General Billotte, commander of the 1st Army Group, charged with coordinating the actions of the Allied forces which had swivelled so confidently into Belgium a few days before, also seemed too shattered by developments to make a decision of any kind. When one was extracted from him, it was soon withdrawn or revised.

This lethargy was infectious. It was communicated right down the line to forces which were not yet seriously engaged. According to Colonel A. Goutard, who later recounted the course of events:

> No one really wanted to counter-attack. It was passed from one headquarters to the next like some unpopular fatigue. The armies, the corps, the divisions, the regiments were never ready. Sometimes, however, some good units – regiments or improvised groups – did attack in real earnest, and met with such astonishing success that the High Command became nervous and called them back hastily.

The inadequacy of their senior commanders infuriated many of the French staff officers. The British liaison officer attached to Billotte's headquarters recorded in his diary that younger members of the staff there 'were quite frankly in despair and poured out to me the measure of their disgust and contempt at the supine futility of their commander and higher staff'. Many broke down in tears as reports came in of the disarray and impotence of their army. Officers of the British Expeditionary Force tended not to show their feelings so dramatically. Gallic emotional display was not their style and it was, after all, not their country which was being invaded and bombed. It was not their magnificent Maginot Line that was being proved a catastrophic folly. It was not their once proud army that was proving feeble and ineffectual. And at first, it was not their troops who were being blasted by German armour and aircraft.

But to the exasperation of much of his staff, Lord Gort, like Gamelin, isolated himself from his major conduit of information on how the battle was developing. While most of his intelligence and operations personnel, receiving and collating whatever reports were available on German movements, remained at BEF headquarters at Arras, Gort had set up a command post at the village of Wahagnies near Lille on the first day of the German offensive, and then moved on May 13th to Renaix closer to the front, and then on May 15th to Linnick St Quentin which was still closer. For communications with his headquarters, he was compelled to rely on dispatch riders and the civilian telephone system, which was abandoned by its operators during air raid alerts. Anxious not to sit back and let things take their own course (which they did nevertheless), the BEF commander was also away from his forward command post for long hours at a time, seeing for himself what was happening. Communications with key sections of his staff were thus impossible to maintain.

Not until the day the Germans had crossed the Meuse did Gort learn that an enemy thrust in that direction – three days in the making – had materialized! And not until the day after they had broken through in strength at Sedan did he learn that it had happened, though by doing so the enemy was positioned for a drive that could slice through his supply lines. The BEF was in serious danger and he had received no warning.

Much of the fault lay with the command structure. Gort was in charge of the British Expeditionary Force but he remained subordinate to the French army command. His immediate superior, Army Group commander General Billotte, was supposed to be coordinating the activities of the Allied forces in Belgium. But Gort had little idea what this coordinator was up to. Battles were raging at various points along the western front but the BEF commander, whose troops were supposed to play a key role in the struggle, was told nothing by his French superior.

The French had much more pressing matters to deal with than the fate of the British Expeditionary Force which for the most part continued at this stage to be spared serious combat. French armies were being pummelled and trounced. German troops were once more thundering over the soil of France. The enemy was dominant in the skies above the country. Paris itself could soon be under threat. These were serious distractions though not serious enough for the British to appreciate being ignored and neglected. Bitterness and recrimination began to creep into relations between the Allies.

In Paris, less than two hundred miles from the front, a different mood prevailed. Parisians had been led by radio and newspaper reports to believe that though there was a battle raging in Belgium, French territory remained inviolate. To American journalist Clare Booth, newly arrived in the French capital, things appeared normal:

> Taxis hooted on the boulevard, glasses clinked on the marble tops of the bistro tables, the flower market at the Madelaine was madly colorful, and the clocks in the towers calmly struck the hours.

Reynaud himself hadn't been informed until the afternoon of May 14th, after German armour had begun pouring across the Meuse, that things were turning very disagreeable for his nation and his people. In addition to the military débâcle, an estimated two hundred thousand civilians in the north were fleeing before the enemy.

The French premier had a message telephoned to London to inform Churchill that the situation had deteriorated: 'The German army has pierced our fortified lines south of Sedan . . . Between Sedan and Paris there are no fortifications comparable to those . . .' France urgently needed more help. Reynaud asked Churchill, who had previously promised the dispatch of four fighter squadrons to beef up RAF forces already in France, to send ten additional squadrons immediately. Without them, Reynaud said, his forces might not be able to stop the Germans from crashing through to Paris.

Though detailed reports had been sparse in London, the War Cabinet already had reason to believe that problems which had arisen at the front were more than the initial battle setbacks for which allowances could be and had been made. Those informed of the heavy losses the RAF was sustaining in France, and of the implications those losses had for Britain's home defences, were particularly alarmed. Though Churchill was a firm advocate of always meeting an enemy at a forward position rather than with his back to the wall, he fully appreciated the dangers of further depleting the country's aerial strength and had reluctantly agreed with his chiefs of staff that no further fighters should be sent abroad.

But that was before London had learned of the German breakthrough at Sedan. Churchill and his advisers had still believed that the main battle would be in Belgium and that the Allied line there would block the enemy's advance, finally bringing Hitler's aggressive adventures to a halt. The Prime Minister was therefore astonished to hear Reynaud's anguished message about Sedan and his plea for help. It was thought possible that the French premier was suffering from a bout of gallic hysterics, triggered by excessively gloomy communiqués reaching him from the front. But at 7.30 the next morning, May 15th, Reynaud telephoned Churchill personally. This time his message to the Prime Minister who, having gone to bed in the early hours as usual, had to be awakened to take the call, was even more desperate. 'We are beaten,' Reynaud sobbed down the line. 'We have lost the battle . . . They are pouring through in great numbers with tanks and armoured cars.'

Churchill could not believe it. He had been dealing with defeatists too long to be convinced that things were as bad as Reynaud insisted. He had 'seen a good deal of this sort of thing in the previous war, and the idea of the line being broken, even on a broad front, did not convey to my mind the appalling consequences that now flowed from it'. He told Reynaud there was no chance that the war would be lost and tried to convince him that the onrushing Germans would soon have to stop and wait for their supplies to catch up. That was when the Allies would be able to administer a savage counter blow. Unable to reassure Reynaud on the telephone, Churchill decided there was no alternative but to fly personally to Paris to discover the true military position and to persuade the panicky French that the outlook was not as bleak as they thought.

But Reynaud was right and Churchill was wrong, as War Minister Daladier discovered to his horror that night when General Gamelin, who had just presented the War Council in Paris an encouraging report, telephoned to change his tune. German panzers, he now reported, had broken out of their bridgehead at Sedan. Not only did he not have the resources to mount any sort of counter-attack, but there was nothing to stop the Germans from roaring on to the French capital itself.

'What you tell me is not possible!' Daladier shouted back over the phone at the French commander. 'You are mistaken!'

Gamelin assured him that he was not mistaken. American Ambassador Bullitt, who was visiting Daladier at the War Ministry when he took the call, cabled Washington, 'unless God grants a miracle . . . the French army will be crushed utterly'. Even if a miracle had been in the offing, it would have come too late for the French 9th Army which was 'in an indescribable disorder, troops are falling back on all sides, Army HQ have lost their heads, they do not even know where their divisions are'.

At times the situation was reduced to the level of farce. Senior members of General Gamelin's staff were gathering protectively round the ineffectual supreme Allied commander. When Colonel Marie-Joseph de Villelume, Reynaud's military adviser, went to Gamelin's headquarters to try to unravel confusing reports on developments at the front, Colonel Petitbon, Gamelin's chief of staff, strongly protested what he considered his excessive curiosity and threatened to impose a news blackout on the head of the French government. 'If this goes on,' he warned de Villelume, 'I will not give any information at all.'

In view of the fact that nothing that was happening at the front reflected credit of any sort on Gamelin, that sort of petulance, though absurd, was understandable. Unperturbable until now, Gamelin was panicking. Having relied exclusively on a strategy of preventing the enemy from penetrating the nation's borders, he had no idea what to do now that those borders had been breached. That night, he urged the French government to prepare to abandon Paris because the capital was in danger of falling to the enemy – and only six days had passed since the first shots had been fired! Plans were set in train to transfer the government to another part of the country. Where it was to go was not decided. In the developing frenzy, a total evacuation of the city – an impossible task – was suggested.

People in London had no idea how the battle was progressing. *The Times* story on the morning of May 16th was almost euphoric:

> Under a seemingly endless torrent of bombs, backed up by an artillery barrage from the French forces, the Germans wavered and then began to fall back. They found the roads to their rear choked and blocked in many places by wrecked and overturned lorries, tanks, armoured cars and supply transport.

It was exactly what might have been happening but was not.

Though his sources were not confined to wishful press reports, Churchill remained unaware of the magnitude of the French setback. But his assumption that the excitable Reynaud had been wildly exaggerating the rout of his army evaporated when he landed in France later that day. To General Ismay, who was in the party accompanying the Prime Minister, the gloom of the French officers who greeted them at Le Bourget airport made it 'obvious that the situation was far more critical than we had suspected'. He was told that the Germans were expected to reach Paris in a few days' time at most. Paris police that day were being issued rifles as well as revolvers, stepping up their raids on cafés frequented by foreign nationals and stopping cars on main roads into the capital to search for fifth columnists.

At a remarkable emergency meeting at the Quai d'Orsay that afternoon, attended by the leaders of Britain and France and their senior aides, Gamelin summed up the situation at the front. He had brought his panic under control and his presentation seemed like a lecture to students at a military academy on how to go about losing a war. Everyone there, all standing throughout, listened in either despair (the French) or astonishment (the British).

Gamelin left no doubt that the plight of the Allies was indeed extremely serious. The Germans had rammed a hole at least fifty miles wide through the defences around Sedan and their armour was racing forward at remarkable speed, heading either for the English Channel or Paris; he did not know which. The French forces in their path had been either scattered or destroyed. 'Where is the strategic reserve?' Churchill demanded. 'There are none,' Gamelin replied. His exact words may have been misheard or misreported. But the meaning was the same. The battle had barely begun but the Commander-in-Chief of the French Army, and officially commander as well of the British Expeditionary Force, the man who at that moment was responsible for the fate of his country, appeared reconciled to defeat.

Believing that the British leader may not yet have fully grasped the gravity of the situation as outlined in Gamelin's stilted presentation, Reynaud recapitulated, explaining, 'The hard point of the German lance has gone through our troops as through a sand hill.' But Churchill needed no elucidation. In case Gamelin's lecture hadn't been enough, he had been treated to a graphic display of the French Government's desperation – through a window of the conference room he could see bonfires being made of Foreign Ministry archives in the courtyard to keep them out of the hands of the momentarily expected Germans. To ward off panic, Reynaud earlier that day had assured his Chamber of Deputies that there was no question of the Government abandoning Paris, but that was exactly what it was preparing to do.

Churchill had no choice but to accept that his confidence in the might of the French army had proved illusory. He was bitter with the French for having neglected the elementary precaution of backing up their front line defences with reserve forces to meet the kind of emergency with which they were now threatened and he was angry with the British War Office for not knowing about that extraordinary omission. 'We had a right to know,' he fumed. 'Both armies were fighting in the line together.'

Nevertheless, the Prime Minister believed that the French leaders were overly despairing and that France should and could fight on. He would not accept that a large and powerful country could win or lose a war in a matter of days. He was not alone in failing to appreciate that France was managing to do exactly that. General Ismay also optimistically believed that getting the French 'into a warlike mood' was only a matter of time.

Churchill had reacted angrily (and foolishly) when one of his senior military advisers had briefed him on a contingency plan for the British

Expeditionary Force to give ground in Belgium because of the panzer onslaught further south. Averse on principle to the idea of retreat except when no viable alternative was possible, he was not convinced that a speedy strategic withdrawal by the Allied forces had become essential.

Seeking to inject the same sort of fight into the French leadership, the Prime Minister reluctantly, and contrary to a War Cabinet decision in London the day before, agreed – with the grudging approval of the War Cabinet that night – to Reynaud's request for six more RAF fighter squadrons to be sent to France in addition to the four squadrons already promised. Despite his concern about frittering away the RAF's stock of fighter aircraft, the Prime Minister was persuaded that 'the first necessity was to support French morale and give them a chance to recover themselves' to deal with the German invaders.

In agreeing to the dispatch of the extra squadrons, the War Cabinet had not suddenly grown less concerned about the danger of jeopardizing Britain's home air defences. Its agreement was an almost reflexive response to the terrifying implications of the German breakthrough, the extent of which it had just learned. Holland had surrendered to the Germans the day before. Brussels was about to fall. The French Army and possibly the BEF as well were in serious danger. And all of that had happened in less than a week! The main thing was to bring Hitler's steamrolling forces to a halt and obviously the place to do that was where they were steamrolling forward. The additional squadrons would help considerably. That British air operations in France and Belgium had so far failed to make any dent in the German advance was not so much overlooked as not yet comprehended.

Fighter Command chief Dowding, deeply distressed by the RAF's losses in France, was appalled by the decision. 'Stuffy' Dowding was less inclined than most to be swayed by the pressures of the moment. For him the primary emphasis had not been stopping Hitler on the far side of the English Channel but defending the British homeland from air attack. He understood that the French might soon capitulate if convinced that the British declined to commit more of their forces to the battle. But he thought that a French surrender was imminent in any case and he believed that the RAF was so outnumbered and outmanoeuvred in the skies over France and Belgium that sending a few more squadrons would just be adding to the futile sacrifice already being made there.

Dowding was already jealously guarding his Spitfires, Britain's most advanced fighter aircraft. He had nineteen squadrons of them but refused to permit even a single Spitfire to be sent to the continent to run the same risk as the Hurricanes he had been obliged to send over. The number of Hurricanes being lost was mounting worryingly. Even more worrying, scores of experienced pilots were being killed. It was understandable that some British leaders had been persuaded by the extreme pressures of the moment to believe that France, as Britain's forward line of defence, had to be saved from defeat at all costs. But Dowding saw his fighters as the only means of Britain's salvation from foreign domination. It was essential, he insisted with nagging persistence, for the country to conserve its air power in order to prevent the Germans, with their larger fleets of bombers and fighters, from achieving the same mastery of the air over Britain that they had seized over Europe.

Others were mesmerized by Hitler's *blitzkrieg* across the Low Countries and the *Wehrmacht's* breakthrough into the French heartland. But Dowding was obsessed exclusively by the danger to the British mainland. He composed a letter to the Air Ministry in London saying that it was necessary to face the fact that the Allied armies in France and Belgium might be defeated. He complained that Britain's home air defences were already well below their previously calculated minimum strength. And he warned that if his fighters continued to be 'drained away in desperate attempts to remedy the situation in France, defeat in France will involve the final, complete and irremediable defeat' of Britain.

It was a statement by an officer who for social and personality reasons was, despite his rank, not really a member of the military establishment. He was overdue for retirement and thought by many of his fellow senior officers to be a tiresome fussbudget. But his warning focused attention on what had become a consideration only within the previous forty-eight hours and on what was still too fantastic for some senior figures to grasp – that Britain's survival as an independent nation could be at stake. The question at issue was reviewed yet again and Churchill this time regretfully ruled that 'no more squadrons of fighters will leave the country whatever the need of France' except, if necessary, to cover an evacuation of troops.

In Belgium, General Billotte, coordinator of the northern Allied armies, remained bewildered by the pace of events. He continued to agonize over the fate of France and the failure of its once glorious armies. Belatedly, instructions emanated from his headquarters for the French 1st Army, on the right of the British Expeditionary Force, to prepare to pull back from the Dyle-Meuse Line to save itself. Lord Gort, whose flank would be left totally exposed if his divisions did not withdraw at the same time, was not informed.

It was not deliberate. It was an oversight that no doubt would soon have been rectified. Billotte and his senior aides had other things on their mind. But not until Gort offered the French on his right a brigade of British reserves to help close a gap the Germans were hammering in their lines did the BEF commander learn that they were preparing to pull out. Outraged by Billotte's inexcusable failure yet to instruct the BEF to do the same, Gort dispatched a senior officer of his staff to demand that the distraught coordinator finally issue coherent instructions. Orders for a coordinated Allied pull-back were then forthcoming. It was to be a staged withdrawal westward, the opportunity to swivel back south to block the German breakthrough at Sedan having by then been lost. The Allied line in Belgium was to withdraw immediately to the River Senne, then to the River Dendre, then to the River Escaut where it was to stand fast and where, if the German advance had not ground to a halt by then, it would be met and halted.

Only after that exercise began did the French command in the north finally provide Gort with a thorough reading of developments as far as they were known. Hard pressed, the French had come to recognize something that hadn't featured much in their thoughts in the two harrowing days since the Sedan débâcle – that the BEF, though a fraction of the size of the French army, might play a role in their increasingly desperate struggle to save their country from being overrun.

But by then Gort had grown irreversibly exasperated with the indecisiveness of his French superiors, and the unreliability of French commanders generally. He later complained, 'It was no uncommon occurrence to agree with the French to retire at say, 9 p.m., and to find that the troops on the line had, in fact, begun to go back at 4.' When his forces had withdrawn to the River Escaut, he found the water level so low that the German tanks could easily have followed his men across because the French had opened sluices to flood regions down river for defensive purposes but hadn't informed the British.

A whole series of major and minor acts or omissions by the French riled Gort, compounding his sense of frustration at how the battle was turning out. He was still under their command but had begun thinking that, under the circumstances, his primary immediate responsibility was not defeating the common enemy, which did not seem a likely prospect in the immediate future. His main concern had become the fate of the BEF.

The orders to withdraw from the positions they had just taken up were not well received by British troops on the line. Their morale had been good. They had been certain they were a match for their German adversaries. But now the confidence with which they had sped into Belgium and had dug in sagged badly. Belgian civilians who had welcomed their arrival with cheers and flowers a few days earlier turned cold and resentful as they watched those same troops abandoning them to the invader with barely a shot being fired. When a company of Grenadier Guards took a wrong turning and had to double back to find the right road, they were cheered once more by people who thought the British were advancing again to meet the enemy. When they turned again to resume their retreat on the right road, those cheers faded into scornful disappointment.

Unlike the French to their right and the Belgians on their left, few of the British had yet been subjected to serious attack. Having unwaveringly held the sector to which they were assigned, they were baffled when told to pack up and move back. Having been nurtured on a diet of regimental pride from the moment they had first donned their uniforms, men of the front-line units felt humiliated at having to cut and run even before being put to the test. And it became one retreat after another. Troops barely dug in at new rear positions when the 'withdrawal party prepare' order was again issued.

> We weren't given much information. We were kept in almost total ignorance. But it didn't need a very bright man to know there was a hell of a fight going on somewhere and we weren't doing very well in it.

In a letter home from Flanders, a soldier wrote, 'We have slept in the most queer places [during the withdrawal] – wine cellars, cow-byres, haylofts, stables.' Rumours of disaster circulated freely. Belgian positions were said to have been blasted by two hundred German dive bombers at a time. The Germans were said to be using a secret weapon which prevented guns from firing. 'Germans have broken through the Maginot Line and are now south of us only ten miles away,' one British officer scribbled in his diary. Another feared that once they had begun retreating, the troops would be 'in no mood to halt'.

Aside from the reproaches and glum faces of the civilians through whose towns and villages they withdrew, the contrast for the troops between their initial arrival and their retreat was depressing. Most had arrived the previous autumn, passing through the pretty French countryside dotted with charming villages, fruit orchards and beech forests in which owls hooted at night. They had been cheerily welcomed in local cafés where the drink was good and cheap. The retreat, along a route further north, was through a dreary industrial landscape, along the cobbled streets of 'endless mining towns . . . blocked with military traffic, guns, lorries and staff cars going one way and refugees going both ways – the position is so fluid that nobody knows where any one German division is'. On their way back, there was neither time nor mood for dropping in on bistros for a beer and a laugh. And when they, like their French comrades-in-arms, were subjected to the attentions of Stuka dive bombers, many of them came to know absolute terror for the first time in their lives.

> It seemed all hell had been let loose. A plane is screaming earthwards; airbrakes wide open, tearing through the sky; then its engines seem to cut-out as it pulls out of the dive, and out of the ensuing silence comes the shrilling whistle of the falling bombs. It is the most hellish experience I have known. For those few seconds the embryo of life hangs suspended on the edge of eternity. The world stands still. The past, present and future is now. Brace your body. Tension every nerve and muscle against the impending shock. For those few seconds, it seems, the soul flits away to a safer place. One bomb falls closer than the rest, shattering the barn roof [beneath which he had taken shelter] and bringing heavy tiles crashing down, narrowly missing my head. I'm lucky. I'm still wearing my tin-hat. Then the planes climb to dive again, and the whole beastly process is gone through over and over again until one wonders how long one can retain one's sanity.

The wretched refugees fleeing the German invader, some for the second time in their lives, were both pathetic and troublesome. Vast numbers of them had taken to the road to get out of harm's way – individuals, couples, whole families with children, young people, old people, many loaded down with as many of their belongings as they could carry. The lucky ones travelled in cars, mattresses tied to their tops in a vain attempt to shield them from aerial strafing attacks. Others were in horse-drawn wagons or farm carts loaded with furniture, cooking utensils and everything else that could fit on board. Some were on bicycles. Hearses, ice-cream vans and other incongruous vehicles joined this desperate exodus. Some refugees pushed baby carriages or wheelbarrows stuffed with their things. But most were on foot and some had walked so far, or had been so ill-equipped for such an excursion, that their shoes had given out and they hobbled along with their feet covered in rags tied with string. Among the refugees were countless Belgian soldiers, fleeing from the German tide either individually or in groups.

The seemingly endless processions of panicking people in flight served German purposes. *Luftwaffe* fighter planes strafed towns and villages to drive inhabitants into fleeing, to clog roads and disrupt the passage of the Allied forces. Once on the roads, they were strafed and bombed and sent plunging for safety into roadside ditches from which, if they were not hit, they emerged covered in mud. The roadsides were dotted with the bodies of those who were not so lucky.

Unable to move quickly along choked lines of retreat, troops withdrawing in vehicles seized the moment when strafing planes zoomed over, and refugees dove to the side for safety, to speed down suddenly cleared roads and make up for lost time. That was, however, a risky stunt for which a price sometimes had to be paid. Later, in France, as the roads grew increasingly clogged, the French High Command ordered that refugees be driven off the roads into the fields, except for limited, specified hours, if they obstructed military movement.

It wasn't only the Allies who were apprehensive about developments. Recalling the disaster which ultimately overtook Germany's invading armies in France in the First World War, Hitler did not trust the enormity of the triumph of his armoured forces. 'The Führer is terribly nervous,' General Halder noted in his diary. 'Frightened by his own success; he is afraid to take any chances and so would rather pull the reins on us.'

General Guderian complained that Hitler, who had strongly backed the *blitzkrieg* strategy, was now 'frightened by his own temerity'. Superstitious, emotional, a gambler who agonized over his rash gambles, he was now convinced that his tanks were moving too far too fast, that their lines were too extended, and that French forces sheltering behind the Maginot Line would rush up from the south to pinch off and obliterate his offensive. As always in moments of stress, Hitler's paranoia shone through. He raged and bellowed and alleged that his generals were well on their way to ruining the whole campaign, almost as if they were deliberately trying to foil him.

The fact was, however, that the *blitzkrieg* was turning into an unstoppable spurt. The Germans were following hard on the heels of the retreating Allied armies in Belgium and the panzers which had crashed through around Sedan had successfully broken out of their bridgeheads across the Meuse and were poised either to rush towards Paris or make for the sea.

In the French capital, Reynaud was trying desperately to retrieve French honour and bolster French morale. After Daladier had informed him that Gamelin had no plan for stopping the Germans, the premier personally took over the War Ministry, shifting Daladier, whom he considered most responsible for French military unpreparedness, from there to the Foreign Ministry. He brought in tough-minded Georges Mandel as Minister of Interior both to put a firm hand in control of domestic matters which also threatened to plummet out of control and to gain another ally against the defeatists in his government. He also recalled the aged Marshal Pétain from his post as ambassador to Spain to become vice premier. The presence in the government of this First World War 'Victor of Verdun' was supposed to demonstrate France's will to win. That, however, was not how Pétain saw his summons to Paris. 'My country has been beaten,' he confided before leaving Spain. He said he was being brought home to sign an armistice with the Germans.

Knowing nothing of this and studying less than candid Allied battlefield communiqués for the slightest glimmer of hope, some Western observers suggested that the German advance was about to come unstuck. It was said that by sending their armour plunging recklessly across northern France, the Germans rather than the Allies were heading for a trap; they would be caught between the Allied armies in Belgium and the French forces shunted up from positions in the south. Besides, too much was being asked of the panzers by their German commanders. They were only machines, bits of metal, which would soon suffer mechanical breakdown or outdistance their fuel supply lines. Cavalry horses could feed off the land and rest up from their exertions without the need for parts replacements. Tanks could not.

For Gort, such musings had no significance. For him the facts were bleakly simple. Having been spared serious German challenge during the first days of the offensive, some of his forces were now being pressed hard by the enemy. Once again he was being told very little by his befuddled French superiors. But he finally became aware that if, as reports indicated, the German breakthrough to the south had not been halted, there was a distinct danger that his supply lines would be cut. Rations and ammunition were already running short. If, as now seemed likely, the Germans were steamrolling towards the sea rather than veering off towards Paris, the BEF could soon be caught in a trap. It was an uncomfortable position to be in, made no easier by Billotte who, instead of producing an emergency battle plan for the northern group of armies under his command, confessed on May 18th, 'I am shattered with fatigue. I have nothing that can deal with the panzers.'

That was tantamount to a confession by the coordinator of the northern armies of his belief that defeat was inevitable which meant that the BEF was in even greater danger than Gort had previously imagined. Though subject to French command, he was not without options. His instructions from the War Office in London, and agreed to by France, had been that if any order he received appeared to endanger his forces, he would 'be at liberty to appeal to the British government before executing that order'. That could certainly be interpreted as applying to a situation in which orders were simply not forthcoming to deal with threatening circumstances.

On May 19th, Gort's chief of staff, General Pownall, telephoned the War Office in London detailing the BEF's predicament. He reported that it didn't look like the French would be able to close the gap the Germans had opened in their lines. The BEF, he said, had three options. It could stand and fight with the danger of being cut off; it could counter-attack southward in the unlikely hope of joining with French forces attacking north to snip off the German advance; or it could withdraw to the Channel coast for possible evacuation. Pownall made it plain to the War Office's Director of Military Operations with whom he spoke, and whom he described as 'singularly stupid and unhelpful . . . knowing nothing of the reports which were being made', that this last option, though extreme, had to be considered very seriously.

The War Cabinet met later that day to consider a response to what was, in effect, a totally unexpected cry for help from BEF headquarters. Gort had not been given authority to make his own strategic decisions. Despairing of his French superiors, he had now turned to London for instructions, advice, encouragement, and support. The response was not what he expected. His warning that the BEF might be driven into the sea shocked Churchill. It was obvious to the Prime Minister that the Germans had pulled off a daring manoeuvre in crossing the Meuse at Sedan and breaking out of their bridgehead there. But no indication had yet reached the British capital that a million Allied troops, including the BEF, might be caught between German pincers. Surely Gort was being irresponsibly premature in suggesting that such a possibility existed.

Those at the War Office and elsewhere in senior positions in London who had never been overly impressed with Gort's command talents were tempted to conclude that their judgment of the man was now being proved accurate. As far as Churchill and the War Office were concerned, evacuations had to be last resorts. The BEF was on the continent not to withdraw but to engage the enemy. It might be momentarily compelled to retreat some distance. It might withdraw to new positions for strategic reasons. But to fall back on the Channel ports was insane. Churchill believed that once it did that, it would be in a 'bomb trap' and its total annihilation or capture would then be inevitable, only a matter of time. Ironside was dispatched to Gort's headquarters to put the BEF commander straight.

However, as a matter of standard policy, all options were to be considered. A meeting was called at the War Office later that same day to examine the points Pownall's telephone call had raised. Two main items were on the meeting's agenda: first, how to supply the BEF through the French English Channel ports – Boulogne, Calais and

Dunkirk – now that the Germans had rendered its supply lines from the coast further south inoperable; and, second, the 'unlikely' possibility of having to evacuate 'very large forces' from France through those same Channel ports.

Contingency planning was set in motion under the supervision of Vice-Admiral Bertram Ramsay, naval commander at the port of Dover, twenty miles across the Channel from Calais. Further meetings on May 20th and May 21st looked more closely at evacuation possibilities. Such a momentous operation was still considered improbable and, if ultimately necessary, unlikely to be overly successful. The hazards involved, both for those being evacuated and those doing the evacuating, would be nightmarish. Nevertheless, emergency options had to be examined, however unlikely they might be.

Admiral Ramsay's staff was to be beefed up to include shipping and transportation specialists, among others. A roster was to be drawn up of all available ships to be put at Ramsay's disposal. These were to include as many passenger vessels as possible, capable of carrying large numbers of troops and of loading them quickly. It was decided also to compile a list of small vessels, including pleasure craft, which could be called upon to participate in an emergency evacuation from French beaches if that became necessary, though it was obvious that lifting great numbers of men from beaches would be an extremely hazardous undertaking, totally dependent on the actions of the enemy, the tides, and the winds. Ramsay's communications facilities were to be improved and he was to liaise directly with Fighter Command for aerial cover if circumstances required. All of this was still considered hypothetical.

Hypothetical or not, the operation needed a code name for convenience and security. Though charged with drama and purpose, the name it was given had mundane origins. Naval headquarters at Dover were situated in rooms built in tunnels which had been carved into the cliffs above Dover city by French prisoners of war more than a century before during the Napoleonic wars. One of those chambers had housed an auxiliary electrical power generator during the First World War and had been known as the Dynamo Room ever since. Hence the name given to what would soon become one of the most critical operations in the Second World War – Operation Dynamo.

Like other paranoiacs whose fears are only partly imaginary, Hitler did have genuine reason to worry about the rapid advance of his tanks. They had covered a lot of ground. There could be trouble if their supply lines proved over-extended, if their infantry back-up did not move up quickly enough to guard their flanks, and if the Allied Command seized the opportunity to do something about it. In fact, on May 19th, in his first decisive move since the day the offensive began, General Gamelin ordered a manoeuvre of the kind Hitler dreaded.

Allied forces in the north were to wheel southward while French forces south of the Somme were to rush north to link up and chop off the German advance. The armoured units which were the vanguard of the German offensive would be isolated and picked off and the offensive itself would be crushed. The concept was sound though it may have been too late for Gamelin's proposed manoeuvre to have a chance of success. His forces in the north were too deeply engaged to be easily or quickly redeployed and the breakdown in communications would have conspired against it.

Whatever the possibilities, the Gamelin plan was never to be tested. Horrified by developments at the front and regretting that he hadn't put Gamelin out to pasture before, Premier Reynaud relieved him of his command that same day. General Weygand, a seventy-three year old First World War hero, was to replace him as Allied supreme commander. Weygand immediately cancelled the north-south link-up operation. He was very much his own man. He wanted to examine the situation before deciding on a course of action. While that was happening, German generals were left to marvel at the failure of the Allies even to try to block their advance.

As instructed by the War Cabinet in London, General Ironside arrived at Gort's headquarters the following day to disabuse the BEF commander of the foolish idea he had floated about withdrawing towards the coast. Neglecting to consult Gort's French superiors, the British chief of staff instructed him to prepare to drive southwards instead. He was to take action very much like that proposed in Gamelin's cancelled join-up plan. The order baffled and infuriated Gort and his staff. Ironside was told the manoeuvre was impossible. Of Gort's nine divisions, seven were in combat on the line and could not easily disengage to move in a different direction. Even if they could, the Germans would quickly rush through the gap that would be left, nullifying the purpose of the proposed manoeuvre. Pownall said it would be 'A scandalous – i.e. Winstonian – thing to do and in fact quite impossible to carry out – it would have involved a flank march across a gap which we knew had some enemy mechanized parties in it'. On the spot to see for himself, Ironside was persuaded that the manoeuvre, which had seemed logical and feasible when examined in the remote, calm setting of the War Office in London, was indeed ill-advised.

From Gort's headquarters, Ironside proceeded to Lens, north of Arras, to consult with Billotte at the headquarters of Billotte's Northern Army Group on what should be done. Also there when he arrived was French 1st Army commander Blanchard. For the first time, Ironside understood Gort's frustration with the chain of command. Neither of the French generals, in whose hands the fate of the BEF lay, inspired confidence. Ironside found them 'in a state of complete depression. No plan, no thought of a plan. Ready to be slaughtered . . . Tres fatigués and nothing doing.' Awe-struck by what seemed to him to be unmitigated defeatism, Ironside, like Gort, concluded that the survival of the BEF rather than beating the Germans had to be the main immediate priority. He saw no grounds for optimism. 'Situation desperate,' he noted in his diary. 'Personally, I think we cannot extricate the BEF. Only hope a march southwest. Have they time?'

Time was, in fact, running out. At seven p.m. on May 20th, a mere eleven days after the Germans had launched their offensive, Guderian's 2nd Panzer Division had reached Abbeville near the mouth of the Somme River, where it empties into the English Channel. One of its battalions had rolled on to reach the Channel at Noyelles in time to admire the sunset. The Allied armies in the north were now closed in on three sides, having only the sea by which their escape might yet be achieved, unless, as seemed unlikely, they could gather the strength to break out southward. Despite Hitler's anxiety, each stage of the swoop of his forces across northern France had been easier than the one before. Resistance had grown weaker rather than stronger. Now the Germans were ready to pivot along the coast to take the Channel ports and close the trap they had so speedily forged.

Word filtered back to the United States of how desperate the Allied position on the battlefield had become. Washington had been shocked by the rapidity of the German conquest of Holland. That shock intensified as reports told of the retreat of the Allied forces in Belgium when the battle had barely begun. 'Worst of all,' said Undersecretary of State Sumner Welles, 'was the increasing apprehension that the German war machine was so overwhelmingly superior in might, quality, strategy, material, and morale to the available forces of the western European powers that Germany might well become the supreme master of all Europe before the summer had passed.'

Churchill and Reynaud continued to press Roosevelt to find ways to circumvent congressional restrictions and release arms and supplies for urgent shipment to their forces. The President was also being urged by Ambassador Kennedy in London and Ambassador Bullitt in Paris to take action, though their advice about what should be done differed fundamentally.

Kennedy sent word that an 'absolutely reliable' informant in London had told him 'nothing can save [the Allies] from absolute defeat unless the President with some touch of genius and God's blessing can do it'. This hint that the United States should intercede to plead for an armistice was not well received in Washington. If achieved, it would have left Hitler with virtually all of Western Europe under either his command or his shadow. A stiff return message to Kennedy from the State Department warned him that the United States was not in the business of trying to solve Europe's problems. With Roosevelt in charge in Washington, it certainly did not intend to do so by undermining Allied resistance to Nazi Germany.

Ambassador Bullitt's forebodings were more troubling. He had been frantically pleading for arms and supplies to be sent to France to enable the French to beat back the Germans. Now, in a 'personal and secret' message to Roosevelt, he said, 'I think it may possibly be of the utmost importance for the future of the United States that you should have in mind the hypothesis that, in order to escape from the ultimate consequences of absolute defeat, the British may install a government of Oswald Mosley and the Union of British Fascists [which Mosley led] which would cooperate fully with Hitler. That would mean that the British navy would be against us.'

The British ambassador in Washington, Lord Lothian, didn't hesitate to draw advantage from American fears that circumstances existed under which the Royal Navy could fall under German control. Lothian stressed that the British fleet was crucial to American national security. He spelled out a predicament which already worried Roosevelt: If the American fleet patrolled the Pacific, American security would be endangered if Britain went under. If the American fleet was in the Atlantic, the expansionist Japanese might grab Hawaii. If the fleet was split to patrol both oceans, it would not be sufficiently strong in either to take on an aggressor. America, Lothian explained, had no logical alternative but to make certain Britain was not defeated.

Roosevelt suggested that if Britain were forced to succumb to Hitler, the Royal Navy could be sent for safety to the United States. Lothian shrewdly replied that it would be difficult to convince the British public to agree to such a plan if America remained proudly aloof in a struggle in which Britain had suffered grievously in the name of freedom and justice. No, the fleet, if it could get away, would more likely head for far corners of the Empire – to Australia, perhaps, or

New Zealand. In such circumstances, the United States would have to do without it. It was a form of blackmail that Roosevelt, not averse to such tactics himself when dealing with congressmen, well understood.

Churchill, whose friendship with the President permitted him certain liberties, was blunter still. He echoed Bullitt's blunt warning about the possibility of the emergence of a regime in London prepared to do a deal with Hitler if the situation seriously deteriorated further. He cabled the President a warning of what might happen if his government were forced out:

> If members of this administration were finished and others came in to parley amid the ruins, you must not be blind to the fact that the sole remaining bargaining counter with Germany would be the fleet, and if this country was left by the United States to its fate, no one would have the right to blame those then responsible if they made the best terms they could for the surviving inhabitants. Evidently I could not answer for my successors who in utter despair and helplessness might well have to accommodate themselves to the German will.

Churchill's suggestion that a government sympathetic to Hitler might actually come to power in London had the intended effect of deeply troubling Roosevelt and others in Washington responsible for American security. But the President knew he was still unable to bring the American public with him in his wish to provide the Allies with substantial material aid. Sympathy for the plight of the Allies soared as word spread of the German *blitzkrieg*, dramatically reported in the American press. However, the news from Europe also reinforced the hope of most Americans that the United States would not be drawn into the struggle.

Still publicly vowing that it would not happen, Roosevelt risked a great deal by maintaining his secret personal correspondence with Churchill. If that correspondence were publicly disclosed, isolationists could claim it was proof that the President was covertly violating the neutrality he professed to be defending. After all, he engaged in no such personal correspondence with Hitler. It could be turned into a serious political embarrassment for Roosevelt and a serious setback for American supporters of the Allied cause. As the position of the retreating Allied armies turned critical, that almost happened.

On the morning of May 20th, Scotland Yard Special Branch detectives, armed with a warrant, went to the home at 47 Gloucester Place, London, of Tyler Gatewood Kent, a code clerk at the American Embassy. As a member of the embassy staff, Kent had diplomatic immunity but that had been waived by Ambassador Kennedy at the request of the Foreign Office. When the twenty-nine year old bachelor, inside in his pyjamas, refused to open his door to police, they broke it down and began a thorough search of his bedsitting room flat. In a closet, they found folders containing copies of 1,500 secret documents which had passed through the embassy code room during the previous seven months. Kent had been handing the documents to Nazi sympathizers in London who had in turn passed them on to the Italian Embassy in London from which they had presumably made their way to the German Embassy in Rome and from there to Berlin. Included had been the Churchill-Roosevelt correspondence.

Kent had been under surveillance for some time. It may have been that Kennedy hadn't been informed of it earlier because, in view of the ambassador's well-known defeatist attitude, he himself was under discreet surveillance by British counter-intelligence. After being arrested, Kent was incarcerated in London's Brixton Prison. The United States did not ask for him to be extradited to stand trial in America. The American government wanted no publicity for the case or for the reasons Kent gave for his actions.

At his London trial *in camera* later that year, Kent maintained that he had acted as a responsible American citizen, that the American people had the right to know about Roosevelt's efforts to provide support for Britain while pretending to be keeping America out of the European conflict. It was hardly a plea that would gain sympathy from a jury in Britain which, at the time of the trial, was being blasted nightly by German bombers. Kent was sentenced to seven years in prison for violating the British Official Secrets Act.

Assistant Secretary of State Breckinridge Long believed that Kent's activities meant 'not only that our codes are cracked a dozen ways but that our every diplomatic manoeuvre was exposed to Germany and Russia'. Of even greater danger to the Allied cause was the possibility that the Germans would make the Churchill-Roosevelt correspondence public and that their propagandists would seek to persuade Americans that their president had been brazenly dragging America into the war against their will. Such a charge could have damaged Roosevelt's chances of winning a third term in the White House. Coming at a time when the President was making up his mind, it might even have discouraged him from running, leaving the candidacy open to someone much less concerned about the fate of Europe. As it was, details of the Kent case were to be kept secret for many years.

Few armies under pressure can retreat gracefully. The better prepared they are for combat, the more cumbersome they become when routed. For the BEF, that meant that thousands of its soldiers – men in the labour battalions, Pay Corps, Dental Corps, support troops of all kinds – though they had to be fed, quartered and transported, no longer performed a pressingly useful purpose. Reconciled to the likelihood that their services would not be needed in the immediate future, Gort ordered some 28,000 'useless mouths' evacuated back to England. From then on, the BEF would travel light – but not always in retreat.

On May 21st, under pressure from London and Paris for the BEF to put up more fight, Gort patched together an emergency strike force consisting of elements of his two reserve divisions and a tank brigade to counter-attack vigorously. The aim was to block roads south of Arras and sever German lines of communications and supply. Two French divisions from General René Altmayer's 5th Corps were to launch a simultaneous attack but failed to do so. Having been heavily engaged and badly battered for more than a week, the French troops were exhausted, though some units did join the counterattack a day late and fought with much spirit until forced to withdraw twelve hours later.

The British strike force was outgunned and outnumbered but in this first major clash between the BEF and Hitler's armoured forces, the Germans took a heavy beating. Many of their tanks were destroyed and four hundred of their troops were taken prisoner, more than the Allies had captured since the beginning of the German offensive. The élite *SS Totenkopf* Division was forced to withdraw in little less than panic before overwhelming German armoured superiority was able to reassert itself. But the British operation was overly ambitious and doomed to be short-lived. Within forty-eight hours, Gort's troops were beaten back and forced to retreat unceremoniously to avoid being encircled.

Nevertheless, their momentary achievement had an important bearing on the course of events. Guderian's newly committed crack 10th Panzer Division was quickly pulled back into reserve to meet any further surprises the British might come up with. Had it been permitted to race directly for Dunkirk as planned, any hope of the Allied escape by sea from the German trap would have been dashed even before the need for it was seriously considered.

From the moment General Weygand had assumed command of the Franco-British forces on the continent, he had been carefully studying the situation. He had even exposed himself to great danger by travelling to forward positions to consult personally with his immediate subordinates. Given the circumstances, it was no casual jaunt for a man of his advanced years. Having examined the possibilities, on May 21st, the day the British Arras counter-attack was launched, Weygand produced a plan to seize the battlefield initiative from the Germans. French forces south of the path the German tanks had blasted open across northern France, and Franco-British forces north of that path, were to launch simultaneous drives to link up, slicing off and isolating the enemy spearhead. It was essentially the same operation General Gamelin had proposed and Weygand had cancelled three days before, on the day Gamelin had been dismissed, except that its chances of success had then been somewhat less remote.

Gort was to be required to commit three of his divisions to play a key role in the Weygand plan. When he learned of it, the BEF commander was appalled. A farcical series of timing and travel errors had caused him to miss the meeting with Weygand at which the north-south link-up was planned so, though suspicious by now of French generalities and assurances, he had been unable to question details of the operation or the operation itself. He was, in any case, unable to comply immediately with Weygand's orders because all the BEF's available reserves were committed at the time to the Arras counter-attack. It was therefore accepted that the link-up drive would not be launched until the battlefield situation had stabilized, not until May 26th at the earliest.

But now Churchill, exasperated by the setbacks the Allied forces had suffered, interceded. Back in Paris the following day, May 22nd, he was characteristically still not persuaded that the situation for the encircled forces was desperate. Reynaud took him to meet Weygand at Vincennes where the new supreme commander vividly and buoyantly outlined to the Prime Minister the campaign he had devised for beating the enemy. Though it clearly resembled Gamelin's cancelled plan, in contrast to his predecessor's despair, Weygand displayed the confidence of a forceful, resolute soldier who knew exactly what he was doing and how to achieve his objectives. This caused difficulties.

Churchill was both relieved and deluded by the sudden, overdue signs of decisiveness, lucidity and fight in the French military leadership. He told the septuagenarian Weygand, 'The only complaint that I have got to make about you is that you are a little too young.' The Prime Minister did not understand that the new commander was offering far more than he could deliver. He did not know that British divisions expected to participate in the Weygand campaign were in the process of being forced by superior German forces to abort their operation near Arras and, their supply lines cut, were too low on ammunition to undertake any new major campaigns. Churchill did not know that the French 1st Army, far from being ready to go on the offensive alongside the British in the north, had been severely battered and was still under relentless German pressure from which it could not disengage to take part in fanciful schemes. And he did not know that the French forces south of the Somme were far weaker than Weygand suggested and that they were nowhere near ready to lunge northward across the German line of advance. Churchill also knew nothing of the agreed timetable for the planned synchronized north-south offensives. But excited by new signs of French resolve, he cabled Gort, ordering him to adhere to what the Prime Minister mistakenly understood to be the Weygand plan.

The BEF commander was instructed to begin his attack southwards in concert with the French 'at the earliest moment – certainly tomorrow with about eight divisions'. It couldn't be done. Even if it could, it didn't make sense. The Prime Minister's intercession provoked undiluted outrage at BEF headquarters. Pownall was particularly incensed:

> Can nobody prevent him trying to conduct operations himself as a super Commander-in-Chief? How does he think we are to collect eight divisions and attack as he suggests? Have we no front to hold which if cracked would let in the flood? He can have no conception of our situation and condition . . . The man's mad.

Pownall had not held Churchill in high regard even before but his fury was doubly understandable. Not only were the Prime Minister's instructions impossible to carry out but one object of the proposed offensive was to prevent the Germans from getting to the English Channel despite the fact that they had reached the Channel two days before and had already begun their drive up the Channel coast. To raise the level of vexation at BEF headquarters to new heights, though disaster was looming for the British forces, London was persuaded by complaints from Paris that the BEF wasn't really pulling its weight. Pownall was bitter about 'criticism . . . that the BEF was not doing enough'.

> Clearly at home they do not understand how much we have done and are still doing. That everyone is in the line, that everyone has been marching or fighting or digging in for sixteen days without rest or relief, that we have held our own ground and inflicted heavy casualties on the enemy.

Whatever appreciation or lack of same London had for the achievements of the BEF, word was passed along to Gort that he ought to stop moaning and get on with his job.

The BEF commander was, in fact, not without partial responsibility for the damage done to understanding and confidence between himself and London. Obedient soldier and gentleman that he was, at no time up to this point had he done more than intimate that he had grave doubts about the competence of his French commanders and their grasp of the situation. Neither Churchill nor Ironside knew what he was thinking. He neglected to take the advice of his friend, Admiral Sir Roger Keyes, who was representing the British government at the Belgian Royal Court and who urged Gort to 'tell the government to go to the devil, and insist on being given a free hand to extricate your army from the appalling situation into which it has been placed, through no fault of yours'.

Confusion reigned supreme in the Allied High Command. Whatever his intentions and expectations, Weygand had little to offer on the battlefield. Proposals, plans, direct orders had little effect on the situation. Commanders couldn't locate one another to convey orders, exchange information and resolve misunderstandings. Many officers and troops were left without orders. Even priority messages arriving at signals sections could not be delivered because nobody knew where to find the units or officers for which those messages were intended. Intelligence on German movements was virtually non-existent. When Weygand instructed the exhausted, ill-equipped Allied forces, struggling for survival, to box in the triumphant German panzer divisions and starve them out, it was apparent that the French command had completely lost contact with reality.

Fighting and running, British troops were bewildered by the pace and direction of events:

> We were making stands of only a few hours in one place [said an artillery gunner]. It was a confused, rambling retreat. We were performing manoeuvres that no artillery battery had ever been known to do. Normally, when you're chasing a target, the movement is a maximum of ten degrees right or ten degrees left. But we were firing at 180 degrees, right around, because the enemy was reported to be behind us, a pretty good indication that things were chaotic.

The Allied armies in the north were enduring agonies of deprivation. The men of the BEF had been put on half rations and were often not even fed those. Many of the troops, both French and British, were living off the land. It was, one officer said, 'a sort of licensed pillage'. The hungry troops did not always respect proprieties as they pulled back but many farmers had joined the streams of refugees and eggs and poultry were up for grabs, as was milk from cows. In towns and villages, foraging soldiers found stores abandoned as well and took what they could use – cheese, canned food, coffee, tea, beer, and wine. However, such scavenging could not satisfy military requirements. Ammunition was increasingly in short supply. For the BEF, it had to be parachuted in from England.

The indecisive Billotte, from whom Gort had received nothing resembling an order in the four previous days, had been fatally injured in a car accident on May 21st. False rumours circulated that he had committed suicide. Blanchard, named to be his successor as coordinator of action in the Northern Army Group, wanted to be formally appointed before getting on with the job. There being no direct communications link between the French Army Command and Army Group Headquarters, that was not easily accomplished.

Nor was it likely that speedy confirmation of Blanchard's appointment would remedy the situation. Aside from the fundamental inability of the Allies to seize the initiative in the battle, the British considered him a dangerous incompetent. At one point, General Brooke saw him standing studying a map of the battlefield and 'gathered the impression that he might as well have been staring at a blank wall . . . He gave me the impression of a man whose brain had ceased to function.' Nor did his senior French subordinates have much faith in his abilities. Shortly after finally assuming command of the Army Group, Blanchard was overheard by a French officer suggesting that perhaps capitulation was the wisest course of action. General de la Laurencie, commander of the French 3rd Corps, one of the few senior French officers to emerge with credit from the débâcle – twenty-five French generals were relieved of their commands by May 25th – urged that Lord Gort take charge of the Army Group in place of Blanchard. He said he believed Blanchard incapable of command. Marshal Pétain also suggested to General Spears, shortly after he arrived in Paris to be Churchill's personal representative there, that Gort take overall command of the armies in the north, though his object may have been to shift the blame to Britain for France's impending defeat.

The retreat of the BEF strike force which had mounted the short-lived counterattack near Arras outraged Weygand. He was convinced Gort had abandoned Arras without being compelled by the Germans to do so. With communications disrupted and the French command in the north completely muddled, the supreme commander had no way of knowing, or any reason to believe, that the retreat had been ordered to save the strike force from annihilation when it was imperilled by enemy flanking movements. What he did know was that it would undermine his plan for snipping off and destroying the German armoured advance. Aside from that, it appeared that the British were abandoning their French comrades-in-arms, thus further demoralizing his troops. To the secretary of the French War Council in Paris, Weygand appeared 'overcome by the defection of the English'. He was wrongly but firmly convinced that Gort would never have acted on his own but must have retreated on orders from London. How could France fight a war when its ally behaved so despicably?

By now, meetings of the War Council were being regularly punctuated by futile moanings about how France had been militarily unprepared for the war, how it had been 'criminal' to have sent its troops into battle without sufficient tanks, anti-tank guns and aircraft. Though Reynaud had to accept some responsibility for that, he did not spare the feelings of the French military command. He told the Senate in Paris that 'incredible mistakes' had permitted the Germans to cross the Meuse and that those responsible 'will be punished'. Reynaud was also beginning to share with his generals growing resentment of the apparent British desire to get their troops out of Europe as fast as possible. He complained that the British 'always made for harbours'. But he made it clear that as far as he was concerned, France was determined to fight on.

The premier's perseverance was not easy to sustain in the climate of despair in Paris, repeatedly heightened by disheartening news from the front. When one of Blanchard's staff officers, Major Joseph Fauvelle, was sent to Paris from Northern Army Group Headquarters to report on the situation, he was brought along by Weygand to a meeting with Reynaud and told the premier, 'In the voice of a seasick passenger asking a passing steward for a basin . . . "I believe in a very early capitulation".' General Spears, who was at the meeting, was appalled:

> I felt cold fingers turning my heart to stone. I have in my time seen broken men, but never before one deliquescent, that is in a state when he was fit only to be scraped up with a spoon or mopped up . . . Nothing short of throwing Fauvelle out of the window would have been adequate.

Spears was also more than a little surprised at that meeting, where the fate of France was being discussed, when Reynaud tolerated seemingly trivial telephone interruptions by his mistress and from someone who appeared to be a politician asking that his son-in-law be transferred to a sector of the front where he was less likely to encounter Germans. Such distractions were perhaps emotionally and politically necessary for Reynaud who was under enormous stress and who realized far better than Spears the extent of despondency with which he had to contend.

Few defeatists in Paris were any longer troubling to conceal their doleful sentiments. At a meeting of the War Council that day, when

Weygand presented a report on the wretched state of what remained of French defences, President of the Republic Albert Lebrun suggested that an understanding with the German invaders might be possible. Lebrun recognized that the French and British governments had agreed that neither would engage in separate negotiations with the enemy without the consent of the other. But, he said, if Germany made 'any relatively advantageous offer we ought . . . to examine it closely and objectively'.

Minister of Marine César Campinchi, who was not numbered among those prepared to give up the fight, was worried that worsening circumstances might lead to the formation of a government in Paris prepared to seek a separate armistice with the Germans. In the spirit of Allied solidarity, Campinchi urged Reynaud to warn Churchill of that possibility. But Marshal Pétain was not overly concerned about British sensibilities. It was his contention that the Allies had a duty towards each other only in proportion to the effort they made in the common struggle, and Britain had contributed far less than France. Air Force Commander General Vuillemin concurred, claiming that while the French Air Force was sustaining heavy losses, little was to be seen of the RAF in the skies over France – exactly the complaint in reverse that RAF pilots made about the French.

Whatever arguments were presented at the War Council meeting, it was evident that what was happening on the battlefield was developing important political dimensions. It was decided that Reynaud would fly to London the following day, May 26th, to confer with Churchill on the possibility of considering German peace proposals if such proposals were forthcoming.

In London, the War Cabinet could not fathom what Gort was up to. Churchill was growing increasingly impatient with the BEF commander. Reynaud had protested angrily to the Prime Minister about the BEF's allegedly unnecessary and certainly unauthorized withdrawal from Arras after its successful counterattack there. Unaware of Gort's reasons, Churchill agreed that the French had grounds for complaint. He said Gort should have informed both London and his French superiors of the action he was taking. He cabled Reynaud, 'We know nothing of the evacuation of Arras, and this would be absolutely contrary to our wishes.' To Ironside, Churchill said, 'I must know at earliest why Gort gave up Arras, and what actually he is doing with the rest of his army.' But while not yet persuaded, Churchill reluctantly allowed that circumstances might make it necessary for the BEF to fight its way to the coast.

Cadogan noted in his diary, 'Gort seems – inexplicably, rather – to have withdrawn 40 kms! But everything is complete confusion: no communications and no one knows what's going on, except that everything's as black as black . . . If *only* that Great French Army could give them a smack on the flank, we should have defeated Hitler. They *may* be preparing something, but there is no sign of it, and I haven't heard of a Frenchman fighting anywhere.'

Frustrated by the dearth of reliable, up-to-date information on what was happening at the front and not convinced that Gort knew what he was doing, the War Cabinet grew increasingly worried, and not only about day-to-day developments. A dazzling, unnerving realization was beginning to fester in the upper reaches of the government and the War Office. It was suddenly conceivable that the BEF, constituting virtually the entire British professional army and all its equipment, might be lost to the Germans! And the fighting war had just begun. Frighteningly awesome in itself, it could also have calamitous consequences for the fate of Britain itself. The Germans were already in a position to cross the English Channel to mount an invasion.

Examination of the enemy's military threat to the country was intensified. The review was not confined to dangers posed by conventional attack. A report to the Chiefs of Staff Committee said that the Germans had large reserves of mustard gas and other poisonous chemical substances and that they had experimented with spraying them from aircraft. Intelligence had reported that on two occasions the year before, German planes had released mysterious, large white balloon-like objects over France. These had disintegrated and covered an area of several square kilometres with a substance resembling cobwebs. It had been impossible for people in the immediate area to avoid getting these cobwebs on their hands and faces though with no noticeable ill effect. There had been no further details or explanation but evidently the Germans were experimenting with new dimensions of chemical warfare. They were believed also to be experimenting with thorium and uranium bombs which could have formidable powers of devastation but it was considered doubtful that the necessary techniques for their development and use were sufficiently advanced to present an immediate danger. Another report said that the Germans might have produced crewless tanks which could be remote controlled from aircraft overhead.

Meantime, rumours were spreading in Britain about the kind of measures to which defence forces might have to resort if the Germans invaded. The War Cabinet was informed that 'there appeared to be a general feeling abroad that, in the event of the enemy gaining a foothold on the East coast, the only means of ejecting them would be to bombard the area with artillery and from the air'. Regional officials felt obliged to put through formal requests for total evacuation of civilians from the targeted region before such drastic action was taken. They were assured that such matters were under consideration.

There could be no doubt that if the BEF was doomed to be captured or destroyed and if the Germans then proceeded with an attempt to invade armyless Britain, the challenge to home defences would be formidable. Arrangements were made for the government to take total authority over all persons and property in the country. The Minister of Labour was given the power to assign anyone in Britain to whatever job he thought would help the war effort.

Belated awareness of the dangers helped concentrate minds in London on the chances of extricating the British forces from France. On May 25th, the War Office sent Gort a telegram telling him what he had known for a week – that he 'might be faced with a situation in which the safety of the British Expeditionary Force would be the predominant consideration'. He was informed that every endeavour would be made to provide ships for an evacuation of his men, as well as aircraft to provide aerial cover, if such an operation became necessary.

Boulogne had already fallen to the Germans which left only Calais and Dunkirk among the Channel ports where an evacuation might be attempted. But Calais was under German bombardment and siege; retreating troops would have to fight their way into the town to be evacuated from its harbour – an unlikely prospect. If an evacuation were to be attempted, it could reasonably be made only from Dunkirk. A message was dispatched to Brigadier Claude Nicholson, commanding British troops holding out in Calais, informing him that his men would have to fight to the end. By holding out, they would delay the German advance up the coast to Dunkirk. Indicating the extent of the sacrifice that was expected, Churchill himself informed Nicholson, 'His Majesty's Government are confident you and your gallant Regiment will perform an exploit worthy of the British name.' A great deal was being asked of Nicholson, who was to die in a German prisoner of war camp. Not only were his forces greatly outnumbered but he had been shortchanged on essential equipment. He had only eight anti-tank guns to fend off German armour; the others with which his troops were supposed to be equipped were still at Dover, waiting for cargo space to be found on ships crossing the Channel.

At this stage – May 25th – the attempt to evacuate the BEF, though increasingly likely, was still no more than that. No one – not Churchill, not Gort, not Admiral Ramsay who would superintend the operation – believed it would be able to produce more than a very limited success of the kind that, while saving some of the men, would underline the enormity of the Allied rout. General Brooke wrote in his diary, 'Nothing but a miracle can save the BEF now and the end cannot be very far off.' It was possible that the evacuation operation would collapse into catastrophic panic. Such was the intimation at Dunkirk where Gort's Assistant Adjutant-General, Colonel G. H. F. Whitfield, had already begun evacuating the 'useless mouths' among the troops. Whitfield was appalled by the conduct of many of them and worried about the effect of German bombing:

> On many occasions both officers and men hurried into the report centre [at Dunkirk] at a speed which made one suppose that the enemy were at least only a few yards behind them. It was clearly impossible for me to check up on the credentials of so many arrivals coming, as so many did, without an authority of any kind to support their application for embarkation . . . Men who belonged to untrained or poorly officered regiments and corps broke to pieces when the heavy bombing raids occurred . . . [But] I am doubtful if even the best disciplined troops could have stood such attacks for long so that I am not surprised that small bands of men, utterly helpless and lost, were reported to me as wandering about Dunkirk trying to find shelter from the next raid . . . In many cases . . . the officers departed for the boats leaving their men behind . . . Officers whom I detailed for jobs which might delay their departure for a day or so disappeared and I have no doubt embarked for England without permission.

Counterattack rather than sending the fighting troops streaming back for evacuation was still officially the plan of operations. Despite Weygand's conviction that Gort had turned tail, and though the BEF commander had grave doubts about its prospects, on the evening of May 25th, he was still prepared to fulfil his allotted role in the Weygand plan. His two reserve divisions were braced to drive southward to attempt the elusive link-up with French forces supposedly preparing to lunge northward. But enemy action once again dictated the course of events.

That evening, the BEF commander received word that German pressure on the sector of the front line held by Belgian forces to his left was becoming irresistible. The Belgians were sustaining tremendously heavy casualties. Some Belgian units had dissolved under German battering. Troop morale was disintegrating. Many Belgian soldiers had personally bowed out of the war – a British liaison officer who had been dispatched to assess the situation had seen some of them knocking back liquid refreshment in cafés without a care about what might be happening at the front barely a mile away.

What was more, those Belgians who did fight on were determined to resist as best they could, but only within the borders of their own country, regardless of the demands of concerted Allied tactics. Instead of preparing to fall back into northern France, they were closing ranks towards Bruges where their general headquarters were situated. As a result, a gap was opening between British and Belgian defence positions. If the Germans rushed through that gap – and captured enemy documents indicated that was their intention – they would be able to cut the Allied line of withdrawal to the coast, trapping the BEF and what was left of the French 1st Army as well as the Belgian army. Indeed, the German High Command declared that evening that 'the ring around the British, French and Belgian armies has been definitely closed'.

Gort was faced with a dilemma. The only forces available to him to prevent that German breakthrough were earmarked for the drive south the following morning, May 26th. If he sent them north instead to block a German breakthrough in Belgium, he would be disobeying orders, undermining the Weygand plan for seizing the initiative in the battle, and confirming French suspicions of British betrayal. The decision had to be made immediately. Delay could be calamitous. An officer found Gort sitting at his table alone at his new command post in a house in Premesque, 'looking rather bewildered and bitter . . .' Uncharacteristically, he voiced his frustration at his treatment at the hands of the French:

> He said . . . not only had their Army continually pleaded that it was too tired to fight, and their staff work broken down, but from start to finish there had been no direction or information from the High Command.

A few minutes later that same evening, Gort's bitterness at being let down found new grounds. He was informed that instead of the three divisions and two hundred tanks that the French were to contribute to the planned joint Franco-British drive south the next morning, only one division would be available. And that was for a do-or-die operation scheduled to be launched in a few hours' time! His conviction that the proposed southward drive was doomed to failure was now unshakable. He no longer had doubts about which course to follow. The two BEF divisions earmarked for the operation Weygand had ordered were instructed to shift north instead to cover the gap opening up between the British and Belgian positions. A line of march to the coast was to be kept open for his troops and, regardless of whatever hopes for counterattack Churchill and Weygand might entertain, that march was about to begin.

The urgency of the situation and communications inadequacies led the BEF commander to make this critical decision without informing either London or his French superiors. General Blanchard, newly confirmed as Northern Army Group commander in place of the deceased Billotte, could not be found by British liaison officers and didn't learn of it until much later that night. The French military command was to see this delay, as well as Gort's unilateral decision, as further proof of the bad faith of their British allies.

Had Gort's decision proved to be a mistake, it might have gone down in history as one of the great military blunders of modern times. Weygand's plan for chopping off the German armoured advance may have been based on a questionable assessment of Allied capabilities but it was the only existing strategy for challenging the German onslaught, and hadn't yet been proved faulty. Now that strategy was in ruins because of the insubordinate BEF commander who hadn't bothered to consult either his French or British superiors before going off on his own. The Allies – and certainly the Allied armies in the north – could not now even attempt to snatch victory from the Germans.

Weygand bitterly declared, 'The defection of the English compels me to abandon finally any offensive movement.' Despite his earlier declarations about saving the honour of France by fighting to the last cartridge, he concluded that it was now necessary to consider how to 'prevent a useless massacre' of French troops. As for the British, a hard-pressed retreat to the coast and the evacuation from France of a comparatively small number of their men seemed the most they could hope for.

Even before Gort had wrestled with the decision to withdraw to the sea, he had initiated efforts to guard the threatened right flank of the shrinking Allied pocket in northern France and southern Belgium. To block a thrust by German panzers across the rear of the Allied armies, a defence line had been established along the continuous chain of canals that ran from Gravelines on the coast through St Omer and Béthune to La Bassée. A remnant of the French army which had rushed confidently into Holland at the start of the German offensive and which had then hastily withdrawn, held the section of this Canal Line closest to the coast. Marshy and streaked with waterways, much of this area was extremely difficult terrain for tanks. Such was not the situation along the rest of the Canal Line. There the German panzers, now poised to bolt forward to close the trap around the Allied northern armies, would encounter no natural obstacles aside from the line itself.

This sector was held by a hastily improvised BEF force in which infantry units, artillery and anti-aircraft troops (mostly without their big guns), and engineer and signal troops were supplemented by an assortment of normally non-combatant soldiers who had not yet been withdrawn to be evacuated as 'useless mouths'. They included medical orderlies, transport troops, technical instructors and even men from mobile bath units. For many of these men – some ten thousand in all – experience in handling weapons amounted to no more than hurried instruction as they took up their positions. All infantrymen now, they fought with desperation but were outgunned, short of supplies and under repeated air attack. By the morning of May 24th, German armoured units had secured four small but dangerous bridgeheads across the Canal Line and were only fifteen miles from Dunkirk! Troops in one of their forward positions could already see the towering belfry of Saint Eloi Church in the centre of the city. Dunkirk appeared to be theirs for the taking.

But the Germans were not without problems. In virtually continuous motion for two weeks, under the strain of battle, their troops were nearing exhaustion. They had suffered heavy losses in equipment, some through combat, most through mechanical breakdown. But victory carries its own momentum. Aside from the momentary thrashing suffered at Arras, the German advance had been relentless. Troop morale was high. Though recognizing the weariness of the men and the equipment problems of the panzer divisions, Chief of Staff General Halder had no doubt that they were capable of one last spurt along the coast to seal the fate of the Allied armies of the north. Cornered, badly mauled and groggy, the bulk of the Allied forces could be closed off from the sea in relatively short order, after which it would be a simple mopping up operation. But on the morning of May 24th, before the final blow could be struck, the advance of the panzers trying to force the Canal Line was suddenly called off.

This strange, totally unexpected development originated with a decision by General von Rundstedt, commander of Army Group A. Rundstedt was worried that his tanks had pushed too far too fast and that his lines were overextended. He thought it would be best to close ranks before bringing the campaign in the north, which was practically won anyway, to a close. What he had in mind was a brief pause for rest and recovery before his panzers resumed their advance. But not only did Hitler endorse Rundstedt's judgment when the destruction of the Allied armies of the north was within his grasp, he turned it into a firm order to halt right across the Canal Line and angrily cancelled an effort by Army Commander-in-Chief von Brauchitsch to circumvent it. He made it clear that the panzers must stay put on the far side of the line.

For the Allies, the order to halt, when it came, was an astoundingly well-timed mercy. It happened just before Gort decided to abandon the Weygand Plan and shift the only two divisions he had in reserve to block the threatening German breakthrough on the Belgian sector on his left. Had the advance of the German tanks on his right not been halted, he would have had to cope simultaneously with closing the gap in Belgium and bolstering his fragile defences on the Canal Line. It is not easy to see how, under those circumstances, the BEF commander could have prevented the Germans from breaking through, either on the Canal Line or in Belgium or in both places, to slam closed their trap on the Allied armies in the north.

Various explanations have been offered for Hitler's halt order. Though the campaign across northern France and Belgium had received his backing from the start, he had been deeply worried about its prospects for success, as demonstrated by his earlier attempt to slow down the panzer advance. As a soldier in the First World War, he had experienced the chaos of combat at first hand and particularly the German battlefield disappointments in the mud of Flanders. He knew that the best laid battle plans could go sour. He realized how great a gamble the entire operation through the Ardennes and northern France had been – with his tanks racing ahead of both their supply lines and the infantry – and had difficulty convincing himself that it was already virtually a total success.

His panzers had not been an unrelieved joy in the past. Some had broken down embarrassingly en route to Vienna during the annexation of Austria in 1938. During the Polish campaign, there had been extensive mechanical breakdowns. Now his tanks had been pushed harder than before and were not bearing up well. Panzer Group commander von Kleist said that fifty per cent of his tanks had been put out of action. Hitler may have feared that his armoured units would grind to a halt or suffer greater losses than they had already if pushed on without rest and repair.

He also feared that the Allied forces had not yet been enfeebled and were still capable of reversing the course of events, that they might recover, regroup and counter-attack as they had at Arras, only in a more sustained fashion. The Belgian, French and British armies in the north still amounted to a million men. It was not beyond the realm of possibility that they would break out of the pocket in which they were enclosed to participate in a modified Weygand Plan. If they succeeded, not only would the German offensive be wrecked but the very survival of his Nazi regime in Germany might be put at risk. Great care had to be taken in this endgame.

It is also true that now that the Allied armies in the north were being pressed against the sea, Paris had become the priority objective. Hitler had already declared, 'The principal thing now is to husband the armoured formations for later and more important tasks.' When Paris did fall to his troops three weeks later, wiping out the shame he felt for the Versailles Treaty two decades earlier, it was to be one of the most ecstatic moments of his life.

In halting his panzers, Hitler was also bowing to pleas from Goering. The *Luftwaffe* commander had been pressing him to permit the German air force to finish off the trapped forces as a token of gratitude for the tremendous contribution it had made in the campaign. Goering reminded Hitler that while few of his army generals were devout National Socialists, the *Luftwaffe* was a Nazi creation. Its pilots were blindly loyal to the Führer and deserved the honour of achieving this triumph over the decadent democracies. Goering told Hitler that if he gave the order that this operation was to be left to the *Luftwaffe* alone, he 'would give an unconditional assurance that he would annihilate the remnants of the enemy; all he wanted . . . was a free run; in other words, the tanks must be withdrawn sufficiently far . . . to ensure that they [would not be] in danger from our own bombing'. Goering said that after his planes had done their work, all that would be required of the army would be to 'occupy the territory'.

There was also the question of Hitler's determination to demonstrate to his generals that he was as much the supreme ruler on the battlefield as he was in politics at home. He insisted on being implicitly obeyed regardless of any contrary thoughts they might entertain. He was increasingly exasperated by senior officers who presumed to engage him in wrangling over strategy and tactics, questioning his grasp of military matters and his judgment. Halder noted in his diary that the 'divergence of views [between Hitler and some of his generals] results in a tug-of-war which costs more nerves than does the actual conduct of the operations'. During his rise as leader of the Nazi movement in Germany and then as German dictator, Hitler had often felt obliged to demonstrate his authority forcefully to prove to recalcitrant subordinates that he was in charge and he may have felt the same as the battle of Flanders neared conclusion.

There is, finally, the possibility that Hitler had been informed that the stars weren't right at that moment for a land operation by his tanks that would have cut the Allies off from the sea. He was reputed to place such great faith in astrologers that later in the war, the British consulted some as well to learn what sort of advice he might be receiving.

Whatever the reason or combination of reasons, the German dictator ignored the complaints of officers who saw no justification for the panzers to be reined in when they had been doing so well.

Guderian was furious. It had been his tanks, in the vanguard of the panzer charge across northern France, which had established bridge-heads across the Canal Line when the order to halt reached him. He noted bitterly in his diary, 'It was forbidden to cross that stream. We were not informed of the reasons for this . . . We were utterly speechless.'

That last wasn't particularly true. They were far from speechless though careful not to let word of the tone of their reaction to reach the Führer. Noting in his diary that the panzer force 'which has no enemy before it' was being 'stopped dead in its tracks', Halder was convinced Hitler's interference was jeopardizing the successful conclusion of the campaign. Word that Dunkirk was to be left to the *Luftwaffe* did not mollify those men who knew the possible consequences. The chief army operations officer called the halt order 'insane'. 'Are we going to build golden bridges for the British?' he demanded. 'Are we going to allow them to embark. This is ridiculous.' Panzer Group leader General von Kleist tried to ignore the order and sent his tanks forward but was emphatically ordered to withdraw them.

Spared the fierce attentions of German armour, the hastily patched together forces which constituted the thin shield guarding the Canal Line could be reinforced. They dug in and consolidated their positions. Hitler's order to halt, tacitly recognized as a mistake, was lifted two days later. But the Germans had to contend with far stronger resistance on the line than they would have met initially as they renewed their attempt to sever what was about to become the Allied corridor to Dunkirk and the sea.

# PART TWO

PART TWO

## Chapter 5 – DAY ONE OF DUNKIRK

# Sunday, May 26th

DUNKIRK IS COMPARATIVELY new upon the face of the earth. Not much more than a thousand years ago much of where it now stands was barely more than a sandbank, slipping in and out of the tide. Soon after the sea receded, a chapel was built and the village of Dunkirk – Church of the Dunes – grew round it. It was a sleepy fishing community on the shore of the English Channel, just north of the narrowest point of that marine trench which separates France from England. Four hundred years ago, when Dunkirk was part of the Spanish Netherlands, the Spaniards turned it into a garrison town for the armada that gathered for an abortive attempt to invade and conquer Britain. In the seventeenth century, it was twice besieged by the English and for a while came under English rule and had to be bought back by France.

Dunkirk subsequently became a thriving port. By the nineteenth century, freight vessels from around the world berthed at its docks. In due course, two long breakwaters were built, converging towards each other in the outer harbour to protect it from the swirl of the tide. The stretch of coast east of the port constituted one of the longest unbroken sand beaches in northern Europe. Backed by wide expanses of desolate, rolling dunes studded with clumps of coarse grass, it extended well beyond the Belgian border eight miles away.

The beach here shelves gently into the sea. At low tide, a person can wade hundreds of yards into the sea with the water reaching no higher than his knees. At high tide, the farther reaches of that same stretch of coast is under several feet of water though still not deep enough for large ships to approach closer than half a mile from the shore.

Though the sea passage to Dunkirk harbour provides little danger to navigators familiar with the sea lanes, it can be treacherous to those who do not know their way or do not have the appropriate charts. Waters even well away from the coast are laced with shallows. Channels between ribbons of sandbank can be as little as twelve feet deep. During most of the year, even on mild, sunny days, the waters off Dunkirk are more often than not buffeted by winds which make crossings bumpy and which can threaten small craft manned by inexperienced sailors with beachings and swampings.

The landscape immediately enclosing Dunkirk city is flat and largely treeless. It would make ideal tank terrain were it not for the impact of the sea on the region. It is a marshy countryside with four major canal systems and many lesser canals and streams. In the spring of 1940 while the evacuation from Dunkirk was in progress, these waterways provided screens behind which defence lines could be established to delay the advance of the German forces which had thundered across northern France.

A National Day of Prayer had been declared in Britain. The BBC broadcast a morning service from Westminster Abbey during which the Archbishop of Canterbury, primate of the Anglican Church, led prayers 'for our soldiers in dire peril in France'. Similar prayers were offered in churches and synagogues throughout Britain that day. In London, the famous Petticoat Lane market was empty for the first time in living memory on a Sunday so that the market traders who tended the pushcarts there could take part.

For many people in Britain, it seemed the first firm proof that things were turning out desperately wrong across the English Channel. It was a very worrying omen. When the broadcast of a prayer service at London's Catholic cathedral was abruptly cut off for no apparent reason, an official explanation was hastily concocted to reassure the public at a time when people were being warned to beware of saboteurs. It was announced that the interruption had been caused by a woman worshipper standing near the microphone who had been overwhelmed by religious emotion and that the incident had no political significance. In fact, she had shouted 'Peace' during the sermon by Cardinal Hinsley and the transmission had been suspended until she had been ejected.

Early that morning, Gort was able to contact London and passed word on that he was shifting the reserve troops which had been earmarked for the drive south northwards to close the gap opening on the Belgian sector of the front. Whatever reservations may have persisted at the War Office, it was pointless for anyone there still to insist that southwards was the way out for the BEF. Gort had made the decision and everyone concerned had to live with it. Later that morning, a cable from Anthony Eden to Gort revealed that London was indeed finally coming to accept that the sea was the only possible escape route for the BEF. The Secretary for War told Gort that he

(*Top, left*) Prime Minister Churchill and Foreign Secretary Lord Halifax. During the darkest days of Dunkirk, Halifax tried but failed to persuade Churchill to determine if an honourable peace settlement could be reached with Hitler.

(*Right*) Left to right: Chief of the Imperial General Staff Sir John Dill, Secretary of War Anthony Eden, and BEF commander Lord Gort, leaving the War Office in London.

(*Above, right*) Vice Admiral Bertram Ramsay, Flag Officer Commanding Dover, was in charge of Operation Dynamo, leading the team that turned an imminent military catastrophe into an historic triumph.

31 May:   As a personal experience D.A & Q.M.G.
embarked with 7 other soldiers at dawn on 31 May.
Every man was most unhandy - not one appearing to
know the purpose of an oar.  The tide was falling and
it was not possible to get the men to understand that
the boat must be kept afloat.  After falling about in
the baot (folding boat R. E manned by one heroic sapper)
saome progress was made in a crab like manner outwards
when after several attempts a tow line was secured to a
naval motor boat.  On arrival at destroyer side the
boat was allowed to charge the ship - no man had an
idea how to fend off.  The boat did not break and the
very dopey and awkward soldiers climbed on board
somehow.  During the tow 2 men in a boat in front
threw away their rifles - it was not possible to
identify them.  The sappers remained and took back
the boat still in tow.  The 'Shikari' Destroyer arrived
at Dunkirk at 0530 & Dover at 0930.

&ast;   &ast;   &ast;   &ast;

(Signed)    J. G. HALSTED
                    Brig

D.A & Q.M.G.    1 Corps

Personal note in the evacuation report filed by Brigadier J. G. Halsted, Deputy Adjutant,
I Corps.

Queues of men waiting for rescue boats extend like human piers into the shallows.

Troops sprawled over the sand dunes behind the beaches when crowds and long queues on the shore made speedy evacuation appear unlikely.

Troops wading out to ships from a beach east of Dunkirk.

(*Right*) Soldiers sometimes had to wade up to their necks in the waters of the English Channel to meet incoming small boats and dinghies and be taken aboard.

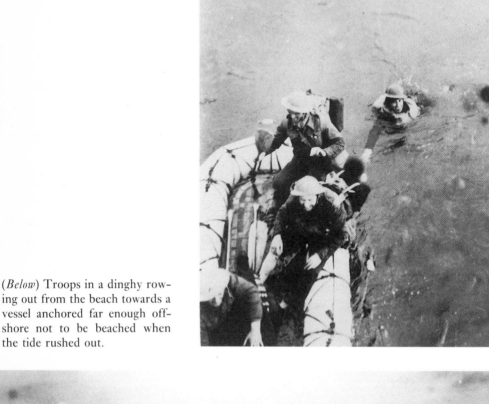

(*Below*) Troops in a dinghy rowing out from the beach towards a vessel anchored far enough offshore not to be beached when the tide rushed out.

The eastern breakwater at Dunkirk harbour, deserted during daytime lull in Operation Dynamo. Sunken vessel in the foreground was but one of the many destroyed by German bombs during the evacuation.

Troops waiting their turn in the sand dunes stare out to sea as the operation continues.

(*Above*) Thick black smoke from bombed blazing oil storage tanks darkened the skies over Dunkirk during most of the evacuation operation.

(*Right*) Troops wading out to a rescue ship. During quieter moments, when evacuation vessels were waiting offshore, the operation proceeded in an orderly fashion. But enemy aircraft could appear over the horizon at any moment.

Low tide shows a pier of trucks built out into the sea to facilitate the evacuation. The trucks were driven and manhandled into position and then planked over where necessary to permit men to move quickly over them to board small ships.

An improvised beach pier at high tide.

(*Above*) Queues of men snake
across the Dunkirk sands. Many
had to wait two days or longer
before being lifted off.

Once aboard ship the ordeal was
by no means over as they had to
run the gauntlet of the *Luftwaffe*
over the channel.

might find himself faced with a situation which, as far as the BEF commander was concerned, already prevailed:

> I have had information all of which goes to show that French offensive from Somme cannot be made in sufficient strength to hold any prospect of functioning with your Allies in the North. Should this prove to be the case you will be faced with a situation in which the safety of the BEF will predominate. In such conditions only course open to you may be to fight your way back to West where all beaches and ports East of Gravelines will be used for embarkation. Navy will provide fleet of ships and small boats and R.A.F. would give full support.

Exasperatingly, this still was not firm confirmation or approval for Gort's unauthorized, unilateral action. Churchill was to review developments with Reynaud when the French premier arrived in London later that day. ' . . . in the meantime', Eden told Gort, 'it is obvious you should not discuss the possibility of the move with the French and Belgians', neither of whom were likely to take kindly to the idea of being abandoned by the British forces.

Gort was relieved that at least London finally appeared to understand his dilemma in remaining under French command while trying to ensure the BEF's survival. He was, however, not convinced that the War Office had yet grasped the full extent of the crisis. The withdrawal to the coast for evacuation, about which London was still dithering, would be an extremely difficult, hazardous operation. A quarter of a million men had to be shifted back fifty miles through a corridor fifteen miles wide with the enemy snapping at their heels and hounding their flanks. Gort cabled Eden, 'I must not conceal from you that a great part of the BEF and its equipment', constituting virtually all of Britain's heavy guns and all its tanks, 'will inevitably be lost even in best circumstances.' To an aide, he confided, 'I never thought I'd lead the British Army to its biggest defeat in history.'

Mutual distrust and recrimination had by now become habitual between the Allied military leaders. The British saw breathtaking incompetence of the French senior commanders as the only possible explanation for the precipitous collapse of the illustrious French Army, to which the BEF had been expected to lend only marginal assistance. The French meantime were bitter that Britain, with a population as large as France, had fielded such limited forces in the struggle against the common enemy – and that those forces made for the sea at the earliest opportunity. And where was the RAF of which so much had been expected? Their essential communications having become virtually non-existent, almost all RAF squadrons based in France had already packed up and scrambled home.

To complicate matters still further, another divergence on strategy developed between the British and French. As far as Gort was concerned, the BEF would be withdrawing for one purpose only – to be evacuated back to England. But Blanchard, even if he had known Gort's objective which he did not, wasn't about to authorize the abandonment of his homeland by the troops under his command, which officially included the BEF. Blanchard believed the pull back was only to shorten defence lines in order to maintain a bridgehead based on Dunkirk for continued spoiling operations against the Germans. 'This bridgehead,' he declared in accordance with instructions from Weygand, 'will be held with no thought of retreat.'

A factor influencing the attitude of the French was their difficulty in fathoming the concept of escape by sea which the British, a seafaring people, grasped instinctively. French navy commander Admiral François Darlan was asked to examine possibilities for 'reembarkation' of French troops caught in the Dunkirk pocket, presumably so that they might be shifted to safety further down the French coast. But that request aroused little urgency – Darlan's reflexive response was that an evacuation was impossible – and none of the commanders in the north were informed that anything of the sort was being contemplated. Attending a meeting of the French government's War Council in Paris, General Spears 'suddenly realized . . . that to [its members] the sea was much the same thing as an abyss of boiling pitch and brimstone, an insurmountable obstacle no army could venture over unless they were specially organized colonial expeditions endowed with incomprehensible powers such as had once been enjoyed by Shadrach, Meshach and Abednego'.

Morale among the British troops drooped markedly as might have been expected from men on half rations if they were lucky, most of whom had done nothing but retreat, dig in and retreat again for the better part of ten days. It seemed a strange way to run a war after messing around for nine months doing nothing. Front-line regular infantry units were highly disciplined and pulled back in good order to new positions when the command came but the same could not be said for reserve and support units. They had neither intensive training nor regimental pride to fall back on. Some units disintegrated under attack when they lost experienced officers and senior NCOs. The men then made their way back as best they could. Many were told, 'It's every man for himself.' Word reaching the men that a National

Day of Prayer had been proclaimed for them at home – 'as though we were an army of the doomed!' – did little to lift their spirits.

Gort's decision to withdraw to the sea did nothing to improve spirits in London among members of the War Cabinet and Chiefs of Staff. Their forebodings about the fate of the BEF were compounded by fear that a German invasion of Britain could be imminent. General Ironside noted in his diary, ' . . . the Germans may try to reduce this country by air-attack alone [before invading] . . . The position is serious.' Many on the fringes of power in Whitehall got wind of what their seniors were pondering in the endless series of top level emergency conferences taking place and also began to fear the worst. Harold Nicolson, parliamentary secretary at the Ministry of Information, advised his wife to have a suicide pill handy 'so that you can take your quietus when necessary. I shall have one also. I am not in the least afraid of such sudden and honourable death. What I dread is being tortured and humiliated.' Lord Weymouth feared what had happened to Czechoslovakia and Poland 'will seem trifling compared to what Hitler will do to the hated English once he gets the chance'.

Senior figures in Berlin were confident that the British as well as the French were on the verge of total defeat. They forecast a British capitulation and the occupation of London 'within a few weeks'. There were hints about a 'great secret weapon' that would bring Britain to its knees. The Germans were not alone in forecasting Hitler's imminent total victory over the Allies. Ambassador Bullitt in Paris cabled President Roosevelt, 'I believe that the British, French and Belgian armies in Flanders will be obliged to surrender within two or three days'. British leaders assumed that Reynaud was coming to London that day to announce his government was considering a separate peace with Germany that would leave Britain fighting on alone against Hitler. Churchill prepared to plead with the French premier not to take that course of action.

Reynaud would be reminded that France and Britain had joined in a solemn undertaking not to conclude a separate peace and that it would be dishonourable to violate that undertaking. Churchill would warn him that France would become a vassal, if not a slave to Germany if it succumbed, no matter how generous were the peace terms Hitler would pretend to offer. He would tell him that if his government did sign a separate peace with Hitler, Britain would have to include France in its maritime blockade of Germany and this might regrettably lead to widespread hunger and starvation among the French people. France would be cut off from its overseas empire – a hint at a possible British seizure of France's territories in Africa, the Caribbean and elsewhere. And it would not be spared death and devastation from military action the British armed forces would be obliged to take against German forces on French soil. French cities would be bombed by the RAF.

At the same time, Churchill intended to try to convince Reynaud that the situation was not as serious as it seemed, that the invading German forces were fully stretched and on the verge of exhaustion, that Hitler was in trouble at home because of domestic economic pressures, and that continued joint resistance to the Nazis by the Allies would soon bring the United States to their side. Finally, if unable to persuade Reynaud, Churchill intended to press the French to make a supreme effort to help the BEF get back to England before the French capitulation and to transfer the French navy and air force to British command so that the Germans would not gain control of them.

As expected, Reynaud did little to lift hopes in London when he arrived. Weighed down with despair, he confirmed the reports the Prime Minister had earlier received from Paris that instead of performing the task for which Marshal Pétain had been brought into his government – to imbue the French with determination to prosecute and win the war – his new deputy premier had revealed himself to be leader of the defeatist faction in France. Reynaud said that he feared the Germans would soon be marching on Paris and said he had no means of stopping them. He said they outnumbered the French defenders 150 divisions to fifty – impossible odds.

Reynaud said France was prepared to fight to the death for its independence. But he pressed the possibility of persuading Italy to undertake diplomatic efforts that might lead to an honourable armistice and save his country from total disaster. He said Mussolini had to be convinced that it would not be in Italy's best interests for Germany to dominate Europe. The Italian dictator had to be persuaded not to join the Germans in their attack on France and instead to use his influence to get peace talks going. France was willing to offer him some of its African colonial empire as an inducement.

Reynaud suggested that Britain might be willing to make similar friendly gestures. It was no secret that Mussolini felt humiliated by British control of the Suez Canal and Gibraltar. They guarded the two portals of the Mediterranean Sea which *Il Duce* liked to think of as an Italian lake, controlled by Rome as it had been during the days of the Caesars. Perhaps Britain would be prepared to internationalize the Canal and Gibraltar, and maybe the mid-Mediterranean island-colony of Malta as well.

Churchill responded cautiously. A staunch believer in the British Empire, he was appalled by the suggestion. Besides, he was convinced that a resort to diplomacy at that stage would only serve Hitler's purposes. But he knew the pressures to which Reynaud was subjected back in Paris. He told him he would have to take the matter up with his War Cabinet, which he did. But he cautioned those of his ministers who were tempted by the idea of an approach to Italy, 'We must take care not to be forced into a weak position' by inviting Mussolini 'to go to Herr Hitler and ask him to treat us nicely'.

With regard to the fate of France, he wasn't sure what would be in Britain's best interests. He knew Reynaud was no defeatist. But the premier's unrelieved despair indicated that France could indeed be on the verge of collapse. German propaganda was already directed at convincing the French that Germany's quarrel was not with them but with Britain and that the perfidious British were determined to fight to the last Frenchman.

It was likely that the French would be offered by Hitler comparatively moderate capitulation terms which, Churchill warned his ministers, 'we would not'. That Britain might find itself alone at war with a triumphant Germany was a painful prospect. But the Prime Minister insisted that whatever happened to France, it would be better for Britain to go down fighting than for it to be enslaved.

That noble sentiment was shared by all in the Cabinet. But a sharp divergence of opinion developed between Churchill and Halifax over whether an effort should nevertheless be made to discover whether an honourable peace could be negotiated before the coast of Britain became the front line in the war. The Foreign Secretary was not yet reconciled to Churchill's style of leadership. Nor was he convinced of the Prime Minister's perspicacity. A clash of personalities figured in their differences but it was more than that. Halifax was not a vindictive man. He genuinely doubted whether the Prime Minister was able to comprehend the extent of the devastation that the *Luftwaffe*, flying from captured airfields in Belgium, Holland and northern France, would soon be able to inflict on British cities.

It didn't have to happen. Halifax believed that the situation had to be calmly appraised and that conclusions should be drawn without resort to emotional speechifying. He told the War Cabinet that, in contrast to Churchill, he believed that if Britain were prepared to make certain compromises, it might be 'possible to get out of our present difficulties'. He said that he attached 'rather more importance' than the Prime Minister to the 'desirability of allowing France to try out the possibilities of European equilibrium' – which very likely meant a peace conference which, by virtue of the German army's conquests, Hitler would dominate. Halifax said he was not convinced that 'the Prime Minister's diagnosis was correct [or] that it was in Herr Hitler's interest to insist on outrageous [peace] terms'. He believed that if terms could be found which did not 'postulate the destruction of our independence, we should be foolish if we did not accept them'.

The Foreign Secretary, who in the House of Lords had been loyally praising the Prime Minister's leadership skills, may by then have regretted not taking over leadership of the country instead of Churchill when he'd had the chance two weeks earlier. He was not alone in his growing impatience with Churchill's rousing war oratory. It did not always have the same morale boosting effect on senior officials as it had on the general public which was cushioned from the alarming details of how badly the situation had deteriorated on the other side of the Channel and of the perils facing Britain.

Sir Alexander Cadogan, the Permanent Undersecretary at the Foreign Office, observed in his diary that he considered the Prime Minister 'too rambling and romantic and sentimental and temperamental. Old Neville [Chamberlain] still the best of the lot.' Apparently dismissing Churchill's obstinacy, 'Old Neville', still active in the cabinet, wrote in his diary, 'If we could get out of this jam by giving up Malta and Gibraltar and some African territories, we would jump at it.'

His country on the brink of disaster, Reynaud also had reservations about Churchill and his talk of the need to struggle on to the last if necessary against tyranny. 'The only one who understands,' the French premier said upon his return from London to Paris that evening, 'is Halifax who . . . who realizes that some European solution must be reached. Churchill,' he complained, 'is always hectoring.'

In Paris, General Weygand, though he bitterly accepted that his plan for a north-south link-up of Allied forces had to be cancelled, was still certain that it would have had a chance of success. But he realized there was now no alternative but for the armies in the north to withdraw towards the coast and he issued the appropriate orders. However, Eden did not intend for Gort to wait for formal pull-back instructions to filter through France's shattered communications. He cabled the BEF commander the official go-ahead.

> Prime Minister has had conversation with M. Reynaud this afternoon. Latter fully explained to him the situation and resources French Army. It is clear from this that it will not be possible for French to deliver attack in the south in sufficient strength to enable them to effect junction with northern armies. In these circumstances no course open to you but to fall back upon the coast . . . You are now authorized to operate towards coast forthwith, in conjunction with French and Belgian armies.

Gort finally had approval for the action he had taken. The BEF had already begun trickling back, as had elements of the French 1st Army. But the Allied command remained plagued by misunderstanding and cross purposes. General Blanchard still did not know, and was not informed, that the British troops were pulling back in order to be evacuated to England. Equally in the dark about British intentions was Admiral Jean Abrial, the French officer in command of the Dunkirk area, whose permission was by rights required before the mass evacuation could proceed. He could only be informed through the chain of command which went through Paris, from which he heard not so much as a whisper on the subject.

Calais was still holding out. For Brigadier Nicholson and the men under his command besieged in the city, it was another day of German air raids, artillery bombardment and ground assaults. The attacks grew heavier as the day wore on and German impatience with the stubbornness of the defenders intensified. Sustaining heavy casualties, the defenders were forced back, fighting as they went, district by district, street by street, separated into smaller and smaller groups in the rubble to which their positions were methodically reduced. Brigadier Nicholson was captured in the afternoon. Though low in ammunition, many of his men fought on until they were over-whelmed. By nightfall, their resistance was crushed and the survivors were taken prisoner and led away in captivity as well.

It is difficult to determine whether the defenders of Calais were needlessly sacrificed. Two days before the city fell, plans had been afoot to evacuate them. But then Nicholson was informed that the French commander of the Channel ports, in accordance with orders from Paris, 'forbids evacuation'. By holding out, the men would disrupt the German advance up the coast. But by the time Calais fell to the enemy, some German units had already by-passed the city on their way towards Dunkirk. The question remains whether the men stayed put only 'for the sake of Allied solidarity', as the War Office put it, at a time when the French were openly indignant about British abandon-ment or whether the Calais defenders served a useful purpose right to the end by tying down at least one German armoured division, giving Allied forces further along the coast more of a chance to strengthen the defence lines between the enemy and the last remaining bolt hole at Dunkirk.

The value of that bolt hole was still in doubt. It depended on whether the BEF could withdraw through the narrow corridor to the sea and then be successfully lifted off. General Pownall noted in his diary, 'Whether we ever get to the sea, how we get off the beach, how many of us survive is on the knees of the Gods. But it's the only thing to be done. We cannot stay here without being surrounded and there is no other direction in which to go.' General Brooke, one of Gort's three corps commanders and later Chief of the Imperial General Staff, believed, ' . . . we shall be lucky if we save 25 per cent of the BEF.'

The Canal Line, guarding Gort's right flank, was now as organized as it would ever be. It was composed of four BEF divisions, none at full strength. Facing them were six German armoured and four motorized divisions of von Rundstedt's Army Group A, still waiting for permission from Hitler to resume their advance. Three of the British divisions on the Canal Line were Territorial reserves; one had originally been sent to France only for training and support duties. Now its task was to stand fast and shield part of the BEF's line of retreat.

On Gort's left sector, four of his other divisions confronted von Bock's Army Group B which, not equipped with any significant amount of armour, was not subject to Hitler's halt order. Guarding the line covering the last twenty miles to the sea on that flank were the Belgians – pummelled, bloodied, and near to collapse. Their condition had been fast deteriorating during the day. A succession of Stuka onslaughts followed by sustained infantry assaults had them reeling. If they caved in completely, the Germans would plunge through and race down to take Dunkirk from up the coast.

Weygand was informed in the afternoon that the Belgian army would fight on to block the enemy advance so long as its supplies held out but that it had 'nearly reached the limit of its endurance'. There was nothing he could do about it. He didn't bother to reply. He was more concerned about the fate of the remains of the badly mauled French 1st Army which was under fire around Lille, at the far end of the corridor to the sea, furthest from Dunkirk to which it still had not been ordered to retreat.

By late in the day, Hitler, ever fearful of an unexpected reversal of his fortunes, was once again agonizing over the progress of the campaign. Though Boulogne had been taken, Calais was about to fall, and aerial bombardment had shattered Dunkirk harbour, the complete destruction of the Allied armies in the northern pocket was taking too long. Despite Goering's promises, the *Luftwaffe* had failed to do the job and Army Group B, which should have been moving in for the kill through Belgium, had not yet crashed through Belgian lines and was meeting very stubborn resistance from British troops protecting most of Gort's left flank.

The crescendo of complaints among Hitler's generals about the immobilized panzers on the Canal Line mounted during the day. 'Our armoured and mechanized forces are standing motionless,' Chief of Staff Halder moaned, ' . . . as though they were rooted to the

ground . . . At this rate it can take weeks to clear up the cauldron . . .'
Hitler found that prospect intolerable. His earlier fears that the Allies
were preparing to break out toward the south to snip off his advance had
proved groundless; no move was being made in that direction. It was
time, he decided, to wind up the operation.

Late that day, he cancelled the order which had kept his armour from
closing the trap around the Allied troops beginning to scamper back
towards the sea. At about the same time, the machinery that would give
the name Dunkirk a unique place in military history was being set in
motion across the English Channel.

At three minutes to seven o'clock at night, Admiral Ramsay at Dover
received a signal from the Admiralty in London – 'Operation Dynamo is
to commence.' A subsequent message told him, 'It is imperative for
Dynamo to be implemented with the greatest vigour.' The object would
be to lift 'up to 45,000 men' from Dunkirk within two days, 'at the end of
which it is probable that evacuation will be terminated by enemy
action'.

No word was given on what was expected to happen to the rest of the
BEF – almost a quarter of a million troops. Were they to be written off?
Things were happening too quickly to give that question the attention it
deserved. Thoughts focused on getting home as many men as possible.
Ironside believed that even the low estimate in Operation Dynamo's
launch orders of the number of men who could be rescued was
optimistic. He thought the BEF would be lucky to evacuate thirty
thousand. The desperation with which Dynamo was launched was
thickly clouded by premonitions of débâcle.

It was also complicated by limited appreciation of what exactly was
involved. Available to Ramsay for evacuation purposes as the operation
began were thirty-five passenger ships (mostly cross-Channel ferries),
sixty-two coasters, barges and flat-bottomed Dutch skoots, and a variety
of supply craft. Ramsay had jumped the gun and had sent rescue vessels
over to Dunkirk that afternoon. But aside from small ships, he was
planning a flow of only 'two vessels every four hours'. At that stage,
comparatively few troops had yet reached Dunkirk to be evacuated. The
order for them to make for the coast was only just beginning to circulate
among units which were not deployed keeping the Germans from
cutting the escape corridor. It was pointless and dangerous to dispatch
vessels for whom no evacuees would yet be available and destroyers were
too badly needed for protection purposes in the Channel and elsewhere
to be earmarked for evacuation duty. It was as if bringing home only a
small fraction of the BEF in the forty-eight hours before the Germans
were expected to close in was to be a self-fulfilling prophecy.

Hopes of lifting men from the Dunkirk beaches, as well as from what was left of the harbour, were dimmed by the fact that at that stage Admiral Ramsay had few craft at his disposal capable of getting in close to the shore without grounding – only some motor boats from the Anti-Smuggling Control Base at Ramsgate, a few fishing drifters and four passenger launches. Ramsay pleaded with the Admiralty to find him additional small craft to work the beaches. But it seemed certain that the bulk of the British army was about to be left in France at the mercy of the Germans, a prospect which Gort, increasingly impatient with his superiors as the situation grew more critical, was convinced London was unable to comprehend.

The experience of ships returning to English ports that day after having run the gauntlet to and from Dunkirk harbour did nothing to convince anyone that Operation Dynamo could succeed. They had been attacked from the air and shelled by enemy guns on the coast, and the harbour itself was a heap of rubble. Arriving off Dunkirk during a heavy air raid, the passenger ferry *Maid of Orleans* was forced to turn back to Dover and had to make a second crossing later to get on belatedly with its assigned task.

Just as Chamberlain had to make way for a more dynamic British leader sixteen days earlier, so General Ironside was required to shift on May 26th from his position as Chief of the Imperial General Staff. Top level military misunderstandings and confusions by the British High Command as well as by the French were recognized as having been partly responsible for the blunderings in France and Belgium. Besides, the Germans were demonstrating that this was a totally different sort of war than had ever been fought before. Under the circumstances, General Sir John Dill, an expert in mechanized warfare, was thought better suited to be Britain's top soldier and was named to replace Ironside, to the relief of many senior officers who believed the move was long overdue.

His extensive command experience still valued, the former chief of staff was put in charge of the British Home Forces instead. It was a much less prestigious post than the one he was leaving but with an invasion threatening, it was taking on ever greater significance. A substantial catalogue of measures for home defence had already been implemented. Now they needed tightening and extension. Coastal defences had to be improved and the expansion of the army – there were only three trained divisions on home ground at the time – had to be rapidly accelerated.

Civil defence measures also had to be more vigorously implemented across the country. Instructions were, for example, issued that day for car owners all over Britain to make certain their vehicles were immobilized at night so that enemy agents landed under cover of darkness would not be able to use them, and for garages to put their petrol pumps out of commission at the end of each working day. Britain was to be ready for the enemy on home ground. Even Buckingham Palace had sand-bagged machine gun emplacements at its gates.

With almost all of the army's heavy equipment expected to be lost in France, the production of war supplies, already receiving priority attention, became an even greater concern. The Minister of Supply, Herbert Morrison, a former chairman of the Labour Party, warned workers against anything that might impede war production. 'In war', Morrison told people working in war factories, 'you are all public servants'. He cautioned them against 'irresponsible mischief-makers who . . . may be "Fifth Column" elements – even direct or indirect agents of the enemy'.

> If any man should come whispering in your ear that you should go slow on your job, that for the nation to demand of you sacrifices for victory is to attack your security and your future – know that man for what he is: a traitor, an enemy more insidious, more dangerous than any parachute trooper.

In Washington, the American government was short on details but President Roosevelt had a good idea of how desperate the Allied position had become. Personal messages from Churchill conveyed a sense of deepest anxiety and cables from Ambassador Bullitt in Paris reported the mood of imminent doom which permeated the French capital. American military attachés in Berlin, Paris and London passed word along of the general state of play on the battlefield. A United States military attaché in Berlin reported that 'whether the Allied forces can counter-attack effectively enough to hold the German advance and stabilize the front is a question which will decide the outcome of the entire war'.

The remarkable speed with which Hitler's forces had smashed through Allied defences and the prospect of an Allied collapse aroused profound consternation in Washington. In New York's Times Square, hushed crowds watched news bulletins about the German onslaught flash around Times Tower. Whatever people thought about rights and wrongs in the war, few had previously considered American interests to be seriously and perhaps immediately imperilled. But now it was realized that Nazi Germany might very soon be in a position to directly threaten the national security of the United States. Until then, the War Department's basic contingency defence plans – codenamed *Rainbow* – had concentrated on the Western Pacific and the threat posed by Japanese expansionism there. Now the Department's Joint Planning Committee hurriedly began revising *Rainbow*.

It proceeded on the worst case assumption that Britain as well as France was about to be defeated and that after that defeat, the United States would be faced by a hostile German-Italian-Japanese coalition. The naval power of this axis of adversaries, bolstered by portions of the British and French fleets seized by the Germans, would considerably exceed that of the United States. Reports circulated that Hitler had threatened to exact a toll of a million British lives if the British fleet was not turned over to him at the time of his victory. While Britain and France pleaded for American war supplies, the White House was urged by its military strategists to consider drastic measures closer to home. Roosevelt was advised to order the 'protective occupation' of the British West Indies and other British, French, Dutch and Danish possessions in the Western Hemisphere if Nazi conquest of the Allies appeared about to be achieved. Roosevelt was bombarded with advice from experts and others on the subject:

> . . . if the bad boys win, or even gain a definite temporary advantage over the more decent boys abroad . . . it is an absolute certainty that we will be baited and badgered and insulted and annoyed with all sorts of incidents of a political, commercial or colonizing nature, which eventually will force some sort of violent unpleasant showdown . . . Nothing the present administration could do would more intrigue both public and press than a sound, vigorous program for complete West Indian control for all time and the center of that control being moved to Washington D. C. – not dictated by squabbling capitals in Europe.

Roosevelt took such warnings and advice seriously. In a message to Congress, he spelled out his worries about the dangers of German incursions in the Western Hemisphere:

> . . . if [the British colony of] Bermuda fell into hostile hands it is a matter of less than three hours for modern bombers to reach our shores. From a base in the outer West Indies, the coast of Florida could be reached in 200 minutes. The islands off the west coast of Africa are only 1,500 miles from Brazil. Modern planes starting from the Cape Verde Islands can be over Brazil in seven hours. And Pará, Brazil is but four flying hours to Caracas, Venezuela, and Venezuela but two-and-a-half hours to Cuba and the Canal Zone, and Cuba and the Canal Zone are two-and-a-quarter hours to Tampico, Mexico; and Tampico is two-and-a-quarter hours to St. Louis, Kansas City and Omaha.

Though most eyes were focused on Europe, Latin America was the area of priority concern for the United States government and military command. There were large and politically active German minorities in several South American countries. Unconfirmed reports said that armed Germans were already in training in southern Brazil where there had been an attempted fascist coup the previous year. Large German embassies were maintained in all Latin American capitals and Germany had developed extensive commercial interests throughout the region, including control of several commercial airlines which flew mostly seventeen-seater, three-engine Junker aircraft, easily converted into bombers.

A War Plans Division memorandum to the State Department suggested that the United States 'initiate conversations at the earliest practicable date with all American republics' for the purpose of defending them 'against all foreign interventions and activity that may threaten them'. It was pointed out that this might 'require the employment of means beyond the present ability of individual American states to provide', in which case, the United States would be ready and willing to lend a hand. The implication was that American dominance in the hemisphere would be invoked if necessary to persuade Latin American countries disinclined to cooperate. 'Assurances should be sought . . . that their existing airdromes, ports and port facilities, as well as anchorages in their territorial waters, will be available to the United States as required'. A War Department general staff memo was even more explicit:

> The only sure way of preventing the surprise overthrow of existing South American governments by German inspired activities is to have adequate force or what appears to be adequate force present on the spot prior to the need for its employment . . . A naval vessel or vessels ostensibly on courtesy visits can be put into critical South American harbours without delay. Detachments of sailors or marines from such vessels might provide the necessary deterrent or the necessary force to accomplish our object.

Countries of particular concern included Argentina, Chile, Colombia, Uruguay and Venezuela. But the primary focus was on Brazil where the US embassy staff reported that many government and army officials were pro-German. Even the Gestapo had established a presence in Rio de Janeiro and German influence was spreading. The *New York Times* ominously reported that a German visitor to Rio de Janeiro had told an elevator boy there to learn to speak the German language because 'You're going to need it'.

The Admiralty in London did nothing to discourage American alarm at German incursions in the Western Hemisphere. On May 24th, it had passed along word – which the United States was in no position to confirm or contradict – that six thousand Nazis had been

boarded on to German merchant ships and might be heading for Brazil
where they could join Nazi sympathizers already there to seize the
government. The following day, President Roosevelt directed his
Chief of Naval Operations to prepare secret plans for transporting an
advance guard of ten thousand American troops to Brazil by air if and
when a German threat materialized there. They were to be followed by
100,000 troops sent by sea. A plan – codenamed *Pot-of-Gold* – was
drawn up earmarking four battleships, two aircraft carriers, nine
cruisers and three squadrons of destroyers for the operation.

On the night of May 26th, Roosevelt went on radio to broadcast one
of his fireside chats. His aim was to prepare the American people for
the disagreeable steps that he believed the United States would
ultimately be compelled to take:

> Tonight over the once peaceful roads of Belgium and France, millions
> are now moving, running from their homes to escape bombs and shells
> and fire and machine gunning, without shelter and almost wholly
> without food. They stumble on, knowing not where the end of the road
> will be . . . There are many among us who in the past closed their eyes
> to events abroad – because they believed . . . that what was taking place
> in Europe was none of our business; that no matter what happened over
> there, the United States could always pursue its peaceful and unique
> course in the world . . . To [them], to those who would not admit the
> possibility of the approaching storm . . . the past two weeks have meant
> the shattering of many illusions. They have lost the illusion that we are
> remote and isolated and therefore secure against the dangers from
> which no other land is free.

The President assured Americans that whatever steps were needed
would be taken to guarantee the defences of their country. 'We shall
build them', he promised, 'to whatever heights the future may
require'. He did not confine his thoughts to domestic defence. 'We
defend', he said, 'and we build a way of life, not for America alone,
but for all mankind. Ours is a high duty, a noble task.'

Roosevelt's comments were derided by isolationists as another of his
moves to nudge the United States into the European quagmire. Frank
Gannett, a candidate for the still-to-be-decided Republican Party's
presidential nomination, dismissed Roosevelt's speech as a charade
meant to scare the American people, much like the famous Orson
Welles radio fantasy about an invasion of Earth by Martians.

Though more concerned about security in the Western Hemisphere, close consideration was indeed being given by Roosevelt to the
incessant pleas from Britain and France for planes and other war
material. But even if Congress would give its approval for the shipment

of war supplies, almost everything was in short supply and could not be spared. The US Army had only 160 P-40 fighter planes for its 260 fighter pilots, and only 52 bombers. The Army's Ordnance Division allowed that it could release five hundred First World War field guns, half a million Enfield rifles, 35,000 machine guns and five hundred mortars. But Roosevelt was barred by law from sending abroad any war material that was not surplus to the defence needs of the United States and questions were raised about whether those weapons could really be considered surplus in view of America's military unpreparedness. So as Britain launched a desperate, apparently hopeless operation to rescue its trapped army, the American government could offer nothing but sympathy and good wishes.

By midnight on this first day of Operation Dynamo, 27,936 men had been brought back to England from Dunkirk. But these were still 'useless mouths' whose evacuation had earlier been ordered. The fighting troops, the men upon whom Britain depended to guard its shores against invasion and form the core of a resurgent army, were still a long way from home and in deep trouble.

## Chapter 6 – DAY TWO OF DUNKIRK

# Outlook Grim

WITH DYNAMO made operational the previous night, the exodus from Dunkirk began in earnest on May 27th. *Mona's Isle*, a Royal Navy armed boarding vessel, was the first back that morning. Its journey was not the kind to raise hopes. It had reached Dunkirk the previous night during a German bombing raid but had managed to take 1,420 troops on board. However, on its return voyage, it was hit by shells from enemy guns on the shore and strafed by German aircraft. By the time it had completed its run back to Dover, twenty-three men on board had been killed and another sixty wounded. Five other vessels sent to join in the evacuation that day came under such heavy fire from shore-based enemy artillery before they reached Dunkirk that they turned back without a single evacuee. And two strings of small boats towed by a tug for use in picking men up off the beaches for transfer to ships offshore were scattered and lost en route after their lines were severed.

German control of the coast below Dunkirk dangerously complicated the rescue operation. Because of the sandbars and shallows that made the waters off Dunkirk a graveyard for ships, the shortest run from Dover, covering a distance of thirty-nine miles, skirted part of the French coast and brought vessels within range of German shore batteries on the coast above Calais. Alternate routes had to be followed. An indirect fifty-five mile route traversed waters that had been mined by the Germans. It had not yet been fully swept and only warships had been degaussed against magnetic mines, but time was pressing and vessels were sent through them anyway to begin loading men. An eighty-seven mile route took vessels into the North Sea before turning south-westward off Ostend to reach Dunkirk. The longer two routes were out of range of the enemy artillery but exposed ships to more protracted danger from German air and torpedo attack. The time factor was also important. Vessels navigating those sea lanes took far longer than the two-hours-each-way more direct run. It meant even fewer men than expected were likely to be evacuated before the Germans moved in to capture Dunkirk and close down Operation Dynamo.

It meant also that it was even more essential than before that the operation be efficiently superintended on the Dunkirk end. A senior officer was needed on the shore to organize the lift-off and maintain direct liaison between the BEF and the Royal Navy. That assignment fell to Royal Navy Captain William Tennant, Chief Staff Officer of Britain's First Sea Lord. Named Senior Naval Officer Dunkirk, Tennant hurried from London to Dover that morning to be briefed and to gather together a staff of twelve officers and 160 seamen, before setting off across the Channel to get on with the job. Given no idea what their assignment was to be but instructed to travel light, one of those officers brought along tennis shorts. Summoned at a church service in Portsmouth, another officer went directly to Dover still attired in full service dress.

Across the Channel, senior Allied army officers met that morning to plan the defence of Dunkirk and its surrounding area. Lieutenant-General Sir Ronald Adam, commanding the BEF's 3rd Corps, was assigned by Gort to organize a defence of the Dunkirk perimeter. At seven a.m., at the Hotel Sauvage in the hill town of Cassel, twenty miles inland from Dunkirk, Adam met with Lieutenant-General Marie Fagalde, the French officer officially in command of all Allied troops on the coast. The two men examined possibilities for establishing the perimeter defence and decided on how to go about it. The British would guard a line stretching from Nieuport on the coast across the border just inside Belgium, and leading to and along the Berques-Furnes Canal running roughly parallel to the coast about six miles inland, as far as the town of Berques. The sector of the perimeter defence held by the French would extend from Berques westward along the canal to Gravelines on the coast. A supply system for the perimeter was to be organized. Ammunition dumps and food stores were to be set up, with ships making the perilous run from Dover ferrying in the needed supplies.

After these arrangements had been made, Adam and Fagalde were joined at the hotel in Cassel by General Louis Koeltz representing General Weygand, Admiral Abrial, General Blanchard, and General Prioux to review the overall situation. None of the French gathered there had yet been informed that the British were falling back on Dunkirk to be evacuated. Adam, who knew, had no authority to confer with them on that question; his assignment had been only to deal with setting up the perimeter defence. Koeltz, Abrial, Blanchard and Prioux still understood that the fall back was only to establish a bridgehead from which the Germans would be unable to dislodge the Allied troops. They had no orders or intention to plan the abandonment of what was about to become the last enclave of northern France which had not fallen to the enemy.

This element of unreality had other dimensions as well. Koeltz transmitted to the assembled officers a proposal from Weygand for a counter-attack to relieve the troops defending Calais, unaware not only that the city had fallen to the Germans the night before but that French forces had even been driven out of Gravelines closer up the coast to Dunkirk. It was from there that German guns on the shore were shelling rescue vessels attempting to negotiate the shortest Dunkirk-Dover route. Even a German bombardment of Cassel itself while their meeting was in session there did not deter Koeltz from harbouring such far-fetched aspirations.

But he was not alone in conjuring up fantasies. Though the French at the Hotel Sauvage conclave knew nothing of evacuation plans and would have been appalled if they had, the story was different in Dover. At a meeting there that morning, during which French naval officers actually conferred with the British on procedures for evacuating both French and British troops from Dunkirk (they hadn't known about the British evacuation plans until that meeting), it was agreed that the Allies should attempt to recapture part of the French coast as far south as Cape Griz Nez, past Calais – a very unlikely prospect given the prevailing situation. It would facilitate the evacuation which otherwise was considered likely to be 'extremely difficult if not impossible'.

At that Dover meeting, the representatives of the British and French navies agreed that Admiral Ramsay would be responsible for regulating sailings of French and British vessels to Dunkirk and that Admiral Abrial, who still knew nothing about Operation Dynamo, would be 'the only authority in charge of all arrangements for berthing and loading ships at Dunkirk and on the coast'. Captain Tennant, on shore at Dunkirk organizing the evacuation of British troops, was to be under Abrial's command. The ground (and sea) rules having been established, accelerating the operation took top priority.

With the realization that great numbers of small craft would be needed to lift men from the beaches came the task of finding those craft and getting them quickly in shape for the operation. That assignment went to the Ministry of Shipping. Early that morning, H. C. Riggs of the small craft section of the ministry contacted Douglas Tough of Tough Brothers Boatyard of Teddington whose family had worked on the Thames for almost a century and who had a comprehensive knowledge of the coast and waterways of south-east England. Empowered to act as agent for the government and escorted by naval personnel, Tough went out to find the small craft and not only those which had previously been registered with the Small Vessels Pool. Many were less than ship-shape:

> There they lay in muddy estuaries and creeks, in deserted moorings, along the coast of Kent and Sussex and in the quiet reaches of the Thames . . . tarpaulined and forlorn, paintwork dirty, brasswork tarnished, water gurgling morosely in their bilges, or high and dry in a builders' yard.

The search went as far north as The Wash on the east coast and as far west as Cornwall. If the owners couldn't be contacted, their craft were taken away anyway. Few who could be contacted objected when informed that their vessels were needed by the navy for an urgent, secret operation. Even if details of the BEF's predicament weren't common knowledge, Britain's growing peril was widely understood. Some owners were asked to deliver their vessels to coastal rendezvous points and hand them over there to the navy. Others insisted on helping out by doing so.

It was one thing for the generals who had gathered at Cassel early that morning to plot out a perimeter defence for Dunkirk and for Admiral Ramsay to calculate how many ships might be needed at what intervals to get the men home. It was another thing to get the troops to the coast for those plans to have any relevance. The harsh reality for the officers charged with that task was that the initiative and overwhelming might remained with the enemy and that their own immediate problem was to find troops to plug gaps in defence lines while trying to manage an orderly, staged withdrawal down the corridor while under fire.

Men under such pressure did not react well to instructions from afar that made no sense. When Gort received a 'personal appeal' from Weygand for strong British participation in unspecified joint counter-attacks – 'Situation demands hard hitting', he was told – it confirmed his suspicion that the Allied supreme commander had taken leave of reality. The only rational objective of counter-attacks now was to keep the escape corridor open. Nor was Gort's confidence in the judgment of other senior French officers restored by General Prioux's announcement that despite the detailed arrangements made that morning for establishing a perimeter defence around Dunkirk, his 1st Army would not withdraw to the coastal area. Prioux declared there would be no further retreat by his troops. They would stand and fight. In view of superior German strength, it seemed a brave but pointless gesture even if it delayed the German advance and helped screen the BEF's withdrawal to Dunkirk.

Gort was now making only the most necessary gestures towards acknowledging French command over himself and his troops. He no longer worried overly much about behaving in an insubordinate fashion. After days of misunderstanding and cross purposes, he and London were finally in full accord. A message from the War Office that afternoon made it 'quite clear that sole task now is to evacuate to England maximum of your forces possible'.

Though Gort agreed fully, it did raise a delicate question. Was he not to concern himself at all with the evacuation of French troops? Some had already pulled back to Dunkirk. What was he to do about them if the question arose? There were differences about that in London. Mindful of Britain's obligations to its ally and still hoping that France would not capitulate, or that it would hand over its air force and navy to Britain if it were forced to, Churchill wanted nothing done to make the French believe they were being deserted by the British. That meant special consideration for potential French evacuees at Dunkirk. The War Office, however, was now concerned exclusively with bringing home as many British troops as possible to fight off the Germans when their inevitable assault on the homeland materialized. In regular contact with the BEF, the War Office was for the moment able to prevail without troubling Churchill and arousing his unwanted advice.

Gort was told that while it was eminently desirable that nothing should be done to suggest a lack of cooperation with the French, the safety of the BEF was to be his primary consideration. The French Admiralty, he was told, was taking steps to provide vessels for its end of the operation. When they appeared, evacuation facilities could be shared equally between British and French personnel. 'Until French ships materialize, however, you are authorized to use British ships for British personnel.'

That was the way the BEF commander preferred it. But from what he had been informed of Operation Dynamo, he was convinced its evacuation plans were totally inadequate. In anguish, he had the previous night dispatched Group Captain Victor Goddard, his air aide, to London to crash a Chiefs-of-Staff meeting in Whitehall in the morning to demand from the navy a much greater effort. 'I have been sent by Lord Gort', Goddard declared, 'to say that the provision made is not nearly enough . . .' In addition to Channel ferries, he said it was essential to send 'pleasure steamers, coasters, fishing boats, lifeboats, yachts, motorboats, everything that can cross the Channel'.

The audacity of this uninvited junior officer presuming to lecture his superiors was not appreciated, especially when neither Gort nor Goddard had full command of the facts. The assembly of small craft from the Thames estuary and south-east coast ports was at that moment underway and preparations were being made to dispatch them to Dunkirk to assist the larger vessels in the evacuation.

Meantime, the two German Army groups which had bludgeoned their way across Belgium and northern France were proceeding with their bid to close the trap around the Allied forces before they could reach the coast. Hitler's order to halt having been lifted late the previous day, the panzers which had been frozen in place the other side of the Canal Line for the better part of three days now launched withering attacks, resumed their forward momentum, and were firmly across the Line well before nightfall.

Once more, the disparity in force strengths was glaringly displayed in set battles. Guarding its sector of the Line, the British 2nd Division, most of whose anti-tank guns had been removed to Dunkirk, faced three panzer divisions, an SS division and parts of two other German divisions. Fighting determinedly nevertheless, it was mauled practically to extinction during the course of the day though its sacrificial perseverance made it possible for elements of four other British divisions and more than two divisions of the French 1st Army which might otherwise have been surrounded to slip back towards the coast after darkness had fallen. Then, still under fire, its battered remnants fell back as well.

It was a hard day for British troops clear across the Canal Line but hardest of all for the men of the 2nd Battalion, Royal Norfolk Regiment. They took very heavy casualties and what remained of the unit was forced to fall back. Enraged by their stubborn resistance and recalling their humiliating setback at the hands of the British at Arras the previous week, men of the SS *Totenkopf* Division took cruel vengeance on the survivors, most of whom were wounded. They had been driven back to a farm near the town of Paradis. Surrounded, outgunned and far outnumbered, they had surrendered only to be marched across the farmyard and cut down by machine-gun fire. Those who were not killed were bayoneted and finished off with pistols. Two of the men succeeded in feigning death, were captured by other German troops and survived to tell the story. After the war, the SS company commander primarily responsible was convicted by a war crimes tribunal with the help of testimony of a woman at the farm and was executed.

At virtually all points of the front, the Germans surged forward, but not without paying a price. A German officer reported, 'At every position heavy fighting has developed – especially at every village and indeed in every house . . . Casualties in personnel and equipment are grievous. The enemy are fighting tenaciously and, to the last man, remain at their posts: if they are shelled out of one position, they shortly reappear in another to carry on the fight.'

German aircraft dropped leaflets on which rough maps had been printed showing how desperate the Allied position in the north had become and calling on the troops to surrender:

BRITISH SOLDIERS!
YOU ARE ENTIRELY SURROUNDED!
PUT DOWN YOUR ARMS!

Except for men who were in no position to do anything but surrender or die, those leaflets had little effect.

Meantime, line troops were receiving orders for their staged withdrawal to the coast. These men had been fighting, retreating, digging in, fighting again, and retreating once more for days without any idea of what their objective was except to stay alive. The instructions they now were given aroused both alarm and relief among junior officers of the 2nd Battalion, Coldstream Guards, who were gathered at their makeshift headquarters in a house they had commandeered just behind the line to be told what they were to do:

> We sat down on chairs making a circle round the room, and waited. The Commanding Officer looked up and, after a pause, said, 'We are to march 55 miles back to the coast' – he paused and looked round at us. Our hearts sank. Fifty-five miles seemed a bit too much. Then he went on – 'and embark for England!' Immediate sensation. No one had expected this. We had had vague ideas of falling back as the armies of 1914 had fallen back until, somehow, sometime, we too should stand and fight our victorious battle of the Marne. But this! There was a sudden loosening of the tenseness we had been living in for so long. We felt a surge of contentment beneath our anxiety about the war news in general and our own immediate prospects in particular. Then we thought again of the 55 miles, and wondered.

Reports began reaching German commanders that a systematic evacuation, such as it was at that stage, was in progress at Dunkirk, that men were being loaded on to British ships in some sort of organized fashion and carried back to England. They did not yet suspect how massive an operation had been launched. But Major General Kurt Brennecke, chief of staff of the German 4th Army, was informed that, 'Large ships are being made fast to the quayside [at Dunkirk harbour], planks are laid across and men swarm aboard'. Brennecke was bitter at the prospect of German troops having to meet those men in combat at a subsequent date, fully rested and once more fully equipped. The *Luftwaffe* was called upon to step up its attacks and German forces pressing up along the coast forced French defenders back to positions a mere four miles from Dunkirk, within easy artillery range of the city.

Further inland, along the escape corridor, road congestion was gravely complicating the withdrawal to the coast. Operation Dynamo had barely begun but already the main roads leading back from the front to the comparative safety of the Dunkirk perimeter were clogged with human and vehicular traffic. In addition to the problem of the refugees, attempts to assign separate withdrawal routes to the British and French commands proved futile. French troops did not appreciate being told that certain roads in their own country were reserved for use by the British. As his report later indicated, Gort was enraged by the resulting muddle.

> The [withdrawal] plan, as agreed [with General Blanchard], envisaged the reservation of certain roads for the exclusive use of the BEF. In fact, however, French troops and transport continued to use them, and this added very considerably to the difficulties of the withdrawal of British troops. The roads were few and for the most part narrow, and . . . they were badly congested with marching troops and horsed transport of French formations, and with refugees.

General Pownall, for whom the tragedy of France at that moment was dwarfed by the BEF's predicament, complained, 'It is no good having boundaries and roads allotted as between ourselves and the French. They pay no attention and do exactly what they damn well like.'

The danger of congestion within the Dunkirk perimeter also posed a problem. If all vehicles heading that way were permitted to enter the perimeter, nothing would be able to move within it. BEF headquarters accordingly ordered that vehicles be abandoned off the road outside the coastal defence zone. Troops heading for evacuation were to be required to make their way on foot the last few miles to the harbour and the beaches. That was easier to decree than enforce.

The withdrawal to the coast came under relentless air attack. Messerschmitt fighters strafed the retreating troops and the positions screening their fall back. Dorniers and Heinkels bombed them. Stukas screamed out of the sky at them to release their deadly payloads. Gort pleaded with London to supply his men with the strongest possible fighter cover but RAF Fighter Command was finding the role it was assigned in the operation impossible to fulfil.

It was instructed to 'ensure the protection of Dunkirk beaches (three miles on either side) from first light until darkness by continuous fighter patrols in strength' and in addition to 'have due regard to the protection of bomber sorties and the provision of support in the BEF area'. Fighter Command couldn't possibly do all of that, not if the skies over Britain itself and British cities were to be guarded against the expected massive *Luftwaffe* onslaught from the continent.

For purposes of air defence, Fighter Command chief Dowding had divided Britain into four geographic areas, each the responsibility of a Fighter Command 'Group'. The task of providing aerial cover for Operation Dynamo fell to 11 Group whose bailiwick was south-east England, closest to the coast of northern France. Air Vice Marshal Keith Park, 11 Group commander, had at his disposal sixteen squadrons – about two hundred planes, depending on serviceability. The Germans were throwing three hundred bombers, with 550 fighter escorts, into this stage of the battle.

To cover the operation, RAF fighters had to fly at least fifty miles from their bases in south-east England – including Biggin Hill, Hawkinge, Kenley and Manston – and then fifty miles back, their planes devouring so much fuel in the process that if they engaged in dogfights they might be limited to as little as twenty minutes over the Dunkirk area before having to head home. They were beyond the range of British radar stations and had to rely entirely on visual contact which meant they had to patrol the area in search of the enemy. Under those conditions, there was no way they could possibly provide uninterrupted cover seventeen hours a day for the BEF falling back on Dunkirk, as well as for the troops already there, and for the ships which were to carry them home.

But cover had to be provided and a system had to be devised to provide it as adequately as possible. None of the three possible solutions was satisfactory. Committing Fighter Command's entire fleet of aircraft, with the possibility that it would be decimated and that mastery of the air over England would thus be delivered to the enemy, had to be ruled out. Dispatching regular large patrols of fighters would mean there would be long intervals between patrols in which there would be no RAF presence at all in the skies over the Dunkirk pocket. Sending smaller patrols would make it possible to shorten those intervals but they would be at a greater disadvantage against the large formations of attacking aircraft the Germans were sending aloft.

The last of these options was chosen. Small patrols of between eight and twenty fighters were dispatched to keep the intervals between flights as brief as possible. That first full day of the evacuation, British fighters, taking off in small groups from first light until nightfall, flew 287 sorties, reverting automatically to on-call status for home defence after and between their missions. Coming up against waves of up to fifty enemy aircraft, they shot down ten enemy aircraft and lost fourteen of their own – an ominous ratio.

Many of the British pilots had never been in combat before. Dunkirk provided a jolting baptism of fire for them. No matter what sort of training they had had, not till their first dogfights did they really learn what their Spitfires and Hurricanes, or the enemy aircraft, were capable of:

> We were jumped by [Messerschmitt] 109s. It was the first time we had met the enemy. All of a sudden the sky was full of aircraft with black crosses on them. It was frightening because I realized for the first time that there was somebody up there who was really trying to kill me. It was a moment of truth.

German squadron leaders took full advantage of the lack of experience of their British counterparts. They would send over a single decoy aircraft. When British fighters roared in to shoot it down, Messerschmitts hovering in the sun thousands of feet above would come thundering down to deal with them.

But inexperience and being outnumbered were not the only problems with which British fighter pilots had to contend. The flight and combat tactics they had been taught, and which still were being drilled into them by their commanders and instructors, added enormously to their difficulties. Unlike the Germans, they flew in V formations so tight that all except the formation leader had to concentrate on staying in place rather than on scanning the skies for the enemy who might be swooping in from above, behind or the side. In addition, back armour for fighter pilots – soon to be provided – was mistakenly thought to add too much weight to the Spitfire and make it less manoeuvrable. Pilots who would have survived were lost as a result. One squadron lost five pilots and five Spitfires during the first two days of Operation Dynamo and had to be pulled out of the patrols to be reconstituted.

The Spitfires and Hurricanes at first approached the combat zone too low – ten thousand feet or lower, to be pounced on by the 109s plunging down at them out of the sun from much higher vantage points. The pilots quickly learned that was a mistake. It took them longer to learn that the Germans were monitoring their radio chatter and would often wait until they told each other they were heading for home before beginning their attack on the troops on the ground and the ships offshore.

Criticism of the RAF had already become a steady refrain among the troops on the ground. They had been repeatedly strafed and bombed but had rarely seen a British aircraft come to their defence. Nevertheless, even on that first full day of the evacuation, despite its problems, the RAF succeeded in disrupting many of the German aerial attacks. Its efforts weren't much observed or appreciated on the ground because of its limited resources and because of the fairly extensive stretch of land it had to cover, both along the coast and inland. But without the RAF's contribution to Operation Dynamo, German mastery of the sky would have gone unchallenged over the evacuation zone and the Dunkirk episode very likely would have ended in slaughter and surrender for the BEF.

In Paris, the sense of impending doom was taking ever tighter hold. Rumours that a German drive to take the city was imminent circulated widely. Police raided hotels and patrolled streets looking for enemy saboteurs and fifth columnists. Thousands of people were stopped and required to produce identification papers. Parisians who could afford to do so fled to the south and south-west of the country to escape, their cars crammed with whatever valuables they could carry. So many left that within the capital, vehicle traffic was down to a trickle.

The government was convinced that Italy, taking heart from Germany's military successes in the north and France's disarray, was about to invade the country from the south-east and that Mussolini's forces could no more be effectively repelled than Hitler's had been. Pétain no longer made much effort to disguise his belief that the war was already lost. He was more concerned that troops be alerted to deal with the danger of domestic disorder, leading to a Communist coup. Beginning to lose heart as well, Weygand spoke openly of Britain's 'refusal to fight' and wondered how France could be expected to struggle on when its allies did nothing but retreat. The countdown to capitulation had begun.

In London, an understanding of the gravity of the situation continued to percolate down through the corridors of government. On learning that the British troops were to be evacuated from France, Minister of Transport Sir John Reith wrote in his diary, 'This is awful and awful the slaughter that will be done them in the process.' Expressions of concern were everywhere in Whitehall. Those who were not privy to restricted information asked questions about what exactly could be happening across the English Channel about which little was being revealed but which continued to engage grim visaged senior officials in a seemingly endless sequence of emergency conferences. Nothing could be learned from the newspapers or the BBC about Operation Dynamo and very little about the circumstances which had brought it into being.

At one of those emergency conferences, Churchill instructed his chiefs of staff to examine how Britain would manage fighting on alone against Germany if that became necessary. The reply later that day was depressing. The Prime Minister was told that Germany held 'most of the cards', that the deciding factor would be air power, and that the German air force outnumbered the RAF in the skies by a ratio of four to one. As long as the RAF could fight off the *Luftwaffe*, a sea-borne invasion of Britain was unlikely. But if the Germans did gain superiority in the skies over England, all might be lost. If the enemy succeeded in landing forces in strength, the country's ground defences, as they then existed, might not be capable of repelling them. It would be essential to deal promptly with initial landings either from the air or on the coast.

Defence plans had to be prepared for any eventuality. They could not be blinkered by conventional thinking. The Germans had shown themselves to be shrewd adversaries capable of imaginative exploits. While it was natural to plan for dealing with scattered landing attempts, it was essential to consider how to prevent enemy tanks which might be landed piecemeal from converging to form an armoured division against which defence on the flatlands of southern England would be difficult indeed.

According to the chiefs of staff, morale of the troops and the civil population would be a critical factor in determining the outcome of the struggle. Churchill was a distinct asset on that score. Building and sustaining popular morale were among his strongest qualities as a war leader. Appearing always to be confident and articulately indomitable, he was determined never to display the slightest suspicion that defeat could be on the cards. However, Lord Halifax remained unswayed by expressions of hope and defiance when the BEF was on the verge of extinction and when the facts threatened death and destruction. A junior official at 10 Downing Street noted in his diary, 'there are signs that Halifax is being defeatist'.

At a meeting of the War Cabinet that day, he pressed Churchill to be realistic. 'Suppose', the Foreign Secretary said, 'the French army collapsed and Herr Hitler made an offer of peace terms. Suppose the French government said [to the Germans], "We are unable to deal with an offer made to France alone and you must deal with the Allies together." Suppose Herr Hitler, being anxious to end the war through knowledge of his own internal weaknesses, offered terms to France and England, would the Prime Minister be prepared to discuss them?' Refusing to be cornered, Churchill replied that in such circumstances, he would not join France in asking for terms but would be prepared to discuss them if told what they were.

Halifax was not at all reassured by either the Prime Minister's response or his general attitude. His own attitude had shifted since he had told Oxford students three months earlier that 'evil must be met by force'. Now deeply anxious about Britain's prospects, he was convinced that Churchill was ignoring the grave danger that confronted the nation and was offering little but emotional responses embellished with fine phrases. After what he called the 'long and rather confused discussion' at the War Cabinet meeting, he wrote in his diary, 'I thought Winston talked the most frightful rot'. He felt that if the Prime Minister continued to act the way he did, 'our views must separate . . . It does drive me to despair when he works himself up into a passion of emotion when he ought to make his brain think and reason'. To Cadogan he declared, 'I can't work with Winston any longer.' 'Nonsense', Cadogan replied. 'His rodomontades probably bore you as much as they do me, but don't do anything silly under the stress of that.'

Reports and rumours of a serious rift within the War Cabinet spread beyond Whitehall. Ambassador Kennedy cabled Washington that, 'If the Germans made Britain along with France an offer of peace there would be a row in the Cabinet between the "do or die" group and the "group that want a settlement".'

> Only a miracle can save the British Expeditionary Force from being wiped out or . . . surrender . . . Churchill, Attlee, and others will want to fight to the death, but there will be other members who realize that physical destruction of men and property in England will not be a proper offset to a loss of pride . . . The English people, while they suspect a terrible situation, really do not realize how bad it is. When they do, I don't know which group they will follow – the do or die, or the group that wants a settlement.

That Britain might succumb, leaving Hitler triumphant and unchallenged, intensified concern in Washington. Secretary of State Welles recalled later, 'Those were the days in Washington when maps of the European front appeared in all government offices. Every morning an officer of the G-2 [Intelligence Section] of the War Department would bring to the Department of State a map of France with the latest progress of the German Armies marked upon it.'

On the Haymarket off Piccadilly Circus in Central London, Americans lined up at the offices of the United States Lines to book sea passage home. The ocean liner *President Roosevelt*, named after Theodore rather than Franklin Roosevelt, was being dispatched to pick up United States citizens paying the £75 fare who could make their way to Galway in Ireland where the liner was due to dock the following week.

Despite prevailing isolationist sentiment in the United States, anglophile White House and State Department officials kept British diplomatic personnel in Washington reasonably well informed of American government thinking and planning. Word that the United States was pondering annexation of the British West Indies and other British territories in the Western Hemisphere for national security reasons did not sit well in London. Lord Lothian, British ambassador in the American capital, cabled a suggestion to London that Britain offer to lease bases in Newfoundland, Bermuda and Trinidad to America so that American forces might merely take over responsibility for their defence, relieving Britain of that obligation. But Churchill, for whom the possibility of American annexation at that stage must have seemed both far-fetched and outrageous, wasn't interested unless Britain was offered something more substantial in return. Despite his intimacy with Roosevelt, he was exasperated at the failure of America to contribute to his righteous crusade against the forces of wickedness in Europe. He told the War Cabinet that Britain had received from the United States 'practically no help in the war'; it appeared to be interested exclusively in its own defence.

Churchill knew that Roosevelt was genuinely sympathetic to the Allied cause and that he was hamstrung by public opinion. He did not take offence at Roosevelt's suggestion that if dire circumstances required and the Royal Navy remained intact, the war against Germany could be carried on by the British from Canada. He and others in London had already pondered the possibility. However, the War Cabinet was not overly impressed when the President suggested that, if the British government and Royal family were forced into exile, the King should go to Bermuda rather than Canada because Americans wouldn't take kindly to the idea of a monarchy based on North American soil. Deeply offended, some ministers wondered whether Roosevelt might be thinking of how nice it would be 'to pick up the bits of the British Empire' if Britain were vanquished. The United States had to be cautioned not to be hasty. Secretary of State for Air Sir Archibald Sinclair said Washington had to be made to understand that Britain intended to fight on despite its setbacks.

Churchill agreed emphatically. But he was more troubled by the possibility that people in Britain itself might be led to believe otherwise and that they might succumb to a desire for a short-cut solution to the country's dilemma – an agreement with Hitler that would leave Germany dominant on the continent and well placed to challenge Britain's independence some time in the future. Halifax, an honourable, patriotic Englishman who could not be accused of underestimating the malevolence of Hitler and the Nazis, was already providing the argument that could easily grasp the popular imagination. The reasoning was deceptively simple: Yes, fight on at all costs if Britain's independence is at stake. But if guarantees can be extracted from Hitler that British independence would not be jeopardized by an armistice, why not consider an offer from Berlin which would save British cities from the kind of devastation that had flattened Rotterdam? What could be lost by just talking with the Germans about it through intermediaries when things otherwise looked so grim?

With preliminary reports from Dunkirk not at all reassuring, with the bulk of the British Army possibly heading for captivity, Churchill was keenly aware of how delicate his own position remained. His speeches were well received but he had yet to show any significant contribution to the cause of Britain's survival. There had been nothing to change the view of many in the Tory Party that he was nothing more than a pushy political lothario and windbag while Halifax remained a much respected figure throughout the land. If further serious setbacks lay ahead for Britain on the field of battle, Churchill knew he could be made to take the route Chamberlain had just travelled to political oblivion. He, and his moving call for an outlay of 'blood, toil, tears and sweat' to ensure Britain's survival as an independent, proud nation, could be brushed aside to make way for Halifax and his passionate but potentially disastrous concern to save Britain from the horror and devastation of the war brought home.

By midday, Captain Tennant had been briefed in Dover on the formidable task that would be his as Senior Naval Officer supervising the evacuation at Dunkirk. That afternoon, he and much of his staff crossed the Channel aboard the destroyer *Wolfhound* to begin the job. They soon began to appreciate the hazards with which they and the evacuees would have to contend. En route, the *Wolfhound* was repeatedly dive bombed and forced to take evasive action while its guns tried to blast attacking Stukas out of the sky. They had no great success at that but it was frightening to realize amidst the din and fury that many of the vessels to be dispatched for the troops would not be well armed and would be capable only of making a gesture at best of fighting back.

Difficult as the crossing had been, it had not been enough to prepare Tennant for the sight that awaited him at his destination. He had never before seen a city on fire. Dunkirk appeared to be an inferno. Flames and a thick curtain of black smoke rose clear across the horizon and the stench of burning oil was everywhere. German bombers had that day unloaded two thousand tons of high explosives and incendiaries on the city. A thousand civilians had been killed as had many of the British,

French and Belgian troops who had been separated from their units and who had converged on Dunkirk over the previous few days to take shelter in its nooks and crannies.

The nightmare continued as Tennant and his party, having debarked, made their way to Bastion 32, Admiral Abrial's harbour-side bunker-like fortress headquarters where the local British command had been given office space, and then went to examine the damage Dunkirk had sustained. Bombed for days, the city was rubble, its streets covered with the wreckage of buildings and the remains of burnt-out vehicles. Dead bodies and the carcasses of horses were strewn about. Tram wires were down all over.

Some British troops had taken refuge in the cellars of buildings and some of them were trapped and killed when those buildings had collapsed. Among those who survived, some were almost unhinged by the experience. An officer told of an NCO, a decorated First World War veteran, crying quietly in the corner of a cellar and how 'several men [there] began to make queer little animal noises – rather like homesick dogs'.

By evening, the troops who had sought these makeshift, dangerous sanctuaries in the city had been ordered to head instead for the beaches and dunes where they would receive further orders. Some soldiers who had thrown away their arms wandered about dazed or drunk. An angry group who hadn't discarded their rifles, apparently crazed by the bombing and angered by the sight of the clean, neat naval uniforms of Tennant's party, advanced threateningly on them but were jollied into submission.

Even more than the city, the harbour had been blasted into wreckage by the aerial bombardment. With deepening dismay, Tennant inspected what remained of the port facilities – the smashed docks and shattered cranes. The two long breakwaters shielding the outer harbour were all that remained reasonably intact. But bringing ships in to berth alongside them would be a risky, perhaps even reckless undertaking and there was nowhere else where vessels could tie up. It was hard at that moment to see how even a small proportion of the BEF could be evacuated.

The only remaining option was for small boats, great numbers of them, to come in close to the beaches east of the harbour to pick men up from the shore. They would transfer them to larger rescue vessels waiting offshore and then go back for more – a long and hazardous process completely dependent on weather conditions, RAF aerial protection, and the ability of the perimeter defence to hold back the enemy. With word reaching Tennant that the Germans had taken Calais, that their forces were moving up the coast, and that their tanks might be no more than thirty-six hours away, he realized that the evacuation plans he had discussed at Dover that morning were already out of date. He urgently signalled Dover, 'Please send every available craft to beaches east of Dunkirk immediately. Evacuation tomorrow night is problematical.'

Misunderstandings compounded the difficulties. When the transport *Canterbury* left Dunkirk after having with difficulty boarded 457 evacuees, it was instructed to turn back other ships attempting to enter the harbour. It passed word to three passenger vessels heading for Dunkirk and they all returned to Dover, although the turn back order was meant only to divert them to evacuation duty off the Dunkirk beaches. Before the confusion was cleared up, the message had been further garbled to become, 'Dunkirk is in enemy hands. Keep clear'. Hearing that, five flat-bottomed skoots turned back to England.

By then, large numbers of men had begun converging on the sands and sand dunes east of the city. Each of the BEF's three corps was assigned a different beach – III Corps was to make for Malo closest to Dunkirk harbour, II Corps was to head for La Panne across the border on the Belgian coast, and I Corps was assigned to Bray Dunes in between. But those who had already arrived were only a small fraction of the number of troops to be lifted off. If evacuation the following night was, as Tennant told Dover, indeed 'problematical', then it was reasonable to conclude that Operation Dynamo, newly launched, was already in its closing phase and that Britain was about to find itself without an army.

Apprised of the situation prevailing at Dunkirk, Admiral Ramsay, like Captain Tennant, realized that it was the wrong time and the wrong place for his plan for a methodically organized, paced flow of rescue vessels. Never before had Britain faced such a crisis. He would have to improvise, with all possible haste. All available craft at his disposal, including the precious destroyers which had been patrolling offshore, were immediately ordered to the waters off the Dunkirk beaches. All told, a cruiser, nine destroyers, two transports, four minesweepers and an assortment of other vessels were ordered to take up positions off Malo, Bray Dunes and La Panne 'with utmost despatch and embark all possible British troops . . . This our last chance of saving them'. They quickly moved into place and lowered their small boats to lift off the men ashore whom Tennant's beach control officers had begun trying, with limited success, to organize into orderly queues.

The evacuation process remained agonizingly, impossibly slow. There were too few small boats and just so much the boats available could achieve. Thirty men were picked up here, forty there, a dozen somewhere else. At the pace the boats were coming in to shore, boarding men, ferrying them out to the larger vessels at anchorage offshore, and unloading them there, the evacuation would be a fiasco. It was already failing.

In desperation, Tennant took another close look at Dunkirk's outer harbour. Its breakwaters, a mile apart at land side, angled out toward each other into open water. Made of concrete pilings, covered with boardwalk, they were about eight feet wide. There was much wreckage in the harbour, but ships could still enter. It still seemed very risky to try to bring them alongside the breakwaters to tie up there. The breakwaters had not been constructed for that purpose. But if large numbers of men were to be loaded on to ships to be taken home to England, there was no other way. The western breakwater was only about five hundred feet long and the water at its near end seemed dangerously shallow. But the eastern breakwater was almost a mile long and might serve as a pier.

A Channel ferry, *Queen of the Channel,* was anchored offshore nearby to board men lifted off the beach by small boats. Tennant signalled it to enter the harbour and tie up at the eastern breakwater. The vessel gingerly eased into place against the breakwater and, to Tennant's relief, was quickly and safely secured to stanchions. There might be boarding problems. The normal rise and fall of the tide in the harbour amounted to a difference of fifteen feet. At high tide, the men might be able to clamber straight from the breakwater on to the decks of rescue ships. At low water, they would hopefully be able to descend along gangplanks and ladders. Dover was immediately signalled that vessels could make for the harbour and Tennant's men immediately went about organizing a flow of men to tramp from the adjoining beach and along the planking of the eastern breakwater to board the ships when they arrived. It was the first hopeful development all day though the overall situation remained less than promising.

The impromptu nature of the operation showed through in various ways. Nothing, for example, had been done or said to indicate to the captains and masters of the rescue vessels that many of the men they would be taking on board would be in need of medical attention and that practically all would have gone with little food and drink for long periods of time:

> The galleys [of the destroyer *Gossamer*] were just as thronged with [evacuated] soldiers as the rest of the ship. However . . . stacks of corned beef sandwiches and gallons of cocoa were produced which were very welcome. In Dover . . . an attempt was made to replenish the stores used [for the next trip] but, apart from fuel and ammunition,

there was an astonishing reluctance to part with anything. Food? Ridiculous! Medical stores? Even more so! However, after numerous phone calls and signals our requirements were met, at least in part . . .

For the Belgian Army, May 27th had been a day of disaster. As it drew to a close, King Leopold had to make a painful decision. His army had been under almost ceaseless attack all day and its situation had become unendurable. It was short of ammunition, virtually defenceless against air attack, and split in two by the enemy. It had already been forced to surrender most of the country to the invaders who bombed Belgium's cities and strafed columns of its pathetic refugees. The resistance of Belgian forces had been overwhelmed by the Germans at each stop line in their retreat. The last of its reserve troops had been thrown into the battle but had failed to have any impact. Holland to the north had succumbed. The forces of Britain and France, which had so recently swept confidently across Belgian territory to save it from the aggressor, were in disarray. King Leopold had been informed that morning that the evacuation of the BEF back to England was in progress. All that fate seemed to hold in store for his own troops was defeat and slaughter.

Shortly after noon, Gort had received a message from Sir Roger Keyes, the British liaison officer at King Leopold's court, which foretold a Belgian collapse: '[The King] wishes you to know that his army is greatly disheartened. It has been incessantly engaged for four days and subjected to intense air bombardment which the RAF have been unable to prevent . . . He fears a moment is rapidly approaching when he can no longer rely upon his troops to fight or be of any further use to the BEF.'

That evening, a Belgian officer crossed German lines to ask for armistice terms. He was told that there would be no terms other than unconditional surrender. King Leopold realized he had no other option. Shortly before midnight, the Belgian Army, which had been guarding the far left flank of the Allied armies, was ordered by the King to cease fire as of four o'clock the following morning. When informed, Weygand exploded in fury, accusing the Belgians of abandoning the Allies without notice, though he had been told of their difficulties and though it had been apparent for at least two days that they would soon be incapable of resisting a determined German assault.

For Gort, the surrender required immediate remedial action. He had from the start been reconciled to the comparative weakness of the Belgian forces. Two days earlier, he had controversially yanked two divisions away from the abortive drive south to cover for them. But, despite General Brooke's belief that they 'seem to have vanished off the map', Gort had been relieved that they had at least held a small sector of the line. Now there would be a totally undefended gap in Belgium twenty miles wide between BEF positions and the sea through which the Germans could pour to seize Dunkirk and bring Operation Dynamo to an abrupt halt.

When the news reached London, the War Cabinet met in emergency session. Minister of Information Duff Cooper had issued a public statement the previous day explaining the failure of the government to release detailed information on developments across the Channel:

> No one in this country would wish to buy news at the price of a single British, French or Belgian life. We must all wait patiently and confidently till news can be given us with safety.

Now Duff Cooper urged in Cabinet that the British public be told how precarious was the position of the BEF. War communiqués issued by the French, and reported in Britain, had a misleading upbeat tone. The minister warned that the British public wasn't yet prepared for the shock to which it was about to be exposed. Churchill agreed but wanted no details released yet. He felt that the disclosure of the Belgian surrender would go a long way towards preparing the public for the extremely bad news it would probably soon have to digest.

As the day ended, there was nothing to indicate that the BEF was anything but doomed. Ill-informed about the pace of the evacuation, Lord Gort believed that a mere two hundred men had been lifted off the beaches by the small boats since morning. The true number, still not enough to arouse great hopes, was actually a little more than ten times that figure. Including the men who had embarked in the harbour, the number brought home on May 27th, the first full day of Dynamo, was only 7,669. Practically all of the BEF was still in danger of being killed or captured.

In a brief missive to his wife, Admiral Ramsay despaired of developments:

> The situation is past belief, frightful, and one wonders how the British public will take it when the full implications are realised. It's all too horrible to contemplate . . . I am directing . . . one of the most difficult and hazardous operations ever conceived, and unless the *bon Dieu* is very kind, there will be many tragedies attached to it.

## Chapter 7 – DAY THREE OF DUNKIRK

# The Long Retreat

THE CAPITULATION of the Belgian army during the night posed a possibly terminal problem for the BEF. By the terms of their surrender, Belgian troops were obliged to allow the Germans to proceed unhindered through what had been their sector of the front, the twenty miles to the sea guarding the British left flank. The pummelled, demoralized Belgians had no intention of doing otherwise. Their soldiers displayed white handkerchiefs to show they were finished with the war even before the Germans moved up. Whatever obstacles to the German advance they had set were removed or left unguarded. If the enemy plunged through in force before the gap was sealed and raced down the coast towards Dunkirk, the perimeter defence for the city, not yet fully established, would prove as useless as the Maginot Line had been. Whatever chance Operation Dynamo had of bringing even a comparatively small number of troops home would be quickly lost. That twenty mile gap had to be covered immediately.

The task fell to General Brooke's II Corps. Though his troops were hard pressed elsewhere on the front, Brooke patched together an assortment of units to rush into key positions vacated by the Belgians. General Headquarters troops were hastily dispatched to do the same. At Nieuport on the coast, the Germans were only just kept from bursting through after they captured a bridge and established a small foothold on the Dunkirk side. At Dixmude, to which a patrol of the 12th Lancers dashed, a Belgian officer – now no longer an ally – had to be forced at gunpoint to reveal how a crucial bridge had earlier been prepared for destruction. The Lancers blew it up only minutes before a strong force of Germans raced up from the east to try to rush across. To Gort's relief, by nightfall, the gap had been sealed and the Germans blocked for the moment from hurtling down towards Dunkirk.

News of the Belgian capitulation came as a shattering blow to French morale. Sanitized official pronouncements had shielded most

French people from understanding the desperation of the Allied position. Many had been persuaded by government pronouncements and their newspapers that with General Weygand and Marshal Pétain back in harness, German advances in the north would be checked and the invaders would be thrown back or wiped out. For them, the capitulation of Belgium was more than a betrayal, as Premier Reynaud told them it was in a doom-laden radio address that morning. It was evidence that catastrophe for France was also imminent.

The British government was, of course, also dismayed by the Belgian surrender. With characteristic hyperbole, former prime minister David Lloyd George told Parliament, 'You can rummage in vain through the black annals of the most reprobate kings of the earth to find a blacker and more squalid example of perfidy and poltroonery than that perpetrated by the King of the Belgians.' However, some in London attempted to extract signs of advantage from French fury at being let down by Leopold. It was suggested that if the French were genuinely appalled by Belgium's 'treachery', perhaps defeatists among them, advocating a similar capitulation to Hitler, would be silenced. 'They must now stand by us to the end', Spears hopefully maintained, 'however weak and vacillating some ministers may be' and Churchill believed it 'might sting the French to anger in which case they would be very much more formidable opponents to the Germans than in their present stunned and bewildered state'. It was clutching at straws.

The withdrawal of the BEF's forward troops was gathering momentum, but not without complications. Lieutenant Colonel A. D. L. Cazenove, commander of the 1st Battalion, Coldstream Guards, which began heading for the coast before dawn that morning, later recalled the difficulties caused by road congestion: 'The move back was extremely trying to the nerves. Endless delays took place, and we stood still for hours on end, not really knowing whether we should be cut off by the enemy or not'.

The 1st Battalion of the Welsh Guards withdrew in single file up both sides of the road as a precaution against air attack and 'because the middle of the road was filled with other troops, both British and French, mostly without any apparent orders, or under any particular control, and frequently without any visible weapons for their own defence, but all with the cry on their lips "which is the road to Dunkirk?"'

At Dunkirk, the navy personnel who had arrived and been assigned the previous night to serve as beach patrols and beach masters had set about trying to impose order on the crowds and clusters of men who were converging on the beaches. A single officer, accompanied by a small contingent of seamen, was posted at intervals along the main beaches – at Malo adjoining Dunkirk city, at Bray six miles further along, and at La Panne, the furthest reach of the planned operation. These officers soon discovered that they were effectively on their own. They had no means of communicating either with other beach masters elsewhere along the sands, with their superiors at navy headquarters at Dunkirk, or with ships offshore to which they were supposed to dispatch the troops congregated on their miniature domains of sand and mud. What was more, there appeared to be little discipline or organization among those troops; nor was there any sign of any organized effort by the army command to establish order or evacuation procedure on the beaches or the dunes. Without giving the matter much thought, the army, concentrating on the intricacies of the withdrawal, had concluded that it was primarily the navy's job to take over once the men got to the shore. Now growing numbers of men were there but the vessels to get them off were still few and far between. Neither the troops nor the navy beach masters had any way of knowing that Dynamo plans were being changed and that the major emphasis would now be on evacuation not from the beaches but from Dunkirk harbour.

When the *Queen of the Channel* had managed to tie up at the eastern breakwater in Dunkirk harbour the previous night, it appeared evident that many more men could after all be embarked there than from the beaches. The vessel, loaded with 950 troops packed into every space on its decks and below, slipped away from the pier as dawn broke, eased out of the harbour and made for Dover. It didn't get far before a near miss from bombs dropped by a German aircraft damaged it so severely that it sank, though not before most of the men aboard had been rescued by other vessels.

Despite this loss, it was clear that the harbour would have to be the primary avenue of rescue for the great numbers of men to be evacuated. Tennant signalled the destroyers which had been ordered during the night to take up positions off the beaches for loading there from small craft – the *Mackay, Montrose, Vimy, Worcester, Sabre* and *Anthony* – to go instead to the harbour and make fast at the breakwater where the pickings would be far better. At the same time, Dynamo headquarters in Dover was advised that many of the other ships coming over should do the same.

Commander J. C. Clouston, appointed pier master at the break-water, set up a tight control system for the troops to be boarded from the breakwater. He posted men to maintain discipline at the foot of the pier and at access points to it. The troops were organized in groups of up to fifty so that they could quickly scamper along in orderly fashion and be boarded as soon as rescue vessels were properly secured. However, though the emphasis of the operation shifted to the break-water, there was no intention of abandoning the simultaneous lift off from the beaches for which small craft remained in desperately short supply.

The small craft which had been requisitioned and rounded up on the Thames and along the south-east coast of England the previous day had begun turning up at Dover early in the morning. Some had been found to be unfit for Channel service and were sent back to their owners and some had gone to the wrong assembly points. Having no radios, they could not easily be redirected. The others were stripped of all unnecessary equipment, fuelled, and made ready for the Channel crossing.

There being a shortage of naval personnel to man those craft, some of the civilian crews which had delivered them were asked to volunteer for a month's duty with the Royal Navy and given some idea of what would be expected of them and their vessels. Most signed on, some with misgivings, never having imagined their pleasure, fishing or ferry boats going to war. Others chose not to:

> Then, and not until then, we were told, not without a certain amount of lurid detail, of the 'stunt' on hand . . . A cold hard lump formed in my stomach and . . . my 'tummy' felt it had dropped to the region of my knees. I dared not look at the others and remembered that I had not even told my wife and the kiddies that I had left London, let alone 'joined up' with the Navy . . . At this point the crew of the 'Queen Boadicea' which had joined our convoy . . . said something about having families and not receiving danger money, whatever that is . . . The three men climbed ashore with their gear amidst complete silence from the other craft and went off. I was glad then that I had not had the pluck myself to make excuses for not going.

Charts were distributed and arrangements were made for the craft to form up in convoys for the crossing as the troops beginning to throng the Dunkirk beaches looked out to sea for rescue.

Since the previous night, Lord Gort had been trying to find General Blanchard who was still supposed to be coordinating the operations of the Allied armies in the north. He wanted to work out joint British-French action in view of the Belgian capitulation. Also trying to remain on top of the situation, Blanchard had been scurrying from one front-line command post to another, without leaving word of his movements. Not till eleven in the morning did they make contact, when Blanchard arrived at the BEF's new headquarters at Houtkerque.

He was exhausted in body and mind but not too tired to be horrified when Gort, assuming the French had similar instructions, told him that the BEF had been ordered by London to proceed to the coast for evacuation. It was the first Blanchard had heard of Operation Dynamo. Weygand hadn't told him, nor had Admiral Abrial. It was wrong, Blanchard insisted, and why hadn't the British informed him earlier? Gort was, in turn, astounded that the information came as a surprise to Blanchard and that the French forces under his command had not yet also been instructed by Paris to make for Dunkirk to be lifted off. Gort assumed, however, that – evacuation or not – the French and the BEF would synchronize their phased fall back toward the coast during the coming night so that there would be no break in the defensive line.

Blanchard wouldn't hear of it. He did not intend for the French to retreat further. He believed it was important to keep the Germans engaged to delay their inevitable drive against Paris. He would thus give Weygand's forces south of the Somme additional time to establish a strong line of defence to repel the enemy assault. Every day saved for that purpose, every hour, could prove valuable for the survival of French liberty. Besides, Blanchard said, his troops were exhausted. They had been under attack and on the move without a break for two weeks and were in no condition to keep going. Even if they did withdraw to Dunkirk, evacuation for them was not an option. Perhaps the Royal Navy had worked out procedures for embarking the BEF. But not informed of the Franco-British naval consultations in Dover the previous morning, he was certain the French Admiralty planned no such evacuation for French troops.

Though not known for his powers of persuasion, Gort tried to convince Blanchard that nothing was to be saved and much was to be lost in standing fast, locked in a closing trap by superior enemy forces. Aside from the absurdity of such a course, he did not want to be put in the position of ordering his troops to abandon their French fellow soldiers while they fought on, gallantly covering what would look like an ignominious unilateral withdrawal by the British forces.

As Gort and Blanchard debated what was to be done, word came from General Prioux, commander of what remained of the French 1st Army – effectively all that was left under Blanchard's command – that his troops were exhausted. No matter what the best course might be, they were in no shape to withdraw. Gort wanted to know how, if they were in no fit condition to withdraw, would they be able to tie down the enemy. The BEF commander pleaded with Blanchard to reconsider his decision:

I . . . begged General Blanchard, for the sake of France, the French

Army and the Allied Cause to order General Prioux back. Surely, I said, his troops were not all so tired as to be incapable of moving. The French Government would be able to provide ships at least for some of his troops, and the chance of saving a part of his trained soldiers was preferable to the certainty of losing them all. I could not move him.

Unable to shift Blanchard, Gort told him that whatever the French did, the British would be pulling back towards Dunkirk to be evacuated. (They were doing so already.) Those were his orders from London and he was obliged to obey them. Besides, he insisted, it would be insane to let his troops be lost to the enemy when an operation to save them was already underway.

Right through the day, fighting on both flanks of the escape corridor remained heavy, as did the casualty levels, inflated that day by an act of murder over and beyond the call of battle. More than eighty men of the Royal Warwickshire Regiment, surrounded near the town of Wormhoudt, surrendered to the *Adolf Hitler* SS Regiment only to be herded at gunpoint into a small barn into which hand grenades were then tossed. Machine-gun and rifle fire cut down most of those who were not immediately killed.

Communications between Allied command positions and the shifting front continued to deteriorate. Remaining radio and telephone links were breaking down and contact had to rely increasingly on motorcycle dispatch riders who tried to make their way through choked traffic to deliver their orders and reports to recipients who often were not to be found where they were expected to be. Aware of the dangers of orders not being received or being received too late, Gort gave his corps commanders a general idea of the fall back defence line for the coming night and authorized them to use their discretion in shifting as many of their fighting units as they safely could back into the Dunkirk perimeter.

The troops withdrew through a landscape of defeat.

> From every house in the villages, from church steeples, farms, cottages, from everywhere where people lived there flapped a white flag, and if not a real flag, a white table-cloth, sheet, towel or handkerchief . . . tokens of surrender which the inhabitants were in a great hurry to have on display by the time the Germans arrived.

Rumours filtered back from the coast of hundreds dead on the Dunkirk beaches and of rescue vessels loaded with evacuees sunk by submarines or Stukas. The routed troops were continually aware of the devastation of which the dive bombers were capable. Under attack, they dove for cover into ditches, 'crawled underneath the wreckage of vehicles, flattened themselves down between the very grass blades in the fields, and stood up to their necks in the water of the canal. In the space of a few seconds . . . not a soul was in sight'.

It wasn't only a matter of making for the coast. The men were ordered to travel light. As they approached the Dunkirk perimeter, they were instructed to make certain their equipment would not fall into the hands of the advancing enemy. An officer recalled, 'We kept enough transport to get us within a mile or two of Dunkirk. Then we finally destroyed everything except one car, which I kept in case of emergency. All along the road our troops were having an orgy of smashing up. Under a clear blue sky, on a quiet country road, it was perhaps the most astonishing sight of all in this queer war.' Vast quantities of equipment were demolished. Men who had been responsible for the care, upkeep and distribution of costly military hardware were appalled by the waste.

> New wireless sets . . . were placed in rows in the fields, twenty in a row, sometimes, while a soldier with a pick-axe proceeded up and down knocking them to pieces. Trucks were dealt with just as drastically. Radiators and engines were smashed with sledgehammers; tyres slashed and sawn after they had been deflated. Vehicles that were near canals were finally pushed in. Some of the canals were choked with wrecks, all piled on top of each other.

Inevitably, there were mistakes, some of them of monumental proportions given the situation. Spare gunners in the anti-aircraft unit which was drawn back to defend the perimeter at La Panne were instructed to take up rifles and join the ground defence of the area. However, the order was misunderstood to apply to *all* gunners in the unit. To prevent their abandoned guns – which were desperately needed to defend the perimeter from air attack – from falling into the hands of the advancing Germans, they destroyed them too before the misunderstanding could be sorted out, to the astonishment, despair and fury of senior commanders.

Despite the road congestion, by the afternoon a vast multitude of British troops had reached the coast and was sprawled on the dunes and along the ten miles of beaches stretching east of Dunkirk where, in more agreeable times, children built sand castles and people frolicked on the shore. To men on the ships arriving to take them home, the troops looked 'like thousands of sticks'.

> The beach was an extraordinary sight. As far as the eye could see it stretched away into the distance, the firm sand of the shore stretching further back into the dunes where the surface was no more than a thin

yellow powder interspersed with parched tussocks of coarse grass. And covering this vast expanse, like some mighty antheap upturned by a giant's foot, were the remains of the British Expeditionary Force, some standing in black clusters at the water's edge, waiting for the boats that were to take them to the two or three ships lying off-shore, while others, whose turn had not yet come, or who were too tired to care whether it was their turn or not, lay huddled together in a disorderly and exhausted multitude.

Queues stretched the entire width of the beaches and into the water. Some of the men had arrived in organized units under command of junior officers and remained as such. Directed into lines for embarkation, they held assigned positions while waiting to be signalled forward to be boarded. But many of the men were from units which had been demolished in battle or fragmented in retreat. Some of these, having been told it was every man for himself, had previously had no idea what was going on – except that things were going badly – and had just 'followed the crowd' back towards Dunkirk.

Survival was the only priority. One officer later wrote, 'We all had one idea now, one impulse – we only wanted to reach the water's edge and be rowed away quietly into the night like King Arthur'. Whether in organized units or 'odds and sods' in small ragtag groups, the troops to be lifted off were exhausted, thirsty and hungry. Some had not eaten for a day or more. On the sand, many were absorbed into organized units which seemed to offer a greater opportunity for survival. Others who tried to join such groups were told, 'You don't belong to us. Get out of here', by men who feared hangers-on would make their own evacuation more difficult. There was nothing for these rejects to do but wander down the beach toward Dunkirk in the hopes of leaving from the harbour or tag on to less exclusive queues from which they might be lifted off home more quickly.

> It would start off as a queue but if you thought you could get to a boat before the others, you were out there in the water. It wasn't really panic but it wasn't a queue any more. You waded out to try to get into a boat. After you failed a few times, you'd get fed up standing in the water and you'd go back and sit on the sand. Then when more boats would come in, you'd try again.

Bodies floated in the water. Most were of men who had been killed by German aircraft strafing and bombing the ships, boats and water line. But some troops had drowned after clinging to overloaded boats which they had been unable to board and then losing their grip.

The undulating dunes with their clumps of coarse grass provided somewhat more protection from the bombing raids and the German fighter planes zooming past a hundred feet above the ground, their machine guns blazing. At least they offered an illusion of cover in a situation in which cover was hard to come by. Men had to decide whether they'd wait on the dunes, where they felt safer, for the summons to embark from an officer or a navy beach master, or on the beach, where the chances for speedy evacuation seemed greater. On both the beaches and the dunes, the sand muffled the bomb explosions and kept the spray of shrapnel to a minimum. But there were bodies on the sand, some covered with discarded great coats, and there soon would be more.

More men arrived all the time, some expecting to be embarked immediately and transported home once they reached the coast. They were shattered to find thousands ahead of them wanting the same. Even on well organized queues, under control of navy beach masters, some declined to wait.

> I saw a man suddenly rush past . . . out of turn. Immediately a determined shout went up from the other men who were in front of him in the queue. 'Get out. Get back, you bastard . . .' There was no mistaking their tone. The man failed to reach the boat which was now putting out to sea. He shrank back, immediately forgotten and unobserved, into the queue . . . In our urgency we forgot things as quickly as animals . . . we had the memories of monkeys.'

To complicate matters, the swell of the sea, though moderate, was enough to make it difficult for the small boats to come in close and take men on board. 'Tired, wet and hungry,' quipped one evacuee, 'we decided that Bray as a holiday resort was much overrated.'

The tide was a problem even when the breeze tailed off. When it raced out, the men tried to move with it so as to be as close as possible to the boats making their way towards them to ferry them out to the rescue ships offshore. When the tide raced in, they were reluctant to back away from the incoming boats, fearing that others would not and they would lose their places at the head of the line. They found themselves up to their knees, their thighs, their shoulders in water.

When they reached a boat, they clambered aboard as best they could. The navy personnel, merchant seamen or pastime sailors manning the boats sometimes had to swing oars at them to keep them from capsizing their craft. More boats were now arriving to participate in the ferrying operation. But there were still far too few to make an appreciable dent in the numbers to be evacuated. It was apparent before mid-morning that the operation directly from the shore could not be expected to achieve much.

At Dunkirk harbour, along the breakwater, things were somewhat more hopeful. Rescue vessels were arriving, tying up, boarding, and departing with increasing frequency. The number of troops being brought back to England was rising. But at the harbour too, only just so much could be done and a few thousand more troops embarked did not make a great deal of difference to the overall picture. Thousands still waited their turn to be lifted off and tens of thousands more still were making their way along the corridor to the coast.

Being rescued from Dunkirk did not necessarily mean getting safely home. In addition to the *Queen of the Channel* which had gone down in the morning, the merchant ship *Abukir* was sunk by a torpedo boat, also after it had set off for England fully loaded. Two other passenger vessels drummed into service ran aground at low tide. A French cargo vessel, the *Douaisien*, one of a small fleet of vessels sent by the French Admiralty to pick up French specialist troops, hit a mine and went down. The trawler *Thomas Bartlett*, searching for German mines off Calais, ran into a British minefield there and sank. Its entire crew was lost. Most of the men on the other vessels were rescued but an unknown number of troops were lost that day after they had been evacuated. Records of who boarded, who was rescued from the water when their ships were sunk, and who was lost would have been impossible to keep.

An early cloud cover and the pall of black smoke from Dunkirk's burning oil storage tanks had provided partial aerial protection for the area through much of the morning. But later in the day, a shift in the wind's direction cleared the skies and German attack aircraft were once more active over the area, though they weren't as much in evidence over the coast as they had been the day before. The *Luftwaffe* that day concentrated instead on the shrinking front of the Allied forces inland. But German artillery, which had been moved up close west of Dunkirk, pounded the harbour area, if not with accuracy, with increasing thoroughness.

The damage inflicted was severe. The potential for even greater damage was great. As the day drew to a close, Dynamo headquarters in Dover ruled that civilian passenger ships participating in the operation should no longer use the harbour breakwater during daylight hours, when they could be sitting targets. Only warships would continue to take that risk. These continued to shuttle in and out of the harbour to evacuate troops. Until nightfall, the civilian vessels taking part in the operation were to concentrate exclusively on boarding men ferried out to them from the beaches. Though exposed to air raids, their anchorages offshore were still out of range of the German guns. For how long, no one dared predict.

Though the story till then had been primarily one of Allied setback, retreat and confusion, German forces had been sustaining heavy losses and facing serious problems as well. General Guderian reported that the equipment of his armoured divisions was 'in urgent need of repair'. Besides, though an armoured breakthrough further inland would have pinched the Allies off from the sea, fighting closer to the coast called for different tactics. 'A tank attack', Guderian said, 'is pointless in the marshy country which has been completely soaked by the rain . . . Infantry forces . . . are more suitable than tanks for fighting in this kind of country'. Further tank attacks would, he said, result in 'the useless sacrifice of our best troops'. The panzer divisions were accordingly withdrawn. Besides, they needed to be rested before turning south for the greater glory of crushing the French forces deployed to keep them from marching on Paris.

Their armies having steamrolled across northern France, the Germans had lost both their momentum and their sense of urgency in the north. The Allied troops in the elongated Dunkirk pocket were trapped against the sea. A mopping up operation was all that was now required to deal with them. German commanders knew that British troops were being ferried home from Dunkirk and they weren't happy about that. But they could not imagine that a truly massive evacuation operation was either underway or possible.

Nor could Churchill, his War Cabinet or the chiefs of staff in London make any accurate forecast of what Operation Dynamo might accomplish. Evacuation figures so far provided grounds for gloom rather than confidence. His mission to the Belgian Royal court concluded by the Belgian capitulation, Sir Roger Keyes returned that day across the Channel with word that Gort, with whom he had spoken, still did not rate the chances of saving the BEF very high. It was known that the men – whether on the shore, manning the perimeter defence, trudging back through the escape corridor, or holding the corridor open – were desperately short of food and ammunition. Not much could be done about it. And what chance could there be of responding satisfactorily to the avalanche of pleas for more ships and boats and for greater aerial cover?

There was growing unease in Parliament as unofficial reports circulated about the BEF's plight and about how the navy appeared to be engaged in some sort of extremely desperate emergency operation. But Churchill, though bracing the House of Commons for bad news, still declined to reveal to it the extent of the crisis. He also refused to leave room for speculation that Britain might be driven by military setback to seek an armistice with Germany.

I expect to make a statement to the House on the general position when the result of the intense struggle now going on can be known and measured. This perhaps may not be until the beginning of next week. Meanwhile, the House must prepare itself for hard and heavy tidings. I have only to add that nothing which can happen in this battle can in any way relieve us of our duty to defend the world cause to which we have bound ourselves, nor can it destroy our confidence in our power to make our way – as on former occasions in our history – through disaster and grief to ultimate defeat of our enemy.

The Prime Minister's refusal even to explore the possibility that Britain might honourably extract itself without further damage from a war in which the country was heading for disaster was questioned once more in the War Cabinet by his Foreign Secretary. Challenging Churchill's obduracy, Lord Halifax, who not long before had resolutely declared he would prefer bankruptcy for Britain to defeat by Germany, insisted, 'We must not ignore the fact that we might get better [armistice] terms before France went out of the war and our aircraft factories were bombed than we might get in three months time.'

Churchill was not moved. He replied that if Britain agreed to armistice talks and then found that Germany's peace terms were unacceptable, the country's war effort would have lost its momentum. He was certain that any armistice terms Germany might offer would be designed to put Britain at Hitler's mercy. By the time Britain then left the negotiating table to get on with the war, 'We should find that all the forces of resolution . . . now at our disposal would have vanished.' Further vexing Halifax by presuming to preach, Churchill declared 'nations which went down fighting rose again but those which surrendered tamely were finished'.

Chamberlain, who was still official leader of the Tory Party and whose views could not be summarily discounted despite his recent ouster, continued to back Halifax on the advisability of exploring chances for honourable peace negotiations. It should be done, the former prime minister said, if only to discourage France from seeking a separate peace with Germany. The two next most senior members of the War Cabinet, men held in high regard by most of the Tory Party, were doing more than merely disagreeing with Churchill. Given the circumstances, they were challenging his leadership. In the history of the war that he wrote subsequently, Churchill makes little mention of their views at that critical moment or of the additional pressure they put him under when the fate of a quarter of a million British troops was very much in doubt. He wrote only of the tremendous support he received from other government ministers who were not members of the War Cabinet, who he said cheered him and praised his stand at a separate meeting that evening:

> Quite a number seemed to jump up from the table and come running to my chair, shouting and patting me on the back. There is no doubt that had I at this juncture faltered at all in the leading of the nation I should have been hurled out of office.

War Cabinet member Clement Attlee, the Labour Party leader who was Churchill's deputy Prime Minister and whose backing was essential if the government of national unity was to survive, was particularly supportive. But Attlee warned that when the public became aware of the fate that appeared to await the BEF, it would suffer a severe shock. No one who knew what was happening believed that Britain would emerge from the Dunkirk episode and its aftermath with anything less than tragedy. The extent of the government's forebodings was revealed by its decision to mark the country off into seventeen food areas. Each would come under the 'supreme control' of a local official 'to ensure distribution of food' if communications broke down in an emergency.

The German propaganda war was stepped up. Gort was said to have offered to surrender and the capitulation of France was reportedly about to be announced. Censorship prevented many such claims from getting through to the British public but couldn't prevent all rumours of impending calamity from circulating and affecting public morale. Steps were taken to deal with any agitation against the war effort that might develop on the home front. A defence regulation was to be introduced in Parliament empowering the government to prohibit the printing, publication or distribution of any newspaper which systematically published material fomenting opposition to the successful prosecution of the war. A particular target was the Communist Party's *Daily Worker* which, following the lead of the Soviet Union, dismissed Britain's involvement in the struggle against Hitler as a capitalist conspiracy.

British fighter planes – Spitfires, Hurricanes, and Defiants – had been in action over the Dunkirk pocket from first light, giving and taking punishment. Fighter Command flew 321 sorties that day, with some pilots shuttling two or three times from their airfields in Kent. Seventeen British fighter planes were lost or damaged in operations before nightfall. Several of the pilots shot down were rescued but seven were killed in action. According to information made available after the war, twenty-two German aircraft were destroyed in combat that day, not all over Dunkirk. But even that total was far fewer than the 'kills' claimed by RAF pilots unable to make accurate judgments in the heat of aerial combat about whom they did or did not shoot down while providing an aerial screen for the evacuation.

Later, when the BBC was finally permitted to broadcast news of the Dunkirk evacuation, it announced, 'Our men can find no words in which to speak of their gratitude to the Royal Air Force'. In fact, the troops on the ground found plenty of words to describe their feelings about the RAF. But few of them would have been acceptable for broadcast as Flight Lieutenant Alan Deere – whose squadron was almost wiped out over Dunkirk – discovered. When Deere was shot down, he made his way to the beaches and sought to board an evacuation vessel so that he could make his way back to his base and get back into the fight. An army major tried to block his way, snarling, 'For all the good you chaps seem to be doing over here you might just as well stay on the ground.'

Admiral Ramsay attempted to redress such criticism at the end of the operation. He declared, 'I and the Forces under my command who have been engaged on the evacuation of the Allied Armies owe a deep debt of gratitude to the Royal Air Force for the support and protection which they have given to us.' But in a subsequent statement on RAF support during the operation, Ramsay was scathing:

> Rightly or wrongly, full air protection was expected, but instead, for hours on end the ships off-shore were subjected to a murderous hail of bombs and machine-gun bullets. Required by their duty to remain off-shore waiting for the troops, who themselves were unable to move down to the water for the same reason, it required the greatest determination and sense of duty, amounting in fact to heroism, on the part of the ships' and boats' crews, to enable them to complete their mission. In their reports, the C.O.s of many ships, while giving credit to the RAF personnel for gallantry in such combats as were observed from the ships, at the same time express their sense of disappointment and surprise at the seemingly puny efforts made to provide air protection during the height of this operation.

Captain Tennant, watching from Dunkirk, was reluctant to be so harsh. 'The sky is a big place', he said, 'and it was often difficult to know if our aircraft were present or not.'

The sky was indeed a big place which partly accounted for the failure of men on the ground to see the RAF in action. To prevent bombers, which did the most damage, from unloading their cargoes on the beaches and on the ships offshore, they had to be stopped before they got there.

> It was no good patrolling over a beach [said one Fighter Command pilot] if you hoped you were going to save the people underneath you. You've got to be 20–30 miles further away. The object was to get in the way of any oncoming German squadrons.

Regardless of their inaccuracy, the inflated kill claims of the RAF pilots did much for morale at home. It gave both the British public and the pilots themselves – if not the troops being blasted by enemy aircraft – the impression that Britain was winning the air war with Germany. Air Chief Marshal Dowding was not at all pleased with the implications. Sensitive to criticism of Fighter Command for not providing more comprehensive cover for the men and ships at Dunkirk, he feared it would now be ordered to do so and that he would then lose more fighters than he could spare before the fight-to-the-finish German assault on the British homeland began.

To neutralize any euphoria that might be generated by the inflated claims of the pilots, Dowding reported that the country's home 'fighter defences were almost at cracking point'. He warned that if Fighter Command's effectiveness was sacrificed at Dunkirk, 'the situation would be serious'. He was saying, in effect, that too much rather than too little aerial cover was being provided for Operation Dynamo – not because less would suffice but because the priority requirement remained keeping aerial home defences intact.

Churchill had a different catalogue of priorities. For him, getting the troops back from Dunkirk was now the prime necessity. He shared the concern of the Fighter Command chief. But the dour Dowding, nicknamed 'Stuffy', had earned a reputation for being constitutionally inclined to issue overly gloomy prophecies. In his diary, Ironside had described him as 'a curious old thing'. Chief of the Air Staff Newall agreed that the Fighter Command chief was being excessively worried. The RAF would continue to provide as much cover as possible at Dunkirk, with the understanding that under no circumstances were Britain's air defences to be denuded.

Gort moved to the coast that afternoon from his inland command post and set up his headquarters in a former Belgian royal seaside villa at La Panne, ten miles north of Dunkirk. His new command post was close to the cross-Channel Brussels-London telephone cable, permitting the BEF commander to remain in touch with the British capital. After touring the area, he informed the War Office that there were about twenty thousand men waiting to be evacuated, that they were exposed to ferocious air attack, and that things looked bleak indeed. 'There can be no doubt that if air attacks continue at present intensities', he warned, 'the area must become a shambles and such a situation could easily arrive in next 48 hours.'

The BEF commander asked London to clarify its instructions to him. He feared that the flanks of the escape corridor – or what was left of it as more men withdrew – would collapse before all his troops could reach the coast and that the defence perimeter would be overrun before the evacuation operation got much further. He wanted definite guidance on what was expected of him if bad came to worst. Was he to surrender the BEF to the enemy to prevent a slaughter or was he to fight to the last bullet? Expecting firm instruction, he had to settle for a pat on the back in the form of a message from Minister of War Eden.

> We have every confidence that you and the gallant troops under your command will continue to the uttermost the grim struggle for our country's safety . . . All possible assistance is being rendered by Royal Navy, and R.A.F. will give maximum cover in their power during these critical days.

Did that mean he was to fight till the last bullet? He wasn't sure.

The evacuation proceeded in greater safety after nightfall when most of the German planes were grounded and when vessels moved in by turns alongside the eastern breakwater to embark troops while small boats continued to work the beaches. But only 17,804 men were brought back to England that day, about a third of them from the beaches. That was more than twice as many as the day before. But it was hardly enough to point to anything but a resounding failure for Operation Dynamo.

Information Minister Duff Cooper finally received Cabinet permission to begin preparing the British public for the worst. In a radio speech that night, he tried to brace people for the trouble ahead.

> It will be necessary to withdraw our army from the positions they now occupy, but it will not be a defeated army . . . It will be an army whose courage is still high and whose confidence is still unshaken, and every officer and man burning with desire to meet the enemy in combat . . . We can all remember the dark days of the last war . . . It seemed that the war was lost. But it never was – and all events which seemed disastrous at the time proved but the prelude to victory . . . As the danger increases so does our courage to meet it.

Not governed by British censorship regulations, the New York *Herald Tribune* reported much more gloomily from London.

> The British Expeditionary Force . . . was all but given up for lost here tonight . . . In this epic tragedy the port of Dunkerque was the only hope of escape, and Dunkerque was under such brutal bombing by the

numerically superior airmen of Germany that the prospect of removing the French-British force in the north was considered in London to be remote. Thus the cream of the British Army appeared, this sad and uncertain evening, to face extinction or surrender. No one in this country thought for a moment that [Gort] would take the latter course.

Under the circumstances, it was difficult not to wonder whether Gort had made a tragic mistake in withdrawing to the coast. 'Poor chap,' General Pownall wrote in his diary that night. 'He feels his position terribly. The most trivial things have always preyed on his mind and now he has a load that he can never shake off all the days of his life. The Commander of the BEF that was driven into the sea in three weeks! So undeserved a fate.'

## Chapter 8 – DAY FOUR OF DUNKIRK

# Journey Through Hell

THE DAY OPENED with tragedy. In the dark early hours of the morning, the destroyer *Wakeful*, carrying 650 evacuees who had been lifted by small boats from the beach at Bray, set sail for Dover taking the longest route to avoid German coastal artillery on the most direct route and the mined middle passage. Before it had got far, it was hit amidships by a German torpedo. The explosion broke the vessel in two and it sank in fifteen seconds. Almost all the men aboard had been asleep below and were lost. The *Wakeful*'s sister ship, the destroyer *Grafton*, with eight hundred evacuees on board, was also torpedoed while searching for survivors. Going down, the *Grafton* opened fire on a small vessel lurking in the nearby darkness which its skipper took to be a German torpedo boat. The *Lydd*, a drifter en route to pick up evacuees, rammed and sank this suspect vessel which proved to have been not an enemy ship but the British drifter *Comfort* which had also approached to try to rescue survivors from the *Wakeful*. It was not known how many men were lost in this series of misadventures. Such tragic farce, chaos and grief had by now become part of the Dunkirk story.

Even before the early morning losses were known at Dover's Dynamo headquarters, personnel on duty there were stricken with intimations of disaster. During the night, some seventy vessels had crossed over, some to pick up men from the beaches, others to embark troops from the breakwater. Where were those ships? They had been expected to begin streaming back to England by three a.m. but by nine they had failed to return. It was more than possible that many had been sunk or disabled. And if so many ships had been lost under the comforting cover of darkness, what prospects could there be for carrying on with the operation during daylight hours – or at all?

As anxiety built up at Dover, word from Dunkirk, relayed by a destroyer, calmed fears somewhat. 'Personnel vessels . . . were having difficulty in making the entrance of Dunkirk harbour in the face of the navigational difficulties caused by a heavy smoke pall over the entrance and in the face of bombing and shelling encountered en route and whilst alongside.' Expectations that passenger vessels would embark great numbers of troops from the breakwater before dawn were as a consequence disappointed. In addition, a strong overnight surf compounded the difficulties of the small craft and of the seamen operating under trying conditions. Any northerly wind whipped up a surf on that stretch of coast. Vessels working the shore had been unable to get on with their appointed tasks until the winds had dropped towards morning light.

Meantime, developments on the eastern sector of the perimeter presented a new threat to the operation. The Germans had moved heavy guns up to the Belgian coast near Nieuport which they had newly captured, forcing the Allied defenders there back toward La Panne. That brought the nearby Zuydcoote Pass offshore, through which the long sea route back to England ran, within range of their artillery and subject to spasmodic fire. The middle Channel passage was about to become the only usable route to and from Dunkirk during daylight hours. It was pronounced swept of mines and all ships crossing during the day were instructed to use it, 'exercising navigational caution' in view of likely congestion.

No matter how diligently practised, navigational caution could not repel air attacks. The Germans had finally realized that British activity on the coast was far more ambitious than they had thought possible. They had previously assumed that except for a comparatively small number who were getting away, the troops locked against the sea had no alternative but capture or slaughter. But air reconnaissance revealed how determinedly and vigorously the evacuation operation was progressing. Once more the *Luftwaffe* was instructed to deal energetically with the situation, specifically to step up its assaults on the rescue vessels. An intensive aerial assault was launched against the ships and continued virtually without let-up until last light. The toll it took was both huge and portentous.

In addition to the two destroyers which were sent to the bottom of the Channel before daylight, another, the *Gallant*, was damaged and put out of action by a near miss, the *Jaguar*, dead in the water after being hit by a bomb, had to be towed back to Dover, and the *Grenade*, loaded with troops at the breakwater and setting off for Dover when she was hit, was turned into a blazing inferno drifting out of control. She was towed clear of the harbour before she could sink there blocking the entrance and exploded just outside. There were few survivors.

A war sloop and two minesweepers were also sunk, as were four passenger ships. Among ships damaged were three other British destroyers, three French destroyers which had joined in the operation though there was as yet no sign ashore of comprehensive French evacuation plans, two minesweepers, and two passenger vessels. Among these last was the *Mona's Queen* which had been the first vessel to run the gauntlet bringing troops back from Dunkirk when Operation Dynamo had commenced, a depressing omen though such grim portents were not in short supply. Many small boats were lost, bombed or strafed while trying to lift men off the beaches. They lay near the water's edge, wrecked, burning or burnt out, evoking premonitions of doom among the troops.

Though badly needed, many of the rowing boats, some of which could carry as many as thirty men, were abandoned and permitted to drift out to sea by the men they had ferried out to the vessels offshore. One naval officer described how, 'On arrival alongside the men would all jump on board and let their boats drift off on the tide. Paddles were lost, rendering the boats useless.' Having waited anxiously for rescue, having so far survived air attacks, and having finally reached a homeward-bound ship, few soldiers were disposed to risk rowing the boats back to the beach for men not yet as lucky as themselves. And sailors from the larger vessels, who sometimes shuttled those small boats to and from the beaches, were normally also the men who manned ships' guns against attacking aircraft. They couldn't comfortably be long spared for boat duty when enemy aircraft might zoom out of the horizon at any moment. Besides, they were exhausted, many of them having been working at full stretch with little time for sleep ever since the evacuation of the 'useless mouths' had begun. Many of them, and particularly the crews of the navy vessels, had been in action and under air attack the better part of a week.

Even when men could be spared from the ships to help organize the evacuation on the beaches, they were not always successful. When the sloop *Bideford*, anchored off Bray, sent men ashore 'in an endeavour to take charge on the beach . . . this was next to impossible. The men rushed the boats and capsized them in shallow water, and then left the boats without making any attempt to right them and use them again'.

Though not an isolated case, such behaviour was by no means universal. Right through the operation, the conduct of the troops varied according to training, personal standards of behaviour, sense of duty, discipline in the presence of officers and NCOs, and emotional reaction to their plight. Some soldiers did row back to shore to ferry more men out to rescue vessels when they easily could have boarded those vessels themselves the first time out, leaving their boats to drift away as most of the others in that situation appear to have done. As many troops as not, patiently or otherwise, waited their turn in the straggly queues rather than rushing to the water line to try to be the first away.

Some of the men who returned after waiting long hours for their turn to be embarked reported that they had seen not a single incident of indiscipline on the beaches. Others insisted it had been every-man-for-himself on the shore unless a navy beach master intervened forcefully, often brandishing a weapon, when men could not be dissuaded from rushing into the water and capsizing incoming boats while trying to scramble into them.

> I took my revolver out and fired in front of the leading man in the water. The sound of the shot and the splash startled them. I warned them back. I told them, 'If you go on like this no one will get away. Now two of you go out and pull the boat into shallow water and turn it around.' A major appeared and asked what was happening. I told him and he asked what I wanted done. I said I wanted two embarkation points with lines back across the beach to the sand hills with the men marked off in blocks of sixty with gaps between them to reduce casualties in case of strafing. In no time, he got it started.

The men – those who were disciplined and those who were not – were worn down and disoriented by being strafed and bombed, as well as by their long retreat. They wanted desperately to be on their way home though most knew from watching German aircraft in action that a hard won place on a ship homeward bound was not automatic deliverance. Ships were ablaze offshore and bodies floated in the water. And indeed the experience of troops as they were being brought home from Dunkirk and the beaches was often more harrowing than that they had endured while under aerial attack ashore. Few had ever been on board a vessel when it was under attack – even worse, below deck:

> At three this morning there was a terrific explosion as a torpedo hit the destroyer. I suppose the force must have knocked me unconscious. First thing I knew I was stumbling about in the dark trying to find the door of the cabin. The whole ship was trembling violently . . . Finding my way out on deck was a bit of a nightmare. Everything was pitch black . . . It didn't occur to me for a moment that any of us had a chance of escape. The sailors last night had been emphatic that a torpedo meant the end of everything. But somehow it didn't matter much. The disaster . . . was still trying to penetrate the outer layer of my brain. I remember similar situations in American films. Gary Cooper always finds a way out.

Many men saved from the German trap on land, and believing they were practically home safe, found themselves swimming for their lives out in the Channel. All knew they could be doing the same at any moment, which accounted for the extraordinary behaviour of some who had taken off their wet clothes when finally boarded on a rescue vessel:

> As one man, we all grabbed our trousers, wet as they were, and pulled them on – there was something undignified about dying with a bare backside.

Fearing a watery grave, a number of merchant seamen engaged in the operation who had already made the perilous shuttle more than once left their ships when they docked at English ports and refused to return. Some others, their ships newly recruited, also bowed out when hearing of the dangers. Their places had to be taken by navy personnel, the reservoir of which was running very dry. Land based personnel and naval cadets were rushed into service.

A half century after the events, the Ministry of Defence declines to release for public inspection documents concerning men and vessels who chose not to take part in the operation and who could not be obliged to. But those days were marked more by extraordinary acts of heroism and selflessness by civilian mariners as well as by navy personnel. Ceaselessly in danger of being torpedoed, or strafed and bombed by enemy aircraft which appeared with heart-jolting suddenness, their vessels scurried back and forth ferrying troops out of the enemy trap, often dauntlessly rushing to the assistance of other vessels when they were hit. When the paddle steamer *Gracie Fields* was bombed after embarking 750 troops from the beach at La Panne, its upper deck was engulfed in steam from broken pipes and her rudder jammed, forcing her to circle endlessly. Ignoring the danger to themselves and their craft, the masters of two barges tied up tight alongside the vessel to take off its human cargo. The minesweeper *Pangbourne*, already damaged by near misses which had claimed the lives of thirteen men on board, and its compass out of kilter, also went alongside the stricken and sinking vessel to lift off the rest of its men and try in vain to tow it back to England.

Just being there had the dimensions of a mythic journey through hell. The armed boarding vessel *King Orry*, arriving at Dunkirk around six that evening, found all the other vessels in the harbour ablaze. It was itself attacked by dive bombers. Hit and badly damaged, it was in danger of sinking in the harbour entrance, blocking further rescue traffic there. But its crew managed to keep it afloat long enough to limp clear of the harbour before it too went down.

Despite intensified *Luftwaffe* operations, RAF Fighter Command stuck to its policy of carefully husbanding its squadrons for the expected massive German air assault on British cities and aircraft factories. But 11

Group commander Park had been persistently and urgently pleading for a change in aerial cover tactics which prevented his fighters from challenging the *Luftwaffe* more effectively. Now able to assess the situation more realistically, the War Cabinet reluctantly accepted that Fighter Command resources were insufficient to provide anything like continuous cover which, in any case, had been ordered when it was believed Operation Dynamo would last only two days. It was agreed now that the operation would 'dispense with full cover at less important periods'.

For the men on the beaches and the vessels lifting them off there were no 'less important periods' except perhaps at night when aerial activity was sharply limited. But it meant that Fighter Command could start sending out larger patrols, up to four squadrons at a time, to cope more effectively with the big formations of attacking German aircraft. The result was longer intervals – sometimes an agonizing hour or more – between patrols when there were no British fighters over Dunkirk. Two of the five concentrated German air attacks on shipping that day between noon and night met no opposition at all in the air. Nevertheless, the RAF claimed to have shot down sixty-seven German aircraft over the Dunkirk area that day against a loss of nineteen of their fighters. It was a vast exaggeration. The *Luftwaffe* lost a total of eighteen planes over all of France and Belgium that day and some of those were brought down over Dunkirk by naval anti-aircraft fire.

However, in flying in larger patrols, when in action in the area the Spitfires and Hurricanes were more effective in disrupting German aerial attacks on the troops and ships. What was more, the stronger British fighter presence had a damaging effect on the morale, confidence and skills of German pilots and air crews. They had been in almost ceaseless action for almost three weeks, ever since the launching of the offensive. Though verging on total physical exhaustion, they were now required to face much stronger aerial opposition than they had so far met in the war. But the troops on the beaches, seeing ships that had come to rescue them blown out of the water, and those on vessels blasted from the air as they crossed back to England, were increasingly bitter about what they believed was the RAF's inadequacy. Few of them knew that the RAF fighters were breaking up German raids which could have inflicted far greater havoc on the beaches and at sea and that RAF bombers were blasting enemy positions, supply lines and communications further back, making it difficult for the Germans to coordinate their attempt to slam shut the Dunkirk escape hatch. Back in England, RAF personnel were cursed out and beaten up in pubs by men newly rescued from France, angrily convinced that the Royal Air Force had disgracefully let them down.

As the day wore on, the beaches and the dunes behind them grew increasingly jammed. British troops were pouring into the perimeter strip by the thousands, and then the tens of thousands:

> On our way to the coast, we thought the navy would have some sense and not make such a balls up as the army seemed to have made of the war. I was under the impression that the navy was out there with heavy guns and they were laying down a barrage behind us and that was protecting us. That was reassuring.

Mostly men arrived in the perimeter on foot but many vehicles of various descriptions came as well, ambulances, trucks carrying needed supplies and equipment. But other vehicles found their way to the beaches too, slipping past military police posted to stop them from congesting the area. With the emphasis on maintaining a strong perimeter defence, few troops could be spared by perimeter command for traffic control.

> There was an awful lot of transport on the beach. People were running up and down in lorries. I don't know if they were on particular missions or just joy riding till the petrol ran out. There was an enormous number of new vehicles, just issued, and some of them were just run into the sea and left there.

Some men arrived clinging to the sides and tops of trucks. Some in abandoned cars they had commandeered. Others used less conventional transport: bicycles they found en route, one man driving a Belgian garbage truck, a few on horses they had liberated from other military tasks or from much drearier employment on farms or the villages they had passed through.

> We ended up at a little seaside resort between Bray Dunes and Dunkirk. There was a road leading down to the sea. We had some idea that we'd get to the port and embark on ships and perhaps be taken down the coast elsewhere in France to continue the battle. There was a captain along with us, and his batman. The captain thought there'd be some sort of officers' mess waiting for him at the beach. The batman was carrying the captain's valise – this great big army valise with the captain's mattress and clothes and things in it – he was carrying it on his head. We came to a gap in the dunes and went up a little rise, looked down and instead of seeing just the sea and sand, it was black with soldiers, rows and rows and rows of them, and patches here and there. The

batman said, 'Bugger this. I'm not carrying that thing any further,' and he chucked the valise down to the ground.

French troops were beginning to pour back through the perimeter line in greater numbers too. When they passed through sectors of the line where the British had established effective traffic control, they were also required to abandon their vehicles and proceed on foot. They did not appreciate being ordered about by foreigners in their own country. Strong feelings were aroused and disagreeable scenes took place in which warnings were exchanged and guns were pointed threateningly. French troops who had been on the run from the moment the enemy had crossed their borders, but who were still determined to fight on, saw the forced destruction of their equipment as another humiliating sign of their impotence.

Friction had built up en route to the beaches. The British repeatedly complained that the French were constitutionally incapable of main-taining essential road discipline. They kept barging through in their vehicles no matter what the circumstances or previous agreements on who was to travel along which routes and French horse-drawn artillery kept trying to turn around in the middle of jammed roads and caused general mayhem. Most of them unaware of or scorning top level route agreements, French troops protested against what they considered British high-handedness in trying to impose rules and regulations as if it were their country. A French officer recorded in his diary, 'A fresh traffic block, a mile long . . . where the British have barricaded all exits so that their columns can pass through with greater ease. The French are wild. Some gunners talk of training their guns on them and shooting.'

When they finally did reach the coast, exhausted *poilus* were enraged to discover that the British had organized the evacuation with consideration only for their own safety. French officers protested to Paris about the way they and their men were treated by the British on the beaches and the French government complained to London. To many of the French, it seemed that not only had the British made a mad rush to the sea when confronted with adversity but that, as if by right, they had taken possession of the beachfront property as well. A French colonel who angrily refused to listen when told which beach he might or might not enter was unceremoniously ordered away at gunpoint. Though, remarkably, there were virtually no incidents in which weapons were fired to enforce beach discipline, a British soldier recorded in his diary, 'A party of about twenty French troops, not used to the British habit of queueing, made a rush for the shore and grabbed a rowing boat. They clambered aboard and started to row. They did not get far for a burst of fire from a Bren gun manned by a naval rating stopped them immediately and we saw the boat floating upside down and some more bodies in the sea.'

Though it was undeniably a British operation, individual French troops or small groups of them (as well as some Belgians and Dutch) waiting on embarkation queues were neither ordered away nor kept from boarding ships or boats when their turn came. But the French command was expected to make arrangements for the greater numbers, the ones in organized units which had fallen back to the coast. Their arrival, beginning that day, caused acute problems for the Royal Navy beach personnel trying against the odds to keep the evacuation process from disintegrating into chaos. To prevent that from happening, part of the beach at Malo was given over for sole French use and the British urged the French to send more ships for their men.

That French officers and troops were outraged by British seizure of control of French beaches was understandable. But none except a handful of French senior officers knew that Gort had been trying for two-and-a-half days to coordinate British-French withdrawal and evacuation procedures only to be informed that the French had no intention of being evacuated. That very morning, Admiral Abrial made 'a big fuss' because the British were proceeding with more than a limited embarkation of selected personnel despite the fact that he, the senior Allied commander in the region, still had received no orders from Paris that there was to be a mass evacuation. Abrial still intended 'to hold on to Dunkirk till the last man and the last round'. He believed the British should help in that task.

Gort was both exasperated and baffled. Time was running out. The Germans could not be held back much longer. Yet, while confused instructions from London indicated that every consideration was to be extended to French troops seeking to be evacuated, Abrial, the senior French officer in the region, a man who rarely ventured from his underground bastion, was acting as if the Allied plan was to stand fast and go bravely down to bloody disaster.

Gort asked London for clarification on how he was to deal with the situation. He particularly wanted a clear reply to the delicate question of whether to embark French troops on British rescue vessels, not something he was anxious to promote. He pointed out that 'every Frenchman embarked is in the place of one Englishman'. The response he received from the War Office was pretty much what he wanted:

> While it is eminently desirable that nothing should be done which might suggest lack of cooperation with French, your instructions that

safety of BEF is primary consideration stand. We have every reason to believe that French Admiralty are taking steps to provide shipping for evacuation of French troops. When they have done so, facilities should . . . be shared equally between British and French personnel. Until French ships materialize, however, you are authorized to use British ships for British personnel.

It sounded straightforward. But nothing was without complications during that turbulent operation. The French command that day finally authorized the evacuation. Trying to bolster French resistance, Churchill sent Reynaud a message of solidarity. He told the French premier, 'We wish French troops to share in evacuation to the fullest extent . . . We do not know how many will be forced to capitulate, but we must share this loss together as best we can and above all bear it without reproaches arising from inevitable confusion, stresses and strains'. Even with the six French Navy vessels that arrived to assist in the evacuation, that wouldn't be easy.

As a result of the communications breakdown, the British had little knowledge of the spirited defence the French were putting up on the right of the perimeter defence line. Their commanders had no reason to revise their conviction that French incompetence was responsible for the Allied predicament. General Brooke, who was about to hand over command of II Corps and return home from Dunkirk, wrote in his diary that the French army had become 'a rabble . . . panicking every time German planes come over'.

Spears in Paris continued to report the increasing inroads of defeatist sentiment there. Among other things, mobilization of French able bodied men not yet called to the colours to meet the enemy threat was considered pointless because the quartermaster had no reserves of rifles or uniforms for them – an 'absurd state of affairs', Reynaud snarled. Weygand urged that 'the British government should be informed that the moment may come when France, against her will, may find herself unable to carry on the struggle in such a manner as to protect her soil'. It was hardly the stuff from which renewed confidence could be extracted.

But surprisingly in view of developments, Reynaud suddenly exhibited a resurgence of hope. Rising from the depths of despair, the French leader now seemed to project the belief that the battle, lost in the north, could still be won in the south. He called for the British forces being evacuated from Dunkirk to be quickly reconstituted as fighting units and shipped back to France to tangle with the enemy, together with three British divisions that had been in training for dispatch across the English Channel when the Germans had launched their offensive. Reynaud further urged that the RAF, both Bomber and Fighter Commands, commit more of their resources to the Battle of France. Orders, he said, had been given for French airfields to be put at the disposal of British aircraft.

Whatever the reason for Reynaud's suddenly lifted spirits, Churchill had by now been forced to accept that France's capitulation was only a matter of time and that a government prepared to cooperate with Hitler might take over from Reynaud when that happened. He wanted France to hold out as long as possible but he signalled Spears in Paris to be less than completely forthcoming when he informed French leaders about details of Britain's plans for continuing to fight on when France went under.

Emergency preparations were, for example, being made to maintain the flow of supplies to Britain from abroad upon which the country's survival as an independent nation depended. More than half of the country's food and much of its raw materials were imported. Ways had to be found to make certain the convoys continued to get through. The plan was to divert all shipping to Britain's west coast ports, furthest from Nazi-occupied Europe. German U-boats were a menace on the high seas, which made the use of so many Royal Navy destroyers in Operation Dynamo a great gamble. But it was believed that if sixty per cent of import levels could be maintained, Britain 'should be able to obtain enough food to feed the population and enough raw materials for essential armament production'. Non-essential imports, 'such as bananas and children's toys', would have to be reduced.

More immediately pressing were preparations to repel a German invasion. Some of the ideas put forward at meetings of the War Cabinet were bizarre, revealing the limits of Britain's home defence resources. The Prime Minister suggested, for example, that old German artillery pieces kept in Britain as trophies of past wars might be reconditioned to be used as anti-tank guns on the country's beaches. In view of the shortage of rifles, thought was given to raiding museums to equip Home Guard personnel with pikes and other primitive weapons, if only to give men something with which to drill.

Nagging anxiety persisted about the sort of new weapons the Germans might have devised. Each day produced a new crop of rumours. One told of an insidious form of genetic warfare – the creation by German scientists of an omnivorous strain of grasshopper which was to be released in hordes over British farms to starve the British into surrender. Another rumour told of German bombs the size of ostrich eggs with tremendous destructive power and of a mysterious device which could put guns out of action and which, it was said, hastened the Belgian surrender.

Home defence forces were alerted to the possibility that the invasion attempt might come in the form of a massive seaborne raid in which up to two hundred fast motor boats, each carrying one hundred heavily armed men, would attack simultaneously at various points along the British coast. Those boats, newly designed, might be able to run right up on to the beaches before disgorging the troops they carried. Such an onslaught might be made to coincide with airborne enemy raids inland so that home defence forces would be hard pressed to cope with both at the same time. The Chiefs of Staff Committee ominously noted, 'We do not consider that by naval or air action we could prevent such a landing'.

Aware of this and other perils, Churchill remained determined to prevent defeatism from sapping British spirits, as it easily could if the wretched news from Dunkirk did not get better. He knew how contagious panic would be if an image of German invincibility took hold of the British imagination. As a directive he issued that day demonstrated, he considered the moods and attitudes of government officials vitally important:

> In these dark days, the Prime Minister would be grateful if all his colleagues in the Government, as well as high officials, would maintain a high morale in their circles; not minimising the gravity of events, but showing confidence in our ability and inflexible resolve to continue the war till we have broken the will of the enemy to bring all Europe under his domination . . . Whatever may happen on the Continent, we cannot doubt our duty and we shall certainly use all our power to defend the Island, the Empire and our Cause.

The war effort was to be intensified. Not only were workers in war factories to be encouraged to increase their efforts but the country was to be scoured for all possible war materials. Antique cannon, pointing out over the Thames at the Tower of London and no longer salvageable as effective weapons, were to be melted down to make bombs and shells. Railings around parks and squares in many cities were torn out and also dispatched to the furnace, as was metal from park bandstands. At the same time, officials thought it was time to make plans to ship Britain's art treasures in the National Gallery and the Royal Collection off to Canada for safe keeping.

At his command post at La Panne, Gort still didn't know what London expected of him if the Germans broke through the perimeter defences, possibly at any moment. At the War Office, Chief of Staff General Dill was worried that the BEF commander might mistakenly interpret the ambiguous message of confidence sent to him the previous evening as meaning that he was to continue fighting to the bitter end, regardless of casualties. Lord Halifax proposed that Gort be told instead that it would not be dishonourable for him to 'relinquish the struggle' – that meant surrender – if the alternative was a massacre of his men.

Churchill disagreed. He said such instructions would only make matters more difficult for the BEF commander. It would be wrong to complicate his understanding of his position by appearing to offer him a difficult choice before it was necessary for him to make one. The Prime Minister maintained that in the absence of precise orders, any brave man was entitled to use his own discretion in a desperate situation. That was the position Gort was in. Churchill insisted that there was nothing in the message of confidence sent to him that conveyed the impression that if the troops were left without food, water, ammunition or hope of rescue, they should keep on fighting. Indulging once more in what seemed at that stage to be unwarranted optimism, the Prime Minister said that a day saved at Dunkirk by not prematurely suggesting to Gort that he might surrender could mean an additional forty thousand men brought home. The decision was to be left entirely to the BEF commander. Churchill told him as much in a personal message that evening:

> If you are cut from all communication from us and all evacuation from Dunkirk and beaches had in your judgement been finally prevented after every attempt to re-open it had failed, you would become the sole judge of when it was impossible to inflict further damage upon the enemy. H.M.G. [His Majesty's Government] are sure that the repute of the British Army is safe in your hands.

This additional message of confidence was appreciated. After commanding one of the most momentous routs in British military history, Gort badly needed it. But his instructions with regard to fighting on to the last were no clearer than they had been before. Why was the emphasis placed on 'the repute' of the army? Was its honour to take precedence over the lives of the men?

The way to the coast was packed with British troops. 'Every road scoring the landscape', recalled one among them, 'was one thick mass of transport and troops, great long lines of them converging towards the one focus – Dunkirk. Ambulances, lorries, trucks, Bren-gun carriers, artillery columns – everything except tanks – all crawling along those roads in well-defined lines over the flat, featureless country . . . Under their greyish camouflage paint they resembled from a distance a slow-moving river of muddy-coloured lava from some far-off eruption.' In the final stage, when they had to destroy their vehicles, almost all of them, thousands upon thousands, though physically exhausted, were walking to the sea.

> Weariness came down like a board on our heads [said a Coldstream Guards officer]. As I marched, my eyes kept closing and I knew that I was walking about like a drunkard. After a little, nausea overcame me, and I fell out for a few minutes. When we halted for a ten minutes' rest, I lay flat on the cold wet road and found a few minutes' relief.

Many units remained intact, some retaining their transport until they reached the perimeter, some élite infantry units marching in columns that were in amazingly good order considering what they had been through and the numbers they had lost. But countless companies and platoons had broken up into smaller groups or had disintegrated altogether. Countless men were on their own or had joined up with a few others, sometimes total strangers, in their trek. Officers, NCOs, and ordinary soldiers trudged forward together. Many had pruned tree branches to use as walking sticks. They all converged on the Dunkirk perimeter.

Even when they passed through the perimeter line, forward momentum was not permitted to flag, even after dark. They had to get to the beaches just a few miles off to be ferried home:

> We continued towards Malo-les-Bains, crossing the railway and marching through the ruined street of Rosendaal whose skeleton walls stood around us like the ruins of some bygone civilization . . . Mysterious shadows flitted about the streets, in and out of broken doorways, and disappearing around corners. They were stray inhabitants who had been cut-off by the swift march of events and were living in cellars. And a few looters. And, probably, a few spies.

By nightfall of May 29th, three days after its pilgrimage to the coast had begun, virtually all of the British Expeditionary Force had completed the trek. Except for stragglers, it had withdrawn into the Dunkirk perimeter. Paying a steep price in casualties, the troops holding the escape corridor open had done their job and now the survivors among them had withdrawn as well. The desperate retreat had been carried out. But for most of the men, the great escape still appeared to be no more than a hope.

Men were dismayed by what they saw as they approached the end of their trek. From a distance, they beheld the pall of smoke from Dunkirk's burning oil tanks.

> [It hung] like Death's hovering wing. Underneath, the tops of the tall skeletons of wrecked buildings and churches were silhouetted in black against the horizon and the lower edge of the dark, threatening wing. Amidst these silhouettes huge fires raged, the long tongues of orange flame leaping high into the air . . . It was a forbidding spectacle. Looked at as a refuge, a gate of escape, it was anything but inviting. We seemed to be heading straight for a holocaust.

And then, to bypass this vision of hell to reach the beach, and see the mass of humanity there, all of them apparently with prior claim to evacuation, seemed another foretaste of doom. Those who had just been fighting the Germans knew the enemy advance guard couldn't be far behind. And all had been under attack or threat of attack from German aircraft and knew their safety was still far from assured. For most who were not now deployed to keep the enemy ground forces from cracking through the perimeter defence, once they reached the coast there was nothing to do but find a place on the beach or the dunes and wait. Some would be there up to forty-eight excruciating hours; a few even longer.

Along stretches of shoreline, rows of summer houses, now abandoned by their owners, squatted just behind the dunes. In some places, they practically fronted on the beaches. Many had been demolished by bombs; others had suffered only minor damage. Some troops settled down within their walls, hoping to be safe there from air raids.

> In the basements of the houses which faced the sea, we took shelter . . . It needed no enticement to make for them . . . There was one man who was so frightened that he had no inclination to leave the shelter. I asked him, 'Don't you want to go home?' His reply was, 'No, I'm staying.'

When not under attack from the air or in immediate prospect of embarking, to shake the tedium some of the men scratched together teams to play soccer on the shore, it being understood that they could always reclaim their established positions in departing queues. Others wandered about if only for a change of scenery or to stretch their legs. The more adventurous ambled back into built-up areas beyond the dunes to scavenge for food and drink in abandoned hotels, stores and cafés, most of which had already been thoroughly cleaned out. One soldier stumbled across some French troops in Bray village huddled around a fire over which they were engaged in serious culinary activity. When he came close, they invited him to take part in their repast which turned out to be baked beans washed down with champagne. He was lucky. Some men went without sustenance till they were aboard ships, and most till they were back in England.

When ships and boats were landing, the lines moved forward at a pace that was agonizingly slow for the men who were furthest from the breakwater or from the water line. Unnerving as the air raids were – both the anticipation and the actuality – for most of the men on the shore they provided the only excitement until their turn for embarkation approached, the only break from the appalling tedium of just being there. It was an excitement laced with terror as men, tensed like twisted steel, pressed themselves into the sand, trying to make themselves small.

> I can still see the hand of the person next to me one time – the hand was only a few inches from my face as we two lay prone – it twitched with nerves, the knuckles gleaming white as his hand clenched and unclenched, the fingers biting into his thigh.

After the planes came over – bombing and strafing – there were always a few more men lying dead on the beach. The others covered them with sand.

Despite warnings from Gort that the Germans might break through at any moment, despite the alarming naval and air losses, despite the suspension of daylight evacuation from the breakwater by civilian passenger vessels, it began to dawn on London and on Dynamo headquarters in Dover during the course of the day that the operation might not be a complete failure. Far more troops were being brought back to England than had been imagined possible when the operation was launched. In the morning, they had boarded from the breakwater at a rate of two thousand an hour.

What was more, despite Gort's forebodings, all reports indicated that the perimeter defence was holding. It was conceivable that it would continue to hold for another day, or even two. During that time, the evacuation could be accelerated. More than half the BEF might be lost – a still daunting prospect. But it might yet be possible to rescue tens of thousands more of those who had fallen back into the perimeter. Tighter, more efficient organization was required on the Dunkirk side of the Channel where the intricacies of the improvised operation continued to be responsible for mistakes and missed opportunities. Many vessels had been made to wait too long outside the harbour for their turn to enter and tie up at the breakwater. On the long stretch of coastline, some ships were waiting needlessly and dangerously off beaches on which, in contrast to patches further along, not many men had congregated. As a consequence, some returned to Dover less than fully loaded.

Captain Tennant and his naval shore party had gone with little sleep since arriving two days before. Supervising and controlling the evacuation of an army under battle conditions was a formidable task. Tennant needed help. That afternoon, Rear Admiral Frederic Wake-Walker, a former battleship commander on the staff of the Admiralty in London, was instructed to make for Dunkirk to speed things up. He was not to supersede Tennant who would remain Senior Naval Officer on land. Instead, Wake-Walker was to command 'sea-going ships and vessels off the Belgian coast'. He was to instruct them where to go when they arrived from England to embark troops. The 'off the Belgian coast' formula was devised so that Wake-Walker would neither come under the command of Admiral Abrial in Dunkirk, who remained the senior Allied officer on the north-west coast of France, nor further ruffle Abrial's already much ruffled feathers when he ignored him as he went about his duties.

Wake-Walker was accompanied by two other senior naval officers who would be in charge off the La Panne and Bray beaches, respectively, and a team of officers and men who were to help maintain discipline on the beaches. Though disciplinary problems remained and would remain till the operation was concluded, they would have an easier time of it than the navy beach masters already ashore. The disorganized crowds of troops which had earlier congregated on the beaches had mostly either already been lifted off or brought to order. The more recent arrivals from inland were for the most part disciplined fighting troops and related units. What was more, officers were increasingly inclined to enforce their authority in unmistakable ways.

> Just as it would have been our rightful turn to board the next returning rowing boat, an officer, with drawn revolver, leapt into the water and ordered our party to the back of the queue, stating we had jumped the queue . . . My party began to argue vigorously against this injustice. The officer threatened to shoot us. I think he meant it, so did the others. In despair, we left the water and tramped wearily up the crowded beach.

More small craft began arriving to lift the troops off, including the first of anxiously awaited landing craft, only eight as yet but a promise of more to come. In London, the Admiralty, responding to anguished pleas from across the Channel, ordered the Small Vessels Pool to requisition more 'suitable motor boats' for immediate service from ports further along England's southern and eastern coasts, from Portsmouth to Yarmouth.

As hopes rose for getting ever greater numbers of troops home, the Admiralty made a decision during the day that sent them plummeting again. Of all types of vessels involved in the operation, destroyers were rescuing most of the men being brought back to England. In addition, of all the vessels involved, they were by far the best equipped to repel German air and sea attacks while scurrying between Dover and Dunkirk. Nevertheless, late that day, the Admiralty decreed that the most modern destroyers in the operation would be withdrawn from evacuation duty.

With a total of ten destroyers sunk or otherwise put out of action in the operation before nightfall that day, the possibilities were frightening for the defence of Britain. If that rate of loss were sustained, Britain's fleet of modern destroyers would be decimated. It was similar to the reasoning that limited the number of RAF fighters committed to battle over Dunkirk. Britain could not be left without adequate naval resources to repel an enemy invasion attempt and to guard maritime sea lanes which had to be kept open if the nation was to survive.

Admiral Ramsay was informed that he could continue to employ his fifteen remaining older destroyers as well as whatever other vessels he could muster. But the modern destroyers would not be permitted to shuttle ceaselessly through the danger zone; nor could they be anchored in place off Dunkirk as troops embarked, sitting targets for the enemy. It was regrettable but, said the Admiralty, it had to be done.

What could not be so easily regulated by decree was the danger of mistake or miscalculation by hard-pressed embarkation control officers. That evening, an officer of the naval shore party whose judgment 'had been affected by the events of the day', sent word back to England from La Panne BEF headquarters, via the War Office and the Admiralty, that because of the tremendous enemy aerial bombardment, Dunkirk harbour was blocked. As a result, further embarkation from the breakwater was impossible.

It wasn't true. The harbour was littered with wreckage and dotted with burning ships but it was not blocked. The breakwater was as usable as it had been before. But direct communications between Dover and embarkation personnel at Dunkirk left much to be desired. Radio contact with the Dunkirk end could be made only through destroyers when they were tied up at the breakwater. Unable to get either confirmation or denial from Dunkirk or other sources and never imagining that so important a message could be mistaken, particularly if channelled through the War Office and the Admiralty, Dynamo headquarters had no option but to order that no further ships should try to enter the harbour. Instead they were again limited to the less effective and more time consuming process of squatting offshore and sending their small boats to ferry men from the beaches. As a consequence, for the rest of that day and during the following night only five small ships entered the harbour to evacuate not the many thousands who might have been boarded from the breakwater but only a few hundred.

The accelerated morning embarkations from the harbour had raised hopes that fifty to sixty thousand troops would be evacuated that day. Instead, because of the mistaken report, only 47,310 men were brought back to England that day – 33,558 from the harbour, 13,752 from the beaches. That made a total of 72,783 evacuated since the operation began, much more than had at first been expected but still leaving much to be done in the little time believed remaining before enemy action closed the operation down.

The rescued men were received as heroes as they came ashore in England, if only for having survived and returned. Cheered as they disembarked at Dover, Ramsgate, Sheerness and other ports in south-eastern England, they were handed sandwiches, tea, beer and cigarettes and bundled into waiting trains. They were cheered again at stops along the route to collecting centres all over the country where they were to be reclothed, fed and sorted out to be dispatched to camps where their units would be reformed.

Churchill passed word to Reynaud, 'As soon as we have reorganized our evacuated troops and prepared forces necessary to safeguard our life against threatened and perhaps imminent invasion, we shall build up a new BEF' to be sent to France. That process would take far longer than the British leader seemed to suggest – more than four years.

## Chapter 9 – DAY FIVE OF DUNKIRK

# Armada in Miniature

Ships out there were sinking. Airplanes were dive bombing. Soldiers were streaming in and down to the water. Two arrived carrying a stretcher between them upon which was the body of a third soldier. They stopped where the sand sloped down to the beach, lowered the stretcher to the ground and, with the butts of their rifles, they scooped out a grave. Then they buried the dead comrade they had carried goodness knows how many miles, as near to England as they could get him. They covered him with sand and made their farewells to him, standing at attention and saluting. Then they went down the beach to take their place on a queue.

The British public still had only a vague idea of what was occurring on the other side of the English Channel. Comfort was drawn from a French report that two thousand German aircraft had been shot down since the start of the battle. That appeared to confirm exaggerated RAF kill claims publicized at street corner news-stands throughout the land. But it was known that things were grim, that Boulogne and Calais had fallen to the enemy, that Belgium had capitulated, and that Royal Navy warships had been sunk. And though it was not commonly understood that the British Expeditionary Force was being driven into the sea – the BBC announced only that a number of troops 'not immediately engaged' had been evacuated from France – it was known that the troops had fallen back to the coast and word was spreading of the large numbers of ragged soldiers arriving at Dover and other ports along the coast of southern England.

Censorship blocked press publication of accounts of the rescue operation. But reports in local newspapers printed when censorship was eased immediately after Operation Dynamo was terminated described what onlookers saw during the days of Dunkirk when the defeated troops were being shuttled home. 'It was a dirty, tired army that tramped to the waiting 'buses [in Dover] that took them to the station and the waiting trains . . .' Florid prose sometimes conveyed the picture more vividly:

> Saturated with sea water, grimed with battle smoke, hungry, thirsty and unspeakably weary, they dragged their tired, war-stained limbs to the sanctuary of the land whose institutions they had given so much to preserve. With brains numbed by incessant bombing, nerves wracked by the inferno of noise which modern warfare brings, and senses crushed by the fearful scenes through which they had passed, there were but two things they craved – comfort and rest.

Unrestrained by censorship, the American press didn't have to wait to publish what its reporters and a lot of other people at Dover saw – that 'dog-tired, wounded and unkempt Allied troops floundered sleepily home from the death trap of Flanders in bomb-raked ships' and that the 'shattered remnants of the BEF – blood-stained, muddy and walking like men asleep' had begun arriving at British ports.

The British public at large was spared the realization that a good part of the BEF might be left on the beaches at Dunkirk when the Germans broke through the perimeter defence. Instead, in the columns of the *Manchester Guardian*, Harold Nicolson, parliamentary secretary to the Minister of Information, who a few days earlier had advised his wife that she, like he, should keep a suicide pill handy, urged the people of Britain not to be dejected:

> The news is bad. We must expect worse news in the days that follow . . . Let us not be down-hearted . . . Sorrow is inevitable but hope is also inevitable. The resources of our Empire far exceed anything which Germany can command . . . It may well be that by employment of methods which did not exist in previous wars [the Germans] may be able to land in Great Britain some thousands of their troops . . . [But] the whole country will rise as a man to resist such invasion and whatever confusion or destruction may momentarily occur the ultimate issue is beyond doubt.

The correspondent of the Associated Press very likely was taking journalistic liberties when he reported to America, 'Invasion of England itself was described by Britain's leaders tonight as really imminent'. But while unlikely to have said anything of the sort to a reporter, that was what British leaders feared. The possibility of a German invasion had become an obsession in the upper reaches of the government and the military. Intelligence services reported that the Germans had intensified their naval activity on the Norwegian coast and were gathering a fleet of motor boats at North Sea ports. And though they had been busily laying mines in British waters, they were also reported to have ominously left a stretch of water off the British coast clear of mines. Admiral of the Fleet Sir Dudley Pound reported to the War Cabinet that he was confident the Royal Navy could deal with a major attacking armada, but he thought it conceivable that some enemy invading craft could slip through the net. They might have to be dealt with on land though it was impossible to say where along the coast they might arrive.

The failure until then to install anti-tank mines on British beaches where the Germans might try to storm ashore aroused both alarm and dismay. Production of those mines was not expected to start until the following week. The War Cabinet and the chiefs of staff were tormented by how inadequate available coastal defences appeared to be. In desperation, Churchill suggested that if the enemy did manage to land on British shores, poison gas should be used against them. Though it was banned by international law, he felt that Britain 'had the right to do what it liked with our own territory'.

Some 25,000 children who had been evacuated from London and other cities considered prime targets for German bombers were to be shifted again. They had been sent to places of refuge on the south and east coasts of England where German landings were now considered most likely. The children were to be moved elsewhere, to the English Midlands and Wales.

Fear of saboteurs and fifth columnists led to a curfew being imposed on all aliens over the age of sixteen who had not already been interned. In addition, unless authorized by the police, no alien was permitted to have use of a bicycle or motor vehicle that might assist him or her in subversive activities.

Civil defence measures were tightened. The authorities began cracking down on people who had neglected to erect miniature air raid shelters of corrugated iron, more than two million of which had been distributed to the public free of charge for erection in their homes or back gardens. A regulation was issued requiring individuals who had been given those 'Anderson' shelters, named after a government minister, either to put them up properly or explain to the authorities why they had not done so.

The day had begun at Dunkirk with Captain Tennant wondering about the whereabouts of ships which should already have arrived at Dunkirk harbour. Unaware that Dynamo headquarters had been mistakenly informed that the harbour was blocked, he had made arrangements to evacuate thousands of troops from the breakwater before dawn. Troops on the adjoining road and beach had been readied to hurry along the pier and clamber aboard for the homeward journey as soon as vessels tied up.

The failure of the ships to appear deepened the sense of nightmare dread for the naval personnel at the breakwater and the waiting troops. Tennant and his staff feared that the vessels might have been sunk or crippled en route, that a replay of the heavy losses of the previous day was in the making. They did not know that Dynamo headquarters, informed that the harbour entrance was blocked, had instructed the vessels which streamed across from Dover under the cover of darkness to make instead for positions off the coast to service boats working the beaches.

For Rear Admiral Wake-Walker, who had arrived off the coast after dark the previous night to make sense of offshore arrangements, the first daylight view of his task was not encouraging. The sloop HMS *Bideford*, with forty feet of her stern blown off, was aground nearby. The paddle steamer *Crested Eagle* lay burnt out on the beach not far away. Other vessels of various sizes and in various states of damage, some still burning, were abandoned in the shallows. Clusters of huddled men were at the water's edge, some of them wading out in search of rescue. Large groups of troops were on the beach. Others were on the dunes. Ships may have been diverted from Dunkirk harbour to stand offshore but few were in sight and few boats appeared to be working the beaches.

A team of navy signals personnel was supposed to be ashore with Aldis lamps to signal the ships to send in their boats and make ready to receive evacuees but not one was to be found on the beaches that morning or at any time during the entire operation. Nor were communications between Dunkirk and Bray and elsewhere along the beach ever established. As a consequence, beach patrols, trying to accelerate the evacuation, at no time knew whether it was or was not advisable to march waiting troops the few miles along the shore to be embarked at the harbour on vessels that might be waiting at the breakwater there.

In many places along the shore, embarkation control procedures remained totally haphazard. 'Any organization for forming groups for the next boat', one naval officer later reported, 'was constantly ruined by streams of stragglers coming down to the water's edge . . . Stragglers were continually arriving and forming batches out of their turn.'

Efforts to fashion some sort of order out of the disarray sometimes served only to contribute to confusion. At Bray Dunes, some soldiers were told that their officers had to get embarkation tickets from embarkation control officers in order to get their men away, and that those officers had to 'get enough men together' in order to qualify for such a ticket. The idea, presumably, was to put a stop to the disorder on the beaches. Whatever the intention, such a system didn't even come close to working; nor could it when there were so many men to evacuate with dispatch under fire, and so few to organize their departure.

Gort's La Panne headquarters called for more boats, and again for more; men under air attack were waiting and had to be lifted off. London was again told that the perimeter defence would not be able to hold the Germans back much longer and that great numbers of troops would be lost when they broke through. Such warnings were now a regular refrain in communications from La Panne to the War Office. With wide patches of beach jammed with weary, hungry men under repeated air attack, the sense of urgency in the Dunkirk pocket was never in danger of wearing thin. German guns found the range of the beaches during the day. They as well as the harbour were being bombarded by artillery, without great accuracy and with limited effect, but some men were wounded and killed and a growing number of bodies lay on the beaches, some covered, others not.

Worse was the news that though the Germans didn't seem to be suffering supply difficulties, some of the troops holding them back at the perimeter defence line were running perilously short of ammunition. It was not inconceivable that positions would be overrun because the defenders did not have enough shells and bullets to fight off the enemy.

Gort's hope was that before that happened, the beaches would be cleared of most of the men already there. Then the perimeter defences would be thinned and the troops withdrawn from the line evacuated, leaving only enough men on the line to hold back the enemy. That final rearguard would then be pulled back under the cover of darkness and lifted off in one carefully prepared swoop. One look at the swarms of men still on the shore made it seem a pipe dream.

At Dover that morning, Admiral Ramsay had no more reason than Gort to be hopeful. With Dunkirk harbour reportedly blocked, without the modern destroyers which had been removed from the rescue operation the day before, with civilian passenger vessels restricted to night-time operations because of concentrated enemy activity, and with several of his larger ships already sunk or otherwise put out of action, there seemed little possibility of doing more than was already being done – except perhaps discover whether the harbour remained blocked and the breakwater remained unusable. The continued loss of the breakwater for embarkation purposes would be a great blow. Tennant calculated that 'A destroyer going full out with her boats to the beaches could only embark 600 men in 12 hours, whereas this could be done in 20 minutes at the Pier'. It was a matter of the safety of the ships and their crews as well as the speed of the evacuation.

Direct communications between Dunkirk and Dover still unavailable, Ramsay dispatched a destroyer, the *Vanquisher,* to take a close look at the harbour soon after sunrise. It reported back that while it had sustained serious damage, it was in fact not blocked at all! Vessels could, without difficulty, enter and leave, something Ramsay might have learned from the five small ships which had done exactly that during the night had arrangements on the England side of the operation allowed such information to percolate upwards from the bustle at the debarkation ports.

After a tour of the harbour area, Wake-Walker confirmed that the breakwater remained usable despite German shelling and that it remained a far better point than the beaches for rapid boarding of troops. Navy vessels – though not civilian passenger ships – were again instructed to make for the pier to start loading. There was such a scramble aboard each and every ship by men who had thought they had been abandoned that when a freighter tied up with provisions for the men in the perimeter, unloading of cargo had to be stopped when it was only half completed.

An extraordinary explosion of activity was taking place on the beaches as well. A vast flotilla of small ships and boats, far more than had been there before, appeared off the coast. The methodical work of the Admiralty's Small Vessels Pool and the requisitioning teams Ramsay had sent out was proving its worth. It was an extraordinary sight. All manner of small and medium sized craft appeared – barges, train ferries, car ferries, passenger ferries, RAF launches, fishing smacks, tugs, motor-powered lifeboats, oar-propelled lifeboats, wherries, cockle boats, eel boats, picket boats, seaplane tenders. There were yachts and pleasure vessels of all kinds, some very expensive craft, some modest do-it-yourself conversions of ship's lifeboats. There were Thames River excursion launches with rows of slatted seats and even a Thames River fire float.

They came from Portsmouth, Newhaven, Sheerness, Tilbury, Gravesend, Ramsgate, from all along England's southern and southeastern coast, from ports big and small, from shipping towns and yachting harbours. Some, from up river, had never been in the open sea before. They were manned mostly by volunteers, men who, without being given the details, had been told that they and their vessels were urgently needed to bring back soldiers from France. Most were experienced sailors – professional or otherwise – but many were fledglings who knew nothing about maritime hazards. Had the weather been bad, some would not have risked going; neither their experience nor their craft would have been up to it. Some mariners would forever be convinced that the extraordinary uncharacteristic calm which ruled the sea during most of the ten days of Dunkirk, permitting the evacuation to proceed – 'the water was like a mill pond' – was literally heaven sent because 'God had work for the British nation to do'.

Some of the vessels which had been requisitioned were manned by naval sub-lieutenants straight from training school. Most who set out had charts to guide them past the shallows and sandbars of the Channel but some of their compasses were of doubtful accuracy which led a few to the now dangerous waters off Calais within range of German guns. One sailor who went ashore at a desolate spot to find out where he was ran into two astonished German soldiers and had to shoot them with his pistol to make his getaway.

Not knowing what to expect when they got to the Dunkirk beaches, these hastily recruited crews were astounded by what they saw – the long lines of bedraggled men winding across the sands and stretching out into the water, looking anxiously, expectantly out to sea. Men who had been standing in the water for long periods of time to guard their places in the queues could barely move. Their boots had become waterlogged dead-weights.

A breeze blew intermittently, tossing boats about and making their approach to the shore difficult and sometimes impossible. When that happened, some of the troops grew fearful that rescue, though so near, might never come. At one point, at Malo, a horde of men broke from the lines on the sand and surged to the water's edge, infected by a fantasy that despite the sea swell, the boats were managing to move in close enough to pick them up. After peering vainly out at craft much too far offshore for them to reach, they turned in frustration sullenly back to resume their places in the straggly queues.

When the winds permitted, the smallest of the boats came practically up on to the beach so that the men only had to get their feet wet. But for most of these craft, the men had to wade out into deeper water and hope they would be dragged aboard. The master of one rescue boat said, 'The snag was that when a rope was thrown to a man, about six grabbed it and just hung on looking up blankly with the water breaking over their shoulders and it was a hell of a job getting any of them to let go so that the rest could be pulled aboard.'

Some of the men seemed incapable of understanding that boats capsized when too many men tried to board them. Other boats were swamped by the loads they were carrying and the men who had piled on board had to wade or swim back to shore to try their luck again. Some men grabbed planks of wood or bits of wreckage, anything that would float and, kicking their legs, tried to propel themselves out to meet the incoming craft. Some men found collapsible dinghies which they inflated and tried to row out to the ships offshore, using their rifles as paddles. Others improvised rafts. Some stripped off their clothes and swam out to be picked up. The crew of a yacht, newly arrived offshore, was amazed to see a man stark naked swim up to them. Other troops tried to swim out fully dressed.

These new arrivals from England quickly learnt the chief hazard with which they would have to contend. The sky would be clear and seconds later a Messerschmitt 109 would roar out of the distance, its machine guns spitting, or a Stuka would scream down to unload its cargo of death. There were other worries as well. Clothes the men discarded, rope and sometimes bodies fouled their screws and rudders and crew members had to go over the side to free them. Most of the vessels, never having been worked so heavily, and some having been laid up for long periods prior to the operation, suffered mechanical and other difficulties which teams of maritime engineers back in southern British ports stood ready to tackle. During the operation, at the port of Ramsgate alone, repair work had to be done on 170 vessels which were stricken with engine, electrical or hull problems which had nothing to do with enemy action.

The problem of getting the men on the beaches to the ships offshore was never satisfactorily resolved. There just weren't enough boats. Motorized craft were finally employed retrieving abandoned rowboats and getting them to the water's edge. But the boats remained in short supply and men continued to wade out as far as they dared to be picked up by small craft which couldn't come in close for fear of beaching.

At places along the shore, engineer troops, among the comparatively few kept busy during their time on the beaches, improvised piers – built mostly of heavy-duty vehicles – to permit men to reach boats unable to come close enough to the shore. Considerable ingenuity and muscle power went into their construction:

> Fifteen or more lorries, to a length of approximately 150 yards, were driven or manhandled through soft sand and positioned whilst the tide was out nose to tail on hard sand thus enabling dinghies and other small craft to be loaded from either side. To 'anchor' the jetty all tyres were punctured, generally by firing bullets through them and when this was completed the backs of the lorries were filled with sand . . . The walkway was made up of decking panels taken from a bridging lorry and

the gaps between the roofs of the three tonners were covered by planks 'borrowed' from a timber yard . . . The military police controlled the numbers embarking at any one time, usually 50 servicemen . . . During our long spells of duty [maintaining this jetty] we were more often than not up to our shoulders in the sea and frequently covered in oil seeping from the chain of lorries.

Efforts to find more small craft to dispatch to Dunkirk continued unabated back in England. The crew of the Margate lifeboat *Lord Southborough* that morning volunteered en masse to go to the Dunkirk beaches. They were provided only with helmets and left 'in the very best spirits'. The Ramsgate lifeboat *Prudential* crossed over with eight small boats in tow. In all, nineteen coastal lifeboats went to Dunkirk, but not with the consent of all their crews. The coxswains of three of the lifeboats, summoned to participate in Dynamo and told they were expected to run their craft on to the beach to embark men, said they were too heavy for that kind of operation and declined to go. The navy then commandeered their craft, putting its own personnel on board. Seven other lifeboats were then commandeered as well to the anger of some of the crews which, though the navy didn't know it, had been prepared to take part. Members of one lifeboat crew had even bought steel helmets for the occasion. Finally realizing that these men were not the recalcitrants they had previously encountered but having already assigned men to the craft, the navy said it would be happy to take along the motor mechanics among those crews. But the offended lifeboat men replied that it was all of them or none. None it was. Under pressure, overburdened, the navy had no time for niceties or even to fully appreciate the situation. As a result, the operation was denied the services of some useful mariners.

Nevertheless, the search for small craft was pursued with unrelieved vigour. Individuals whose names were on file with the Small Vessels Pool were personally contacted. For Charles Hunt, the owner of the yacht *My Quest*, it was a visit from two naval officers at his Putney home:

He was told to consider himself and his boat at the disposal of the Naval authorities, given a brief outline of the situation and told to keep it 'under his hat'. His instructions were to get underway as soon as possible. He mentioned the affair to a friend, Mr Ted Avery, who volunteered at once . . . Naval crew took over at Sheerness.

The little ships and boats were doing far better work than had been thought possible when the operation began, or seemed likely even that morning. Now that they were there in profusion, they were able to

(*Above left*) Survivors of the rescue passenger ship *Mona's Queen* which sank in less than two minutes after hitting a German mine off Dunkirk on day three of Operation Dynamo. They were rescued by the destroyer *Vanquisher*.

(*Above, right*) French and British troops embarked at Dunkirk aboard a vessel heading for England.

(*Below*) Evacuated troops watch smoke rise from bombed Dunkirk oil storage tanks.

A row of British army trucks outside Dunkirk destroyed during the BEF's retreat to the sea to keep equipment from falling into enemy hands.

Abandoned vehicles on the beach. X in left background marks the remains of an abandoned ship put out of action by enemy aircraft.

Sunken and beached vessels and beach litter turned what had once been a seaside pleasure area into a surrealist vision.

British soldiers lying dead on the beach, a few of the many killed in air raids and by shelling during the operation.

Post-evacuation beachscape – desolate and deserted, the sands of Dunkirk were dotted with abandoned and destroyed vehicles and the discarded gear of rescued troops.

The still smoking ruins of Dunkirk, almost completely flattened by German air raids and artillery shelling. Thousands of its inhabitants were killed, as were many British and French troops who took shelter in its buildings and cellars.

Dunkirk harbour, a place of sunken or abandoned vessels, after the last of the rearguard was withdrawn from the perimeter defence and the Germans arrived to seize the port.

Silhouette of some of the first German troops to enter Dunkirk, resting in the ruins of the city's main square.

Conquering Germans marching along the beachfront, now abandoned by British and French troops who had either been evacuated or led off in captivity.

A party of German troops on the Dunkirk beach next to the remains of a British tent, still flying a battered Union Jack. Bombed out and beached vessels in the background.

After completion of Operation Dynamo, German soldiers inspect a pier of trucks British troops built to master tidal problems.

(*Below, right*) Left behind. British and French troops being led as prisoners away from the Dunkirk beach.

(*Below, left*) A cup of tea for a wounded soldier after his return home. Trains waited at Dover and other ports in south-east England to whisk the evacuees to bases inland for rest and recuperation and to be regrouped to help repel the expected German invasion.

Prime Minister to General Weygand
most immediate

Crisis in evacuation now reached. (Stop)

Five Fighter Squadrons acting almost continuously is most we can do, but six ships several filled with troops sunk by bombing this morning. (Stop) Artillery fire menacing only practicable channel. (Stop) Enemy closing in on reduced bridgehead. (Stop) By trying to hold on till to-morrow we may lose all. (Stop) By going to-night, much may certainly be saved, though much will be lost. (Stop) Situation cannot be judged by Admiral Abrial nor by you or us here. Nothing like numbers of French troops you mention in Bridgehead now, and we doubt whether such large numbers remain in area. (Stop) We have therefore ordered General Alexander Commanding Bridgehead to judge for himself whether to try to stay over to-morrow or not. Trust you will agree, again.

Draft of message from Prime Minister Churchill to General Weygand on June 1st. The original said that General Alexander would 'judge for himself' on timing the closing phase of the operation. In acknowledgment of French susceptibilities, Weygand was instead told that Alexander would consult with Admiral Abrial on the 'best line to follow'.

ferry thousands of men from the shore. But it remained a cumbersome, inefficient procedure. The sinister likelihood remained that unless more large vessels were immediately available to board great numbers of troops from the breakwater, the operation, for all its achievements so far, would fail and long columns of bedraggled British troops would be marched off into captivity.

Admiral Ramsay contacted the Admiralty to plead for the urgent return of the modern destroyers removed from evacuation duty the day before. He understood that those fighting ships were needed to guard Britain's lifelines but insisted that the country's lifeblood might depend on the safe return of the men from the sands of Dunkirk. If Dynamo failed, the future of the country would be very bleak indeed. Ramsay was persuasive and within hours six of the modern destroyers – *Harvester, Havant, Ivanhoe, Impulsive, Icarus* and *Intrepid* – were back on rescue duty, dodging bombs, boarding men from the breakwater and ferrying them to England.

Gort's chief of staff, General Pownall, had returned from Dunkirk overnight to report to Churchill, military service ministers and the chiefs of staff. He said some sixty thousand British troops – his rough guess – had still not been evacuated and pressed for efforts to be intensified to bring them home as soon as possible. Churchill once more asserted that it was important to embark French as well as British troops. Pownall told him he thought the French should be responsible for saving their own men. He was bitter about the blunderings of the French Command which he held exclusively responsible for the BEF's predicament. Ignorant of the fact that French ships had begun participating in the evacuation, though not in great numbers, he repeated to Churchill the refrain that so long as the French failed to provide ships to carry their men to safety, 'every Frenchman embarked [on a British ship] meant one more Englishman lost'. This was an inconvenient truth which Churchill, stung by French charges that Britain had turned tail, was not happy to hear. He conceded that embarking French soldiers might reduce the number of British who would be saved but, he insisted that, 'for the good of the common cause, this must be accepted'.

Convinced that Churchill still failed to grasp what had happened and what was still happening on the far side of the Channel, Pownall tried to convey to the Prime Minister a picture of the confused conditions with which Gort had to contend in the Dunkirk perimeter. Aside from the British troops, he said the entire area had become a 'congested mass of disorganized Frenchmen, refugees and Belgians'. The difficulty of maintaining discipline under such conditions had not been resolved. At one point, he said, it looked as though about 1,500 Frenchmen were going to try to storm the boats on the shore instead of queuing up to wait their turn. After a beach area had been allotted to the French at Malo, the situation on the shore had eased. But problems persisted and the defence line remained under pressure.

The British did not know that the Germans were withdrawing their tanks from the assault on the Dunkirk perimeter. They were haunted by a vision of the panzers crashing through to the troop-congested shore. No one at the meeting believed that it would be possible to bring many more men home 'if the German armoured divisions supported by the *Luftwaffe* pressed their attack'. It seemed inevitable, Pownall said, that 'the perimeter would be broken as it thinned out and there would be carnage on the beaches'. It was a terrifying prospect and an awkward one for a Prime Minister, new to his job, who might have to explain to Parliament and the British people how the bulk of the British Army had been lost.

Nevertheless, anxious to sustain French morale, Churchill sent a message to Reynaud promising that French troops would share in the evacuation from Dunkirk 'to the fullest possible extent'. But a renewed plea from General Weygand that the men evacuated from Dunkirk be shipped straight back to bolster French forces preparing to repel the expected German drive against Paris couldn't be treated seriously in London, even if Britain could rely on a home defence force larger and better trained than the one available. The men brought back had no guns, no tanks, no transport. All they had were their rifles, and many not even those. Britain no longer possessed a fighting army of any significance. It had to be rebuilt, rearmed and reinforced. Besides, no one knew how many men would finally be rescued. The War Office in London, accepting Pownall's estimate of sixty thousand still to be evacuated, hoped that 45,000 might be disengaged from the perimeter line that night and ferried home before dawn, the remainder to be lifted off the following day. In fact there were still more than 100,000 British troops in the Dunkirk pocket.

Conferring later that day with Admiral Ramsay, Pownall advised him to consider the dark early hours of Saturday, June 1st, the morning after next, as being the last 'reasonable date' by which the rearguard could be expected to hold back the enemy. That did not rule out the possibility that the Germans might break through before then. But by 1.30 a.m. on Saturday it was hoped to have reduced British forces ashore to four thousand men of the final rearguard, all the others having by then been disengaged, marched back to the beaches or the pier and brought back to England. Special attention was to be paid to assembling and holding ready ships, boats and tugs for the climax of the operation, lifting off that last four thousand troops between 1.30 and 3.30 a.m. on Saturday. Special effort had already been made to separate senior sergeants and other experienced cadre from most other units to bring them back to England to start rebuilding the British Army. But these last troops were élite fighting men. They had to be brought home!

Final plans for closing down Operation Dynamo would be reviewed the next afternoon, Friday, May 31st, in the light of conditions prevailing at that time. But at that moment, said Pownall, the Royal Navy was not doing enough to bring the troops home. He warmly praised the navy's efforts and achievements but he expressed doubts about whether the Admiralty had initially fully understood the magnitude of the task to which it had been assigned. He was in fact saying that it had still not caught up with events – it was essential to get still more ships and more boats over to Dunkirk at once!

For operational and morale reasons, Churchill had earlier been reluctant to tell Gort what to do when the final moment at Dunkirk approached. But he now agreed that specific instructions had to be issued to the BEF commander. A brave man, and mortified to have led an army that was being driven into the sea, Gort had indicated that he intended to stay with his troops till the end. But his capture would be a propaganda coup for the Germans. Churchill accordingly told him to forget any notions he might have of superintending a heroic last stand by the BEF and ordered him to prepare to return to England:

> Continue to defend the present perimeter to the utmost in order to cover maximum evacuation now proceeding well. Report every three hours through La Panne. If we can still communicate we shall send you an order to return to England with such officers as you may choose at the moment when we deem your command so reduced that it can be handed over to a Corps Commander. You should now nominate this Commander. If communications are broken you are to hand over and return as specified when your effective fighting force does not exceed the equivalent of three divisions. This is in accordance with correct military procedure and no personal discretion is left you in the matter. On political grounds, it would be a needless triumph to the enemy to capture you when only a small force remained under your orders. The Corps Commander chosen by you should be ordered to carry on the defence in conjunction with the French and evacuation whether from Dunkirk or the beaches, but when in his judgment no further organized evacuation is possible and no further proportionate damage can be

inflicted on the enemy he is authorized in consultation with the senior
French Commander to capitulate formally to avoid useless slaughter.

The BEF's III Corps had already been mostly evacuated and II Corps
had begun to embark. Their commanders – Generals Brooke and
Adam – were departing for England that day, handing over their
commands to subordinates. That left General Michael Barker as the
only original BEF corps commander remaining in France. Gort told
Barker he was to stay behind to oversee the closing act of the Dunkirk
defence and evacuation. He was to be expendable. His instructions
were to hold out as long as he could. When no other option remained,
he was to surrender.

The appointment of Barker for this endgame assignment raised
objections from General Montgomery who, having succeeded Brooke
as III Corps commander, was himself being evacuated. Never one to
hold his opinions of others to himself, Montgomery told Gort that the
appointment of Barker, a high-strung man given to bouts of anxiety,
was a serious mistake. He said that Barker 'was in an unfit state to be
left in final command', that 1st Division commander Major-General
Harold Alexander, though junior to Barker, would be a more
appropriate choice, and that Barker should be evacuated back to
England. Alexander was much respected for his cool, methodical
approach to problem solving. Montgomery suggested that such a man
might even be capable of performing the miracle of keeping the enemy
at bay till everyone could be evacuated.

Like many who came in contact with Montgomery, Gort found his
arrogance irritating. But he realized that he was right about Barker, an
aging soldier no longer up to the strain of combat, and agreed that
Alexander should take final command of the rearguard instead. When
Barker was informed by Alexander the following day, he broke down
and wept.

Developments in the war threatened to complicate further the perpetu-
ally fragile relations between Britain and Ireland. It was realized in
London that the Germans would be pleased to use Ireland for
backdoor entry into Britain. It was believed German intelligence had
established an espionage network in the country. A report by Sir
Charles Tegart, a counter-insurgency specialist, claimed that Ireland
was crawling with German agents and that the Germans had a detailed
plan for taking over the country. The week before, the Dublin police
had raided the home of an Irish businessman of German ancestry and
had found details of Irish airfields, harbours, bridges, and military
installations, as well as a radio transmitter and receiver. German

submarines were active in Irish waters and it was believed that they were used to make contact with agents on the shore and to supply them with the paraphernalia of espionage.

A quasi-fascist Irish 'Blueshirts' movement, which had never had much of a following, had largely fizzled out by the time war had started. But the violently anti-British Irish Republican Army, though believed by London to be a greater threat than it actually proved to be, was very much in evidence. The previous Christmas the IRA had demonstrated its daring and capacity for action when it had subdued the sentries and garrison at an Irish Army arms warehouse near Dublin and made off with a million rounds of ammunition. Contacts between the IRA and German intelligence had long been established; indeed they had existed even in the First World War. There could be no doubt that the organization was ready and willing to help the Germans conquer Britain. The fear in London was of an IRA-assisted German landing in Ireland as a prelude to an assault on Northern Ireland, which then as now was a province of the United Kingdom. An attack on the British mainland could well follow.

The previous day, Churchill had received intelligence reports that 'the Germans have concerted detailed plans with the IRA and that everything is now ready for an immediate descent upon the country'. Chamberlain maintained that the IRA was almost strong enough to overwhelm the Irish army which had as its core only 7,500 regular troops. The former prime minister urged that British forces be readied to be sent to Ireland to help suppress internal subversion and repel external aggression. In fact, a column of British troops based in Northern Ireland had already been secretly alerted to cross the border into Ireland when given the order. But it was recognized as likely to be counter-productive to take any action until a German attack on Ireland actually materialized.

Thousands of Irishmen had enlisted in the British armed forces and many were at Dunkirk. But the legacy of anti-British feeling remained so strongly implanted in their country that Irishmen in the British armed forces were advised to wear civilian clothes when they went home on leave. No government in Dublin could have survived permitting British troops to deploy on Irish soil until a German assault had been launched. Prime Minister Eamon de Valera informed the British that Ireland would fight if attacked by Germany and would call for British assistance if that became necessary. But if British forces arrived without being invited, the Irish government would not be held responsible for the consequences.

London was told that the government in Dublin was confident it could deal with the IRA without outside help. Nevertheless, a top secret two-man official mission – Joseph Walshe of the Irish Department of External Affairs and Colonel Liam Archer, chief of staff of the Irish Army's intelligence branch – had been dispatched to Britain a few days earlier to seek specialist military advice for preparing for the possibility of a German invasion attempt. When they returned to Dublin, they were accompanied by a British Army defence expert – in mufti – assigned to offer on-the-spot advice on defence precautions. Word of his presence in Ireland was a nervously guarded secret.

The chiefs of staff remained anxious about Ireland. They believed that 'until [Ireland] abandons her attitude of neutrality she cannot fully safeguard herself against danger of enemy activities within her territory, nor obtain the full cooperation of our forces to anticipate and resist attack. Unless this security can be achieved, Eire will remain a serious weakness in the defence of these islands'. Churchill shared those misgivings but always probing to pluck advantage from adversity, he said that if the Germans tried to move against Ireland, Britain would 'have the greater part of the [Irish] population on our own side for the first time in history'. He also maintained that if the Germans did seek a backdoor entrance to Britain through Ireland, it would not necessarily be a bad thing for Britain. He pointed out that the RAF would then be able to take on the *Luftwaffe* in an air war over Ireland 'under conditions specially favourable to us and costly to them'. The suggestion must have shocked Fighter Command chief Dowding whose squadrons were already spread frighteningly thin covering Dunkirk while preparing for the expected onslaught against Britain from newly seized forward *Luftwaffe* bases in Europe.

With the British army, navy and air force all actively engaged in the evacuation, interservice rivalry and recriminations were inevitable. Criticism of the RAF for the limited aerial cover it provided was persistent. But the Royal Navy, which was also paying heavily for its part in the operation, did not escape censure either, despite the remarkable feat of improvisation in which it was engaged. When Admiral Wake-Walker met with Gort at La Panne that evening to review the situation, he was surprised to be called upon to answer for the navy's performance, something which he had assumed to be worthy of nothing but praise. It was made clear to him that the army felt it had done its job in bringing the BEF back to the coast; now it was up to the Royal Navy to bring the men back to England but, in view of the persisting congestion on the beaches, it didn't seem to be doing too well. Caught by surprise, Wake-Walker made no reference to the failure of the army to plan for or provide adequate beach organization or control or, for that matter, to maintain greater discipline in the ranks. He explained that much of the navy's performance depended on weather conditions which hadn't been unrelievedly favourable and on the intensity of enemy action. But to his exasperation, he could not dispel mutterings about the 'ineptitude of the navy'.

German generals were also muttering about ineptitude – that of their own forces in failing to close down the Dunkirk bridgehead. Halder complained about standing by and watching 'countless thousands of the enemy get away to England right under our noses'. Brauchitsch moaned that the 'effects of the blunders forced upon us by OKW [Armed Forces High Command] . . . are beginning to be felt now. We lost time and so the pocket with the French and British in it was sealed later than it could have been. Worse, the pocket would have been closed at the coast if only our armour had not been held back.' Everyone was busy blaming someone or something else – the *Luftwaffe* for failing to wipe out the bridgehead, the order to halt for preventing the tanks from doing the job, the diversion of troops and equipment to knock France out of the war.

That day Army Group A, which had made the running all the way from Sedan, was withdrawn from involvement in the Dunkirk episode. Its armour, which was useless anyway in canal-laced terrain that was being flooded after the French opened protective flood gates, was to be regrouped, repaired and rested for the attack south to bring France to its knees. The operations officer at Army Headquarters insisted that it was necessary to intensify efforts to disrupt the evacuation but complained that 'no one is now interested in Dunkirk anymore'.

That wasn't true. The bridgehead had become a serious embarrassment to the commanders still assigned to wiping it out. So anguished did they become at their failure to do so that they considered landing troops from the sea to accomplish the task. They also contemplated pulling their forward units back from contact with the perimeter line to give the *Luftwaffe* a free field of attack against the defenders. But finally it was the ground troops, pressing against the perimeter, who remained responsible for trying to break through and they found the defenders 'fighting back very stubbornly'.

Like the Allies, the Germans were plagued with communications problems and had difficulty coordinating their attacks. Their commanders worried about the danger of their troops firing at each other. To add to their frustration, they were intercepting British radio communications which indicated that, despite Gort's repeated urgent pleas for more boats, the evacuation operation was proceeding with considerable success and was even being stepped up.

By midnight, 53,823 troops had been brought back to England that day, most of them from the beaches. Many more would have been evacuated had embarkation from the breakwater resumed earlier in the day once the report that the harbour was blocked was proved to be mistaken. But a total of 126,606 troops had now been brought home since the start of Operation Dynamo.

Hope began to percolate through the War Command in London that the unbelievable was taking place. It looked like far fewer troops would be left to the Germans at Dunkirk than seemed likely even the night before. But this surge of cautious optimism was balanced by a growing flood of demoralizing rumours circulating among the public. It was said that German saboteurs were being caught all over Britain, indicating that the enemy was readying a major assault on the homeland. It was said that the Irish government had signed a secret alliance with Germany that would expose Britain to attack from across the Irish Sea. Most worrying of all for morale purposes, it was rumoured that the War Office was offering the public such limited information on what was happening across the Channel because British troop losses there were devastatingly huge. It was decided that the British public should finally be told what actually was happening.

## Chapter 10 – DAY SIX OF DUNKIRK

# The People are Told

ON THE MORNING of May 31st, the people of Britain were finally told by the BBC and their newspapers about the desperate operation to evacuate their army from France. 'Under the guns of the Allied navies,' the *Daily Express* reported, 'under the wings of the Royal Air Force, a large proportion of the B.E.F. who for three days had been fighting their way back to the Flanders coast have now been brought safely back to England.'

'Eyes hollow from lack of sleep,' the *Daily Mirror* said, 'days' growth of beard on their chins, some without food for forty-eight hours, they were utterly weary as they stumbled into train after train.' A newspaper cartoon described BEF as standing for Bravery, Endurance and Fortitude.

There was no mention of how many casualties had been sustained by the forces which had kept open the retreat corridor for almost a week or of the men killed or wounded on the Dunkirk beaches and while being ferried home. Making a rough estimate, Pownall had told Churchill the previous day that the casualties amounted to a very substantial number – between sixty thousand and eighty thousand men. But that morning's news, as released by the Ministry of Information, was dressed up to generate a mood of relief after all the worrying rumours that had spread about the fate of the men. It was reassuring for the British to hear that so many of their boys were already back home, safe behind their English Channel moat, and that the others were following.

There had been a steady flow homeward during the night. But winds of up to force three blew up from the north-west during the early morning. These were moderate by textbook definition but the strongest since the operation began and fresh enough to disrupt embarkation from the shore. Many of the small boats capsized or were swamped. All the boats, and larger craft as well, were bounced about by the waves. The coxswain of the lifeboat *Lord*

*Southborough*, which tried to get in close to the beach, called it 'a nasty surf':

> Troops were rushing out to us from all directions and were being drowned close to us and we could not get to them . . . It seemed to me we were doing more harm [than good] by drawing the men off the shore, as with their heavy clothing, the surf was knocking them over and they were unable to get up.

Some troops who considered themselves fortunate to have been lifted off despite the surf were thrown back into the water when their boats capsized. They had to wade or swim back to the shore. All along the coast, boats blown ashore or unable to pull back fast enough when the tide raced out were stranded high and dry in the mud.

For the men manning the small craft, endurance had become problematic, as the naval reserve officer put in charge of the motor boat *Triton* recalled soon after:

> My crew and myself were drunk and stupid with exhaustion. My body ached all over and I was almost hoping I would be knocked out to escape my weariness. The lad working the engine was sleeping, the cox was steering anyhow . . . My arms feel; as if they had left their sockets [from hauling men aboard] . . . I drove [my men] when they were crying with exhaustion. May God forgive me for the hell I put them through.

There was no telling how long the winds would blow. It could be hours before there was a let up, or longer. It was not unusual for the surf along the coast to act up for days without a break. Wake-Walker despairingly reported to Dynamo headquarters from a destroyer offshore that a change in operation procedures was once more essential: 'Majority of boats are broached to and have no crews . . . Consider only hope of embarking any number is at Dunkirk'. In case that message wasn't fully appreciated, he followed shortly after with another: 'Dunkirk our only real hope'. Believing the perimeter defence could collapse at any moment, Dynamo headquarters at Dover nevertheless insisted it was important to go on trying to use the beaches as well as the Dunkirk breakwater as long as possible. Wake-Walker responded curtly, 'Dunkirk our only hope', and acted accordingly, diverting arriving vessels to the harbour.

Men on the beaches were formed up and directed westward along the sand towards the breakwater, some in military order, others straggling along in groups or knots, some all alone, trudging wearily to where they hoped rescue could be found. Like much that happened during the ten days of Dunkirk, it was a remarkable sight and an even more remarkable experience for those who took part:

> Long columns of men three or four deep, wandering irregularly along like vast serpents – somehow faintly reminiscent of the Children of Israel in the wilderness! . . . The move up was the most devastating business we ever had. At first we moved along fairly quickly, and did as much as 300 yards at a time with perhaps ten minutes rest. This got slower and slower till in Dunkirk we moved 20 yards and rested for anything up to half an hour! . . . One had to keep awake to avoid losing one's unit at the next move, as well as the risk of not being taken on by another if one did lose touch.

Dunkirk remained a dangerous place to be. From their positions west of the city, the Germans had intensified their artillery bombardments while the *Luftwaffe* continued to pay special attention to the harbour as well. At nine that morning, Tennant reported to Dover, 'We have been continuously and heavily bombed and they are finding the range of our loading berth'. In fact, casualties were already being inflicted on the breakwater itself.

> Half way along the mole [breakwater], a solitary, khaki-clad figure lay on the wooden staging. We could not see his face for a great-coat had been spread over him, hiding the stark reality with an illusion of sleep. A helmet, pierced with shell splinters, lay close by on the edge of a gaping hole of shattered timbers and concrete below which the sea lapped. Poor sod! What rotten luck! So near, so very near and he almost made it. Without pause and without comment we filed ahead.

Gaps blasted in the pier by shells were quickly spanned by loose planking though places remained along its length where troops had to vault over the holes. Wake-Walker sent messages to Dover pleading for the enemy guns to be bombed and silenced and those messages were passed on. But despite RAF efforts, the shelling was sustained for much of the day. It added considerably to the pressures not only on the evacuees but also on the navy pier masters keeping things under control at the foot of the breakwater, rushing the men along it when vessels berthed, and getting them aboard quickly so that the turn-around of the ships could be expedited.

> Why the jetty was not blown [a pier master said] I shall never understand; one good bomb at the inshore end would have completely held up the embarkation and it is doubtful whether we would have got off half the number we eventually did.

Gort reported from La Panne to the War Office by telephone that morning that the Germans appeared to be preparing a major attack to crack through the perimeter defences and descend on the harbour and the beaches. In view of that, the question of how to deal with French evacuees came up once more. In an extraordinary phone call at midnight the previous night, Churchill had personally ordered Gort to accelerate the evacuation of French troops. Now the BEF commander wanted clarification.

He had earlier been told how important it was for élite British fighting troops mounting the rearguard to be brought home; indeed, Dynamo headquarters was making special arrangements to get them away. Now Gort wanted to know from London whether, when it seemed unsafe to delay any longer, he should order those troops to fall back for speedy evacuation, even if such a move would expose great numbers of French soldiers to capture. The alternative was for the British rearguard to hold their positions till the last possible moment, exposing themselves to even greater dangers than they already faced, in order to cover the evacuation of many more French troops than might otherwise be lifted off. Put that way, the question left London with no real choice. Secretary of War Eden told Gort that if it came to that, his main concern had to be getting the British rearguard to safety.

Departure arrangements for Gort himself were now finalized. His request that, contrary to the orders he had received the previous day, he be permitted to remain with his troops till the end was turned down. He thereupon called on Admiral Abrial at his Bastion headquarters near the harbour to coordinate the remainder of the evacuation process, to inform him that he was leaving later that day, and to report that General Alexander would be assuming command of what was left of the BEF in the area. He offered to take senior French officers back to England with him but that offer was declined. Only a pretence remained that the BEF was under Abrial's command so it was not an overly agreeable leave taking. Though increasing numbers of French troops were being evacuated, Abrial could not be shaken from the conviction that to save their own skins, the British were abandoning France in indecent haste.

In Paris, it appeared that the mills of fate were grinding inexorably towards catastrophe. In his desperation, Reynaud urgently renewed his earlier pleas to Churchill for troops to help block the impending German drive against the French capital. The French premier also again asked for increased RAF involvement on the continent and for joint appeals for American help of the kind Washington had already made clear would be rejected. Aware of Churchill's francophile inclinations, King George felt inclined to remind him that he was

Prime Minister of Britain, not of France. But it wasn't necessary. Churchill had no intention of agreeing to any of Renaud's requests.

He feared, however, that blunt rejection would be seized upon by defeatists in Paris to press for immediate armistice terms. To boost French spirits, he flew to the French capital that morning to attend a meeting of the War Council there. His plane and its fighter escort had to take a round-about approach to avoid German fighters but he arrived looking 'as fresh as a daisy' and glowing with confidence.

The French leaders made no such pretence. National calamity seemed around the corner and they were bitter about it. They were openly resentful of what most considered Britain's puny contribution to the struggle. And they were angry about how the Dunkirk evacuation was proceeding. When Churchill boasted that the evacuation was turning into an historic success, that far more men had been evacuated than had been thought possible, Weygand asked acerbically, 'But how many French? The French,' he charged, 'are being left behind.' It was said this would cause much ill-feeling in France if it came to the attention of the public. Churchill tried to tone down French bitterness. 'We are companions in misfortune', he said. 'There is nothing to be gained from recrimination over our common miseries.'

Weygand was not easily soothed. Reynaud, upon whom Churchill was counting to keep France in the war as long as possible, was also bitter about evacuation statistics. He extracted from Churchill the estimate that of 220,000 British troops, 150,000 had so far been evacuated, while of 200,000 French troops, only a mere fifteen thousand had been taken off. Churchill maintained that much responsibility for the disparity rested with the French. He said that the French forces in the north still appeared not to have received orders to be evacuated. He suggested that Weygand immediately rectify that situation.

Speaking with deep feeling of the common sufferings of France and Britain, the British leader then declared that his troops would not receive priority treatment in the evacuation but that the troops of the two countries would leave Dunkirk 'arm in arm'. What was more, he said that it would be the British who would constitute the final rearguard for the evacuation, even though they would inevitably suffer heavy losses as a result. That would permit the French rearguard to disengage and be evacuated first. 'I will not', the British leader declared grandly, 'accept further sacrifices from the French.'

Churchill's princely gestures and backbone-stiffening oratory partially mollified the French, but not everyone in the Prime Minister's own party was pleased with his performance. Spears, for one, objected to Churchill's magnanimity:

His emotions were leading him too far, I thought. He was being too generous. After all, if we were in such dire jeopardy, it was due to colossal French incompetence and, steeped as I was in the French atmosphere, I knew that in French eyes we only came into the picture in so far as could help France. Perfectly natural perhaps, but we, on the other hand, ought not to sacrifice our chance of survival to the French, who certainly would not do so for us. The idea that we might be invaded because we had absolutely no troops to resist even a weak landing was unbearable.

Churchill appeared to have no such qualms. On the verge of tears, he told the assembled French leaders how deeply he felt the suffering and loss of the men in the north. He declared that Britain was determined to fight on to the end. 'England did not fear invasion', he said, 'and would resist it most fiercely in every village and hamlet. It would be better . . . that the civilization of Western Europe, with all its achievements, should come to a tragic but splendid end, than that the two great democracies should linger on [under Nazi domination], stripped of all that made life worth living.'

His voice breaking with emotion, Churchill said that in order to make certain that as many combat-ready men as possible would be brought back from Dunkirk to be reorganized immediately into new fighting units to continue the struggle against the enemy, he had ordered that the British wounded be lifted off last, which probably meant leaving them to be taken prisoner. The neutral Americans would be asked to try to see to the well-being of the casualties that had to be left behind. Churchill declared that his country would never accept slavery and that 'if one of the two comrades fell during the course of the struggle, the other would not lay down his arms until his friend was on his feet again'.

This declaration of undying friendship did not have the intended effect. Some found it considerably less than encouraging. War Council secretary Baudouin felt that it implied that 'England has already coolly assumed that [France] should succumb in this strug-gle . . . England has already put on mourning for us.' Not for the first time, Baudouin was led to wonder whether France should continue to fight a war that was as good as lost, as Churchill seemed to indicate, as well as expensive in lives and money.

His doubts were reinforced by Churchill's refusal to be shaken from his insistence that he could not immediately send additional troops to help France fight off Hitler's armies when they turned towards Paris. The Prime Minister explained that the men being brought back from Dunkirk could not be regrouped and reequipped overnight and he had no other forces which might be sent at once. Besides, at that moment, there were no more than five hundred heavy guns in all of Britain. That was not enough to mount a nation-wide defence against a German invasion, much less adequately arm a new expeditionary force.

Churchill insisted that Britain had not been remiss in its contribution to the common struggle against the enemy. He pointed out that ten of its precious squadrons of fighter aircraft – of which a great many had been lost – had been sent to France. Its remaining twenty-nine squadrons were barely enough to guard Britain's cities and aircraft factories against German attack.

There was a tense moment at the Paris meeting when Spears responded sharply to the suggestion of a French official that continuing military setbacks might force France to modify its foreign policy. The implication was that it might find coming to terms with Hitler the only suitable way out of the impasse. Aware that some of Reynaud's ministers were already advising such a course of action, Spears warned that if the suggested policy change meant what he thought it meant, Britain not only would feel obliged to blockade France but also to bomb strategic French centres which came under German control. The two Allies would, in fact, become enemies.

Despite the differences of views and emphasis of those present, it seemed to the British delegation that Churchill's strength of will had in the last analysis done its magic. By the time the meeting had concluded, the senior French figures in attendance appeared to agree with the British Prime Minister that the struggle with the enemy not only should be maintained unflinchingly but that it would lead to ultimate victory.

However, this transfusion of hope, if it actually occurred, proved short-lived. Once mutual assurances of fighting on to victory had been exchanged, the French leaders were compelled once more to come to terms with the unpalatable facts being created on the battlefield, as Churchill soon discovered. He spent the night in Paris and at dinner at the British Embassy, Reynaud and the Prime Minister's other French guests seemed much more subdued than they had been at the conclusion of that afternoon's War Council conclave. After his French guests left, Churchill 'realized in his heart that the French were beaten, that they knew it, and were resigned to defeat'.

It had been easy enough for Churchill to promise that the British and French would leave Dunkirk 'arm in arm'. But Gort, preparing to leave for home, realized that the pressure of events might not permit him – or General Alexander when he took over from him – to be so generously disposed, even if they wanted to. Greatly increased numbers of French troops had received evacuation orders and were pouring into Dunkirk and on to the beaches. Though reliable signal communications had finally been established between Dunkirk and Dover, neither Tennant on the shore nor Wake-Walker coordinating from offshore had been given any idea of how many there would be. It was therefore impossible for them to provide information to Dynamo headquarters on the size of the rescue fleet that was needed, an important consideration in view of the continuing hazards involved. Nor was information available on how many French vessels, of what capacity, would be available to take part in the operation.

The weather, which had caused difficulties for the little ships and boats that morning, improved considerably during the afternoon. The wind dropped off and a high tide refloated boats driven aground earlier. Wake-Walker was again able to direct vessels to positions off the beaches and the boats resumed ferrying troops out to them.

> Behind the dunes, we could see bayonets rising and falling in unison. Then the men came in sight, tall men led by a captain who was shorter than they were. They marched straight down across the sand into the sea. So orderly and confident was their marching that we thought the Red Sea would open for them. It didn't. As they entered the water, their rate of marching slowed and the men behind took smaller steps, their rifles all still going up and down together. The chaps behind, who hadn't got in the water yet, marked time. It was a magnificent sight, a marvellous show. We thought we'd get those chaps on board straight away. Not so. A Dutch skoot, which took less water than we, swung right around, went to where they were, picked up the whole lot and off she went. One of our sailors called out to the men, 'Who are you?' 'The Irish Guards!' someone replied.

No matter where Wake-Walker instructed ships to position themselves, many dropped anchor as soon as they spotted lines of men on the shore and boats picking them up to be ferried out. The result was that some vessels which had been sent furthest east to stand off Bray and La Panne didn't get that far. Troops on the beaches furthest from Dunkirk waited in vain until German artillery bombardment sent them scurrying over the sand towards greater safety on beaches nearer to the harbour.

The result was that some ships that did go as far up the coast as instructed infuriatingly found few men waiting there to be picked up. Wake-Walker began receiving bewildering messages from ships that there were no troops on the shore when, in fact, there were thousands. At the same time, he was receiving messages from the shore that not enough boats were coming in to pick up the troops, when further along boats were turning back empty from the beaches. The absence of direct ship to shore communications meant that much effort was wasted that day.

The weariness of ship's crews, the intermittent congestion, the floating wreckage and sunken ships, and the need often to swerve quickly in the offshore waters produced increasing numbers of accidents at sea. At midday, the destroyers *Icarus* and *Scimitar* collided and the latter had to be ordered back to Dover for repairs. Other vessels in collision, either in the harbour or off the beaches, were less lucky. Some had to be towed back to England; others sank to add to the litter of sea wreckage.

A particular danger to small craft and the men they lifted off the beaches was the need for larger vessels to take quick evasive action when they came under sudden air attack.

> Our motor yacht went alongside a destroyer. They had scrambling nets down the side. Our chaps were scrambling up when all of a sudden she shot ahead. We were tied up to her so she towed us with her. A lot of the soldiers fell from the nets into the water. They were shouting for help but we couldn't do anything about it. We were being pulled along. A few seconds later we knew why. They'd seen a dive bomber coming down. The bombs fell just astern of where she'd been. We never saw those men who fell into the water again.

During the day, the situation at the La Panne beach aroused new concern. The Germans had moved their guns closer around Nieuport and, resorting to a primitive but effective device, had sent up a manned observation balloon to direct artillery fire. Wake-Walker signalled Dover for aircraft to shoot the balloon down. But the Germans kept raising and lowering it and it reappeared through much of the day, enabling German gunners to zero in more accurately on targets in the La Panne area. The beach there, crowded with troops, was getting to be a serious liability to the British. Men were being hit but still few facilities existed anywhere along the beach for caring for the wounded and no facilities at all for properly interring the dead:

> A horrible stench of blood and mutilated flesh pervaded the place. There was no escape from it. Not a breath of air was blowing to dissipate the appalling odour that arose from the dead bodies that had been lying on the sand, in some cases, for several days. We might have been walking through a slaughter house on a hot day.

British intelligence reported to the War Office that day that the Germans were building amphibious tanks capable of rolling up from the sea on to the beaches of England. It deepened the anxiety felt in London at the continuing loss in the Dunkirk operation of warships and planes needed to repel the expected invasion. Senior figures – newly baptized in the murky, chill pond of realism – were not reassured by accounts of trouble in Germany where shortages in consumer goods and raw materials were said to be causing widespread resentment, where news of heavy casualties on the Western Front were said to be arousing alarm, and where the Nazi command was said to be terrified that it would not be able to fulfil promises made to the German people that the war would be brought to a rapid conclusion. All of that sounded encouraging, but so had pre-battle assurances about Allied might.

In fact, to an observer on the spot in Berlin the German people appeared to be largely untroubled by the war. Correspondent William Shirer noted in his diary, 'The Kurfuerstendamm jammed with people meandering along pleasantly. The great sidewalk cafés on this broad, tree-lined avenue were filled with thousands, chatting quietly over ersatz coffee or their ice-cream . . . The war has not been brought home to the people of Berlin.'

It had, however, been brought agonizingly home to Wake-Walker watching his rescue ships blasted and sunk, pleading with Dover for more vessels and still more, and finding his methodical way of dealing with problems frustrated by the chaos in which he found himself:

> It was always impossible for me to do more than deal with the situation
> of the moment. I did not know what ships were coming or when . . .
> Nor was it possible for Dover to give me much information. Ships got
> back there, unloaded, and were off again, the stream was constant but
> irregular and it was not possible to see any way ahead.

When Gort left for England that evening and General Alexander took charge of British troops remaining in the perimeter, he, like Gort before him, officially came directly under the command of Admiral Abrial. Like Gort, he was given the escape option of appealing to London if any of Abrial's orders were likely, in his opinion, 'to imperil the safety of the Force under your command'. No matter what Churchill had promised the French, Alexander's primary task was to wind up the evacuation of remaining BEF troops in France as expeditiously as possible. He was, however, authorized, in consultation with Abrial, to capitulate to the Germans to avoid useless slaughter if it appeared that 'no further organized evacuation was possible and no further proportionate damage could be inflicted on the enemy'.

No sooner had Alexander taken over from Gort than Anglo-French differences about evacuation procedures resurfaced. It was now accepted that the deadline for completing the BEF evacuation early the following morning as planned could not be met. There were still too many troops on the beaches and dunes and, amazingly, the defence line was still holding. But Alexander told Abrial that he believed it was unlikely that the operation could be sustained more than one more day and night. He urged a concentrated effort during the coming night to lift off the troops already awaiting embarkation and to disengage and evacuate the rearguard during the night after. The plan now would be for the curtain to come down on Operation Dynamo by first light on June 2nd, twenty-four hours later than planned earlier.

Abrial did not approve. He thought such a deadline would be a total miscalculation. He did not believe French troops holding rearguard positions could disengage so quickly. He maintained that the Dunkirk bridgehead had to be held until all troops could be embarked.

> His idea [Colonel William Morgan, Alexander's chief of staff, later recalled] was that . . . the troops were to remain and, as far as we could see, were to remain for some time. Of course, we knew this was impossible. The British troops were absolutely finished. They could not go on much longer . . .

Outraged by British haste to abandon France, Abrial threatened to use his authority as commander to close Dunkirk harbour, though it is unlikely that he was serious. 'General,' he scolded Alexander, 'you must stay. It is a matter of England's honour. French soldiers have let themselves be killed to protect the embarkation of the British army. Now your last troops must take part in the defence of Dunkirk to permit the evacuation of the greater part of our troops'.

What he was asking was, in fact, less than Churchill had offered the French in Paris earlier that day. He wanted the British only to share final rearguard duties, not take on all of them. He did not know of Churchill's offer but he did know that when taking leave of him, Gort had promised – in the confusion which attended his departure – that the British rearguard would continue to hold its sector of the perimeter line so that the evacuation of French troops could continue.

Alexander had heard nothing of that promise. Gort had neglected to inform him. The new British commander focused on what he considered his primary duty as spelled out in his orders – to do nothing to imperil the safety of his troops. If that meant letting the French down, that was regrettable. He told Abrial that in his opinion, any plan to delay final evacuation past first light of June 2nd 'did not take into account the true military or naval situation'. Abrial conceded that the perimeter defence line was unlikely to be able to hold where it was. He proposed drawing it a mile or two closer to the coast (in fact less than four miles from the beaches) and reconstituting it there to stand fast.

Alexander thought that was nonsense. He protested that such a new stop line would be so near the coast that close range enemy artillery fire on the harbour and the beaches would rapidly render further evacuation impossible. It was not simply a matter of differences of opinion. The British commander had no confidence whatever in Abrial's judgment. He believed that his continuing reluctance to venture forth from the protection of his subterranean fortress headquarters to see for himself what was happening coloured his understanding of what was possible and what was not. When Abrial insisted on having his way, Alexander said he would have to invoke the escape clause of his instructions and refer the matter to London.

Hurrying back to BEF headquarters at La Panne, he was relieved to see the telephone connection with London was still intact despite enemy bombing. He quickly contacted Secretary of War Eden by phone – the last call that could be put through. He told Eden that the delay Abrial had in mind would lead to the loss of some of Britain's finest fighting troops. Eden – who had not yet heard of Churchill's offer in Paris to have the British rearguard take last honours at Dunkirk – agreed. He authorized Alexander to proceed as he had proposed, aiming to wind up the evacuation of British troops by dawn the day after next.

But the formula wasn't to be as simple as that. Alexander was instructed to embark Britain's remaining troops at Dunkirk 'as rapidly as possible *on a 50-50 basis* with the French army'. *Fifty-fifty* could be interpreted in two ways – current or retrospective. But 'as rapidly as possible' had only one meaning as far as Alexander was concerned. His intention was to get the British troops out by then no matter what. He returned to Abrial's headquarters to tell him as much. He said he hoped that the French commander would get his troops also to work towards the new deadline so that the final evacuation could be even handed. But he made it clear that the last of the British would have left by then even if they did not.

Abrial resented being confronted with an ultimatum, especially one handed him by a subordinate. But all he could do was complain to Paris. To make things personally awkward, it was already night and Alexander did not want to risk trying to get to his new headquarters, now moved closer to Dunkirk city, in the dark. He and his aide overnighted at Abrial's Bastion, stretched out on a cold concrete floor.

Instead of the expected forty-eight hours, Operation Dynamo had now lasted almost three times that long. But the incessant fears that the perimeter defence line would not be able to hold the enemy back much longer now appeared on the point of being justified. It was time to wind the operation quickly down, starting with the tricky task of shortening the perimeter line.

The plan was for the left of the line, just inside Belgium on and near the coast, to be shortened and reestablished by a rearguard further back towards Dunkirk, on the Franco-Belgian border. La Panne and its beach were to be evacuated of troops. First the troops abandoning the far left of the perimeter in Belgium were to disengage after last light and fall back on La Panne beach from which, they were told, they would be speedily evacuated. Speed was essential because, as the Germans would soon realize, the area was about to become no man's land.

But traversing La Panne to the beach had become a perilous undertaking despite the cover of darkness. Much of it now in ruins, La Panne had been a prosperous, modern city, its main streets lined with new buildings of concrete and glass. It was a strange place for the ragged remains of an army to be trudging through.

> The streets of La Panne were an amazing sight. The roads were nearly blocked . . with every conceivable type of vehicle . . . Houses were crashing down and tramway cables and standards all over the place. The civilians were rightly in the cellars.

German spotter planes dropped flares to light up the scene. Soon after came 'the thump of distant guns followed by the whine of approaching shells'. Being out in the open seemed distinctly hazardous to well being and orders were shouted to get the men under cover:

> 'Off the streets! Into the shops!' came the orders, shouted along the street, and no one required second bidding. Great plate-glass windows, still intact in our part of the street, shattered under the impact of rifle butts, heavy glass clanging tunefully to the pavement. Soldiers hastened through . . . One little cameo of the moment was the abrupt appearance behind his glass of a restaurateur, gesticulating excitedly to the troops to desist. Such is the inherent respect for property, that several [men] paused, butts poised, while the owner hastily unlocked his glass door; and in they streamed, plate glass still intact.

For those troops and for thousands of others, as the day drew to an end, rescue back to England still seemed a long way off. But despite the difficulties and delays, the anguish and the casualties, by midnight on May 31st, the sixth day of Dunkirk, 68,014 more men had been brought back to England, more than on any day so far – 45,072 from Dunkirk harbour, 22,942 from the beaches. Most of the BEF was home again, accompanied by thousands of French and some Belgian troops. Almost 200,000 troops had been rescued since Operation Dynamo had been launched.

Satisfaction in London at 10 Downing Street and the War Office was severely blunted by the realization that tens of thousands of men were still to be brought home and that the chances of saving them were growing slimmer by the hour. Concern about the fate of those troops was heightened by German press allegations of cruel treatment of German soldiers who had escaped or had been liberated after having been captured by the British. It was charged in German newspapers that British officers and men had acted as if their German prisoners were 'cannibals or murderers'.

> They were subjected to vile insults, beaten, threatened with death and robbed of all personal possessions. Chained hand and foot and thrown into a corner or left out in the street to be exposed mercilessly to artillery fire. On the march, those who could not keep up with the column because of wounds or fatigue were driven with big clubs in the hands of sadistic officers. When questioned, they were subjected to blinding light to weaken their resistance when asked for military secrets. Germany will not forget nor allow such conduct to go unpunished.

With perhaps sixty thousand British troops still stranded across the Channel facing capture or death, such allegations and threats were alarming. For the War Cabinet, the possibility that those men were about to become hostages of Hitler, perhaps a bargaining factor, remained chilling.

## Chapter 11 – DAY SEVEN OF DUNKIRK

# Death from the Skies

FOR MEN MANNING the vessels fully engaged in the operation from the beginning, the strain was approaching breaking point. Many aboard destroyers which had so far not been put out of action by enemy attack had been on duty, except for brief snatches of sleep, for five straight days or more and were reaching the limits of their endurance. For those who had briefly been rested while their vessels underwent quick repairs, the prospect of a return to Operation Dynamo was agonizing. For all, going back to Dunkirk meant venturing once more into an inferno in which their senses would be stretched to the limit and from which the chances were they would not return.

There was no let up in the hazards the vessels had to face on each crossing – shelling, bombing, strafing, German submarines and torpedo boats on the prowl, squatting at anchor exposed to the enemy for long periods of time while troops boarded at the breakwater or off the beaches. None of this was made easier for ships' personnel by the crush on board during each trip home, with evacuees crammed into every possible cranny and cubbyhole.

Crews grew anxious and jittery and some men were stricken by mysterious afflictions as a result of their efforts and experiences. The chief officer of the Channel steamer *St Seriol*, working his ship's remaining lifeboat, frantically rescuing men from a sinking vessel before they drowned, pulling survivors from the water, was stricken with a form of nervous paralysis from the waist downwards which made him incapable of standing for any length of time for some time afterwards. Deprived of sleep, under virtually constant pressure, many men's minds wandered:

> We were standing on the bridge of the destroyer [said a naval officer] and one of my fellow officers said to me, 'Look through these binoculars. I can see camels on the shore. I think there are five of them. It might be four . . . or maybe six.' He might have been

pulling my leg. But it was entirely possible that he was hallucinating.

A growing number of reports were filed about men losing control. Ships began returning to English ports carrying their cargoes of evacuees with almost every crew member, including most officers, fast asleep. In warship wardrooms as vessels crossed the Channel to get on with the job, hands shook as men lifted glasses and cups to their mouths. Aboard the destroyer *Whitshed*, two seamen who had been 'jocular, robust men' were reported to have turned 'sullen, morose, depressed, hard-faced and silent. Occasionally they wrung their hands'. They said they would jump over the side rather than face another night at Dunkirk. The minesweeper *Hussar* had to be removed temporarily from the operation when a bout of weeping broke out among the crew. Thirty crew, including officers, of the minesweeper *Hebe* had to be put ashore for treatment after an outburst of what was described as 'mass hysterical epilepsy'. Dynamo headquarters had anticipated problems. Spare naval personnel had already been rushed to Dover to fill in for men incapacitated by the horrors of Dunkirk.

None could escape being affected in some way or other, even those known for self-control in crisis situations:

> We were just about to cast off and this French sergeant – he was standing on the fo'c'sle – he turned to the captain [Mark Thornton, captain of the destroyer *Harvester*] who was on the bridge, raised his hands in the air, said, 'All is lost,' in French and threw his rifle over the side. The captain was furious. He leapt up and tried to scramble over the top of the bridge. Two of us grabbed his legs and held him back. There is no question, even with his bare hands, he would have done something pretty nasty to that man.

For the civilian crews of the passenger vessels which had been committed to the operation, the hazards were somewhat less than for most navy personnel. Now crossing only by night, they were no longer exposed to enemy targeting. But these men were not trained for battle nor under any official obligation to keep returning to a war zone. Like warships, their vessels still risked being shelled by enemy guns firing at random at Dunkirk harbour while tied up at the breakwater and they risked being sunk by torpedoes while traversing the Channel. Collisions remained a constant danger, particularly in the dark. And though doing a reasonably thorough job, Admiral Ramsay's minesweepers were unable to clear away all the mines German planes continued to lay in the Channel and off the English coast each night. The crews of small, fragile passenger ships which had never ventured far from the English coast were undertaking journeys that tried the nerves of personnel aboard heavily armed warships. The master of the *Malines* explained why he was withdrawing his vessel from the operation:

> It was evident that my crew was on the edge of revolt . . . I considered the odds against a successful prosecution of another voyage too enormous and the outcome too unprofitable to risk the ship. My draught does not permit me to reach the beaches at Dunkirk, and the quay appears to be untenable.

For the little ships, the strain was severe as well. Most were new to the operation. Indeed, Ramsay's scavenging parties were still out along the south coast of England rounding up more small craft to send across. But the pressure was mounting sharply on those working the beaches. The perils of navigation in waters that were often congested compounded the dangers of enemy attack. Smaller ships were continually exposed to buffeting when caught in the wash of larger, faster craft and repeatedly had to swerve sharply to avoid being swamped:

> The effect of the consequent plunging on the troops below in a stinking atmosphere with all ports closed can well be imagined. They were literally packed like the proverbial sardines – even one in the bath and another perched on the W.C., so that all the poor devils could do was just sit and be sick.

Some of the civilian-manned craft which had volunteered or been drummed into service, their engines groaning under the strain of the operation, the nerves of their crews shot, now slipped quietly away to their home ports after unloading the men they had rescued. The masters of others simply announced that they had done their bit, were dog tired, and would not cross the Channel again. In several cases, Royal Navy vessels were instructed to 'force them back to their duty'. Increasing numbers of naval officers and seamen, many drawn from other commands, were put aboard civilian vessels, either to take charge of them or to stiffen the morale of the civilian seamen reeling under the Dunkirk experience.

That night some ships were spotted returning empty from France under the mistaken impression – which their masters and crews had formed with gratitude and relief – that the operation had been concluded:

> We were running this RAF launch in and out from the beach. Night came and day came and night came and day came. One evening things seemed to quieten down. Somehow the bustle and banging

had eased off. We got the impression that this was the end of the road. We were tired out. We thought we'd done our bit. There didn't seem much more to do. We thought, 'Let's go home.' We didn't discuss it. It just came to the three of us. We were so bloody tired, we didn't have the sense to pick up another dozen soldiers to bring back with us. But we didn't even know if we'd be able to get back. It was getting dark. We had no compass, no charts, no weapons, no lights, no food, no nothing. We didn't even know if we had enough fuel to get home.

The tide on the coast continued to prove dangerously mischievous to sailors unfamiliar with its fast-in-fast-out perversities. With scores of small ships and boats crewed by inexperienced mariners, many beached at each low tide. Tugs and other vessels capable of towing them free were in great demand. Spotting a tug making for Dover with a cargo of evacuees, Wake-Walker called on it to turn back to tow off a minesweeper which was stranded deep in the mud off Bray. Paying no attention, the tug master continued on his course back to England. He had volunteered for his vessel to serve as a transport to bring back the troops and he intended to abide by that understanding. But with so many men still to be evacuated, Wake-Walker was determined to maintain as much control of the situation as he could. He had a gun trained on the tug and instructed a naval reserve sub-lieutenant aboard the vessel to take charge of it and go to the assistance of the beached minesweeper. The tug captain was outraged to be treated that way but he was not the only man in the operation who found that far more was demanded of him during the Dunkirk days than he imagined would be.

Despite assurances to the contrary from their officers, forward troops who had fallen back after dark the previous night towards La Panne beach from the now shortened perimeter line in Belgium were to have no easy passage home. They discovered that no quick evacuation awaited them. They and other troops making their way through the debris-strewn streets of La Panne found nothing but muddled hopelessness on the beach. Hordes of men were already congregated there but not many were being lifted off – no more than three hundred an hour – by the few boats working the shore in that sector. A mood of despair and dread prevailed, compounded by the effects of the random shelling of the beach by German guns and by the virtual absence of beach masters and beach patrols to explain what should be done.

Navy personnel on the shore had been ordered under no circumstances to allow themselves to be captured by the enemy and most had by now been evacuated, some reluctantly in view of how much there was still to do. Confusion and bewilderment reigned as newly arrived troops proceeded along the beach in search of rescue, shells falling around them claiming dead and wounded, most of whom were left untended where they were hit. Recollection of the horror stayed with many of the men for long after the fact:

> To my right and left lay three still figures; a fourth, propped on one hand, spoke. His voice carried an entreating note of despair . . . 'Help me. Help me,' was all he said, face indistinguishable except in outline in the darkness, a stranger whose voice has ever since accused – because I slogged on without pause. Those were the orders. But the main drive was that of self preservation, and whether the medics ever found him alive I could never know.

Senior officers on the spot decided that there was no alternative to marching troops down the beach towards Dunkirk. They might find transport while on the way to Bray or at Bray beach itself. But the supply of boats appeared to have dried up all along that stretch of the shoreline as well, as demonstrated by the sequence of messages that flowed across the Channel in the early morning hours:

0243 – Minesweeper *Gossamer* to Admiral Ramsay: 'We must have more boats west of La Panne'.

0324 – Ramsay to *Gossamer*: 'It is now impracticable to send more boats. You must do your utmost with yours'.

0341 – Tanker *Niger* to Ramsay and Wake-Walker: 'Situation on beaches is critical . . . More boats urgently required'.

0358 – *Gossamer* to Ramsay: 'Thousands more (?moving) from La Panne westward. No boats'.

0430 – General Whitaker, 7th Guards Brigade, to General Dill at the War Office: 'Absolutely essential provide many more small boats with motor boats to tow if grave losses are to be avoided and remainder BEF cleared. Matter utmost urgency'.

0611 – Wake-Walker to Ramsay: 'All craft used for towing boats have returned in the night. They must be sent back'.

The troops who had converged on La Panne beach after dark the previous night, mostly disciplined infantrymen, had formed up and made off towards Dunkirk along the soft sand under command of their remaining officers. They picked up stragglers on the way. Men who had been separated from their units shouted out in the dark, trying to find them again: 'A-Company, Green Howards!' 'C-Company, East Yorks!' Most finally found rescue from the break-water at Dunkirk harbour though some were lifted off the beaches before dawn by small craft which had worked right through the night:

I saw what appeared to be a causeway about eight feet wide leading out into the water, so [my ship] made for it and hoped to find the men at the end of it. Imagine my surprise when I found that it was a perfectly straight formation of men standing in line about six deep as if they were on the Guards Parade! When I came right up to them and not before did a sergeant step out to say, 'Yes, sir, sixty men.' He walked down the line, the straight unmoved line . . . and told off sixty men to follow me out.

In desperation, in frustration, some men stripped down, discarded their weapons and tried to swim out to ships they spotted offshore. Some succeeded. Some were lucky enough to be picked up by boats heading in towards the beach. But many were never seen again. At one point thirty soldiers making their way along the beach swam out towards a warship when an officer accompanying them said anyone who thought he could reach it could 'have a go'. It was early morning light by then – 4.30 a.m. – and soon after they set off, German fighters swooped low out of the horizon to strafe them and the ship they were heading for, the minesweeper HMS *Halcyon*. The *Halcyon* managed to avoid damage but of the thirty swimmers, only four were saved, and two of those had been wounded in the water.

Right through the dark earliest hours of day, men had filed steadily along the breakwater at Dunkirk harbour on to vessels which had tied up there. At one point during the night, ten thousand British and twenty thousand French troops waited to load at the pier. 'A solid block of troops' jammed the pier and access to it and extended on to the beach for about two miles. Some of the men had been waiting most of the previous day; some since the previous night. Here too the Germans continued to lob shells at random. Aside from the casualties they claimed, the damage they did, and the fear they generated, they served to magnify the eeriness of a mass embarkation of ragged, weary men illuminated by a backdrop of the still blazing Dunkirk oil storage tanks, Dunkirk ablaze and an occasional German flare.

French troops arriving in great numbers complicated matters on the beaches for cultural as well as language reasons. Either by experience or heritage, many of the French were farmers from far inland for whom the sea and sea-going craft were impenetrable mysteries. Having reached the coast, many declined to go further even when given a chance and just milled about aimlessly, adding to the congestion on the shore. Others, like many of the British troops, piled into boats at the water's edge, paying little heed to space or weight limitations. Some of those craft just settled deep into the mud and were stuck there. Having found sanctuary of a sort, those aboard just settled in and waited. Some sat there long enough for the tide to come in and lift them away.

Even along patches where great numbers of troops were not congregated, the shore stretching up the coast from Dunkirk was no longer the tidy seaside playground it had been a few days earlier.

> The litter on the beach was indescribable: rifles, Bren guns, kits, everything lying all over the place. Destroyers and large and small boats of every description were lying on the bottom quite close to the shore, with masts, bridges, and funnels standing right out of the water. One destroyer was actually beached, cut completely in two by the bombs.

Dawn of June 1st, the seventh day of Dunkirk, had risen clear and bright and not long after came the first of the German bombing raids of the day. A second wave was mounted about an hour later and a third about an hour after that. Again and again right through the day, flocks of bombers, dive bombers and fighter planes roared in to attack the rescue vessels as they arrived from across the Channel, as they loaded, and as they headed back to England, their holds and decks crammed with evacuees. Once more the *Luftwaffe* shifted priority attention to the task of pounding the ships and disrupting the rescue of the Allied troops remaining in the perimeter strip, now some 100,000 French and forty thousand British – a course of action which, if systematically pursued from the start, would have wrecked Operation Dynamo days earlier. Some of the men saw the specific ships they expected to be ferried out to from the beach – and to which men before them in queues had already been carried – hit, set ablaze and sinking:

> The troops on the shore were watching the Navy being bombed [recalled a civilian volunteer yachtsman] . . . The really astonishing thing was that there was or appeared to be nothing . . . happening to the troops. I thought that this was an excellent bit of German terror-psychology . . . bombing the Navy, letting the troops watch the 'might' of the Waffe, making them think twice before being sure that was the way they wanted to go home.

For the men on the beaches it must indeed have looked like Armageddon out at sea, with the forces of evil prevailing. It must have seemed that way to many British mariners as well. As if being dragged to his doom, the captain of the destroyer *Ivanhoe*, damaged and under attack, shouted out to the destroyer *Havant* which had come close to render assistance, 'Get out of here or you'll end up the same as us!' The *Havant* was soon also hit and went to the bottom near the entrance of the harbour. Out of control, the *Ivanhoe* was taken in tow and managed to be hauled back to England.

The destroyer *Basilisk* was hit off La Panne and sank while struggling home. The minesweeper *Skipjack* had picked up between 250 and three hundred men off La Panne when a bomb struck her amidships. Before the order to abandon ship could be obeyed, 'she turned turtle' and sank. Most of the evacuees aboard were below and were lost. Those who were flung into the water or managed to jump overboard were machine gunned.

The French destroyer *Foudroyant* was sunk, as was the gunboat *Mosquito*. Ship after ship was sunk, crippled or damaged. Once again, in the midst of this deadly turmoil, hundreds of men were saved from certain death by ships which, despite the danger to themselves, moved in close for evacuees and crew to transfer from stricken vessels.

The German onslaught from the air continued right through the day. During intervals between attacks, hasty emergency repair work on damaged vessels was undertaken, men were transferred from rescue ships which had been hit, survivors were fished out of the water, and the wounded were treated. Those intervals also were periods of dread expectation because no one doubted that the Stukas, Dorniers, Heinkels and Messerschmitts would soon be back. The waters off Dunkirk had been turned into a special kind of maritime hades, dotted with vessels ablaze or burnt out, some beached, some half sunk, their bows pointing skyward, with bodies and wreckage flowing in and out with the tide.

As before, bitter complaints were voiced at the failure of the RAF to provide anything like adequate aerial cover. But RAF Fighter Command was at a fundamental disadvantage. The Germans could pick time and place for their ferocious aerial forays. By keeping the intervals between patrols as brief as possible and through sheer luck in timing, British fighters were able to challenge and disrupt some of the enemy raids. But, though the RAF lost thirty-one aircraft that day (to twenty-nine for the Germans), more than once it was conspicuous by its total absence, leaving the enemy unchallenged mastery of the skies over Dunkirk.

When not challenged by British fighters, German attack planes had to contend only with anti-aircraft fire, mostly from British destroyers. The planes came over low and fast, too fast for the gunners to distinguish Spitfires from Messerschmitts. They fired at both, usually with little effect, but kept firing nevertheless. Under the exposed circumstances in which they found themselves, there could be no holding back, no husbanding of resources. HMS *Keith*, like other destroyers in the operation, had turned around so quickly at Dover to get on with the job after unloading its complement of evacuees that it arrived back at Dunkirk down to its last thirty anti-aircraft shells. Attacked from the air, it twisted and turned at speed but was hit, crippled and sunk. It was turning into one of the most tragic days in the history of the Royal Navy.

Resentment and humiliation must have coloured Gort's feelings when, back in London that morning, he arrived to attend a meeting of the War Cabinet. He had reason to believe that much of the guidance and instructions he had received from the War Office and Churchill himself over the previous two weeks had been ill-informed and confused. At the same time, being commander of an army which had done little more than retreat and which was being driven into the sea was not likely to reflect credit on his abilities, regardless of circumstances. But so greatly had the evacuation already exceeded expectations that despite the numbers of men still locked in the German trap on the north-west coast of France, Gort was warmly received at the meeting. Had the national security situation not been so grave, he probably would have been given a hero's welcome, if only for the sake of public morale.

The War Cabinet was anxious to hear the latest about conditions prevailing in the Dunkirk perimeter and the prospects for the continued evacuation of fighting troops. Gort told the assembled ministers and service chiefs that the defence line probably would hold till the following morning but it might be a near thing. Every effort should be made to complete the evacuation that night. Churchill's unceasing insistence that as many French troops as possible should be rescued, even if it might entail British losses, still did not impress him. Unaware of the heroism and determination displayed by the French rearguard, now keeping the Germans at bay as it took responsibility for ever longer stretches of the Dunkirk defence line, Gort doubted if many French troops of fighting quality remained in the area. He could not refrain from voicing his conviction that the French command had been massively and overwhelmingly responsible for the dilemma in which the BEF had found itself and implied that, therefore, French troops were unworthy of any additional perilous effort by the Royal Navy to save them.

Gort's belief that Dynamo would have to be wound up that night was echoed by the service chiefs. Profoundly alarmed by the punishment the Royal Navy was continuing to sustain, Chief of the Naval Staff Sir Dudley Pound had no doubt that there was little chance of embarking any men after sunrise the following day. Pound reported that nearly all the destroyers engaged in the operation had suffered at least some degree of damage. What was more, the Germans had now moved guns into position to shell the last Channel route through which ships had been able to reach Dunkirk with a measure of safety. Few of the one hundred fishing vessels which the French had offered for participation in the operation had appeared and some of the French vessels which had been taking part were heading for Le Havre down the coast with the troops they had embarked, to unload there rather than making for England.

The RAF, also reeling from its accumulating losses, supported the navy's urgings that the operation be brought rapidly to a halt. Britain's fighter plane strength was said to be 'already considerably below the minimum essential' for the defence of the country. The War Cabinet was told that for the previous three weeks, Fighter Command had been operating at a rate far in excess of its ability to replace lost pilots and aircraft. In addition, sending the Spitfires and Hurricanes aloft might soon prove a futile gesture. Machine-gun ammunition for the aircraft was being used up faster than new supplies were becoming available. A serious shortage was looming.

Having returned that morning from Paris where he had the previous day assured French leaders of Britain's everlasting camaraderie, Churchill was reluctant to be swayed by the arguments and warnings of his military chiefs into downgrading the importance of evacuating French troops. He maintained that it was essential to hold on at Dunkirk as long as possible, even at the cost of naval and military losses, so that the French might be disabused of their belief that the British were abandoning them. The Prime Minister was, however, persuaded that General Alexander, as British commander on the spot, was best situated to know what the possibilities were and that the decision on when to wind up the evacuation should be left to him.

Alexander had no doubts about the timing. That morning, he had met with Abrial at the Bastion to confirm that the reduced British rearguard would hold what remained of its portion of the defence line only till nightfall, after which maintenance of the line would be completely in French hands. Informed of the decision, senior officials and officers in Paris were enraged. It confirmed the belief of many of them that, having rescued its own troops, perfidious Albion couldn't care less what happened to those of its ally. To soften the blow, Churchill cabled Reynaud and Weygand to explain the factors influencing British actions:

> The critical point of the evacuation has now been reached. Five fighter squadrons are practically continuously in action. This is all we can provide [to cover the evacuation]. Six ships, several of which were packed with troops, were sunk this morning. The only practicable channel is under artillery fire. The enemy's grip is tightening, and the bridgehead is narrowing. By attempting to hold on till tomorrow we may lose everything. If we close down tonight much will certainly be saved, although much may be lost. The situation cannot be assessed as a whole by Admiral Abrial, alone in the depth of his fortress, nor can it be by you, nor by us here. We have therefore ordered General Alexander, commanding the British sector of the bridgehead, to examine with Admiral Abrial the best line to follow. We are relying on your agreement.

The original draft of the Churchill message to Reynaud and Weygand, said that Alexander had been ordered 'to decide for himself' exclusively on how to proceed. But even when toned down, the message did nothing to mollify Reynaud. The French premier icily informed General Spears that it seemed that Churchill's assurances the previous day that Britain would not act unilaterally had lapsed with remarkable rapidity. His anger was fuelled also by reports that French officers were being grossly abused by the British at Dunkirk. He had heard that a French general and his aide had been manhandled away from a rescue ship and told that if they embarked, it would mean that two less British soldiers would be evacuated and that could not be tolerated.

Spears had by now stopped trying to smooth over differences between Paris and London. The Allies had developed fundamental differences. While Dunkirk appeared to be turning into something of a triumph for the British, it was a symbol of defeat and disgrace for France. Instead of trying to explain things away, Spears was now answering charge with countercharge. As for the French general allegedly mistreated at Dunkirk, he suggested that by trying to flee France alone, he had been using his rank to save his own skin, and not the lives of the troops under his command, and that was wrong. Spears also firmly rejected criticism by Reynaud of Gort's performance as BEF commander. He asserted that Gort's failing, if he had one, had been not to complain about 'the abysmal collapse of the French Staff and French generals'.

The matter of Admiral Abrial's jurisdiction and judgment remained a delicate issue. The British – first Gort and now Alexander, with Tennant acting for the Royal Navy – had repeatedly consulted Abrial as they went about running the Dunkirk end of the operation on land. However, those consultations had for the most part been mere gestures in recognition of Abrial's rank as Dunkirk commander. Abrial and the French in general were keenly aware it was largely only a formality, devoid of substance, and they were not at all happy about it. But the British – as Churchill made plain in his cable to Paris – were convinced that Abrial couldn't manage events if he chose never to emerge from the seclusion of his Bastion fortress. It was, of course, also a convenient excuse, permitting them to continue acting in accordance with Britain's own needs which, at that moment, were thought to involve national survival.

The end of the road was fast approaching for British troops still holding rearguard positions. Aside from running low on ammunition, they knew they had been reduced to comparatively few in number and that the Germans could not be held back much longer. Orders and instructions were sometimes neither clear nor consistent. Under intense enemy pressure, some officers understood that they were to pull their men back to the coast at their discretion when it seemed to them that the situation was hopeless. Others understood they were to hold fast no matter what until specifically ordered back. An officer of the 5th Borderers was shot dead by command of a Coldstream Guards major when, following superior orders, he defied the major's command not to withdraw his unit from the line. It was a futile gesture because the unit soon had to pull back anyway.

During the day, the rearguard was forced from several previously secure positions, taking heavy casualties in the process. A serious German penetration which developed on the eastern rim of the perimeter, near the Franco-Belgian border, cut sharply into beach embarkation possibilities. Easternmost beaches had to be abandoned and evacuation of men directly from the shore was restricted to the sands extending only for about a mile-and-a-half up the coast from the base of the breakwater. Beyond that, beaches from which thousands had been evacuated over the previous days, were now no-man's-land. The few reserves available were thrown into the battle to stop a German breakthrough that appeared to be developing. By evening that enemy advance had been checked. That meant the elaborate embarkation plans for the coming night had not been in vain, though they so easily could have been. The great escape was still in progress. However, men still on the line were hardly confident that they would get away.

Stories filtered back to them of hundreds lying dead on the sands and of ships fully loaded blasted out of the water. They were close enough to the coast to hear the explosions and gunfire off the coast. Some doubted whether they'd even get the chance to be embarked. From experience, from limited knowledge of what was happening elsewhere on the line, and from ingrained prejudice, they had little faith in the French soldiers who were assuming ever wider responsibility for defence of the shrinking perimeter.

But the French were fighting with unflagging spirit and determination. Each breach the enemy was able to force in their positions was quickly sealed though General Alexander remained cynical about the new defence line they were trying to establish closer to the remaining evacuation areas, little more than three miles in from the coast. The remaining British rearguard would withdraw to the beaches through that line after dark but Alexander believed it would crumble under the first serious German assault, probably early the next day, after which Dunkirk itself would quickly fall, city, harbour, beaches and all.

Nevertheless, the British commander was instructed by London that evening to 'hold on as long as possible in order that the maximum number of French and British may be evacuated. Impossible from here to judge local situation. In close cooperation with Admiral Abrial, you must act in this matter on your own judgment'. The last of the British were still due to be lifted off before dawn but clearly London was prepared to continue Operation Dynamo as long as there was any reasonable chance of saving more French troops. If that were the case, the new deadline Alexander had set for ending the evacuation by the coming sunrise was also no longer valid. Now it was up to the French to prove he was wrong to doubt their ability to hold back the Germans.

As reports of the day's enormous naval and maritime casualties accumulated at Dynamo headquarters in Dover, Admiral Ramsay realized that the operation could not be sensibly sustained along the lines it had been proceeding. The pace of the evacuation had not diminished. The one remaining cross-Channel route used by the rescue vessels was kept busy:

> It was almost like a motorway with ships going up and down in both directions, with different lanes for faster ships and slower ships. That's where the Spitfires were [said an evacuee who hadn't seen much of them before]. It was a protected line.

But the price was mounting frighteningly. Before nightfall, thirty-one rescue ships, including six destroyers, had been sunk or otherwise put out of action that day.

> In these circumstances [Ramsay later reported] it was apparent that continuation of the operation by day must cause losses of ships and personnel out of all proportion to the number of troops evacuated, and if persisted in, the momentum of evacuation would automatically and rapidly decrease.

He decided therefore that starting the following morning, the operation would be suspended during daylight hours for all larger vessels, including warships. Big ship embarkations still to take place before Operation Dynamo ran its course would be confined to hours of darkness. Little ships, the loss of which would neither damage British defence capabilities nor take great numbers of troops down with them if they were sunk, could continue working the beaches by day.

As darkness settled again over Dunkirk, ships once more began entering the harbour to tie up and load. As many as seven vessels at a time made their way into the harbour, gingerly trying to navigate paths clear of the debris to which so much had been added that long, savage day. There was no dawdling on the pier. The waiting troops were rushed along it and on to the ships as soon as vessels were made fast. They quickly loaded and made off again leaving berthing space for other vessels. Ships berthed two or three deep at the pier. Many evacuees used some of those up against the breakwater, as well as burnt out wrecks, as pontoons to scramble over to get to the vessels that would carry them to England.

By midnight, 64,429 more men – almost half of them French – had been brought back that day – 47,081 from the harbour, 17,348 from the beaches – a total of 259,049 since the operation had begun. And more were already en route. Word of this remarkable exploit was spreading quickly to other parts of the world. Across the Atlantic, the *New York Herald Tribune* paid its tribute:

> There have been trapped armies, terrible retreats, perilous embarkations, and heroic rearguard actions in the past, but no combination of them on a scale like this. Defeat sustained with such fortitude is no disaster . . . . These are soldiers of civilization, enrolling themselves imperishably among those who will save by suffering everything that makes civilized life of value.

The *New York Times* added its acclaim with Churchillian grandiloquence:

So long as the English tongue survives, the word Dunkirk will be spoken with reverence. For in that harbor, in such a hell as never blazed on earth before, at the end of a lost battle, the rages and blemishes that have hidden the soul of democracy fell away. There, beaten but unconquered, in shining splendor, she faced the enemy.

## Chapter 12 – DAY EIGHT OF DUNKIRK

# Thwarted Hopes

A DECISION HAD TO BE made about the wounded fortunate enough to be under medical care in the perimeter. Most were at Rosendael just inland from Malo, where the single remaining Casualty Clearing Station in the bridgehead was located. Churchill had assured the French that wounded British personnel would not be evacuated so that only men able to return immediately to battle could be saved. But no orders to that effect had been passed down and many wounded troops had been lifted from the breakwater and rushed to hospitals when they had been brought back to England. However, the intensity of German bombardment of the harbour had led to a decision to embark only casualties who could walk and could therefore be evacuated quickly and without difficulty.

An effort was now made to bring home the more seriously wounded before the Germans overran the area. Two British hospital ships, clearly identified as such, were sent across by daylight after an uncoded radio message, meant to be intercepted by the Germans, was transmitted announcing their mission. Both vessels were attacked. One was sunk; the other was badly damaged and had to turn back. The 230 remaining stretcher cases at Rosendael would have to stay behind.

However, they were not to be abandoned. Medical staff consisting of one officer and ten men for every hundred non-ambulatory casualties were to remain behind to care for them. A ballot was taken. The first names out of the hat left for home by way of the breakwater. Three officers and thirty men stayed on to care for the wounded and be captured by the Germans.

The wounded that had to be left behind at La Panne when it was abandoned to the enemy appear not to have been so fortunate. Four American army officers, neutral military attachés based in Berlin, were taken by the Germans on a tour of La Panne early that day. Their report to Washington indicated that because of the frenzy during the last hours before the area was abandoned, the casualties there had been left to their own devices.

> We entered the town [La Panne] a few hours after the British forces had completed their attempt to evacuate by sea . . . German troops . . . were still in the process of mopping up. The British had left some of their dead unburied (we saw approximately 100 bodies on the beach and the beach boulevard) and had left no medical personnel with their wounded. The latter were reported to number 700 of which 50 died almost immediately after the town was captured. The Germans report that no British medical officer had remained behind.

The post-battle scene beheld by the American officers at La Panne was one of death and destruction.

> That the British put up a desperate and stubborn fight is admitted by the Germans. Most of the British dead were found in small groups beside trucks or guns . . . Some bodies of drowned soldiers were seen. All had overcoats on and are believed to be from wrecked transports. Large numbers of British transports and some anti-aircraft guns of all calibre as well as abandoned equipment and ammunition were found scattered on the beach and in the town in great disorder . . . A single British destroyer was lying broadside on the beach. The Germans claim she was put out of action earlier in the day by a Stuka attack . . . German artillery was firing over us . . . in the direction of Dunkirchen. The combined fire of German artillery and air bombing on the town was terrific . . . [A] rate of about 100 explosions per minute . . . was still being maintained.

Boarding had been brisk from the breakwater in the harbour in the darkness of early morning. Troops, both British and French, proceeded down it in a seemingly endless flow. Rescue vessels had arrived in goodly number and continued to do so until just before dawn. Columns of men moved along the pier four abreast, two columns of British troops, two of French, boarding in good order. Despite the great numbers of men and ships in motion and the hasty overloading of the vessels, there was not a great deal of noise. The men were too weary for chatter and too pleased finally to be homeward bound in the seeming safety of comparative darkness to grumble. Ship's engines rumbled as, full up, the vessels headed out to sea. Ship's sirens hooted, though not as often as the heavy traffic seemed to warrant. Shells bursting sporadically in the harbour during the night were now part of the Dunkirk scene and caused no special excitement, except when one exploded close to the breakwater or a vessel, after which it was soon as if it had never happened.

But a problem arose. Though the road and beach approaches to the breakwater, and the breakwater itself, had been jammed with men when the previous night had fallen, those waiting were boarded and taken away well before dawn. Suddenly a strange lull interrupted the brisk pace and mood of the operation. The breakwater was empty except for a few ships' officers and men, aware that they could be blasted to smithereens at any moment, nervously peering down the pier for more men to board.

Inadequate communications prevented word of passage availability at the harbour from reaching the throngs of troops further along the sands who were hoping to be lifted off there before the imminent German arrival. Officers from destroyers which tied up at the pier during the night scoured nearby beaches and dunes to find evacuees, without great success. Equally unsuccessfully, the navigator from the destroyer *Malcolm* wandered through the streets of Dunkirk playing the bagpipes to lure troops out of cellars in the devastated city in which they might have hidden for safety.

The last four thousand British troops of the rearguard had disengaged from the line after dark the night before but they had miles to go, most of them on foot, before reaching embarkation areas. As they headed, tired and hungry, for the coast, they passed through the new French stop line which Abrial said would hold the Germans back when ground fighting resumed come the morning. For many of them, the rescue was to be totally haphazard:

> A still close dark night, lit dimly by a steady glow from Dunkirk . . . and intermittently by the gun flashes of French artillery firing lots of ammunition. French sentries kept challenging from the darkness; we were none too certain we were on the right road, when suddenly we reached the beach and turned left toward the Mole. Into the final straight at last, but the finishing post – the Mole – a most unpleasant looking place seen from a mile or so. Apparently blazing like Hell from end to end (this was really the oil tanks behind it); crashes and bangs near the shore told us that it was being steadily bombed and shelled. Pick up the step there, chaps – left, right, left, right. Suddenly a young Staff Officer was reached: 'Take your party down to the beach and get away in boats; lots are coming in.' Order obeyed with alacrity. Not so good when one paddled in, found many others paddling, no boats in and nobody knowing anything. Like a traffic jam this muddle sorted itself out eventually, and before dawn most of the Regiment [18th Field Regiment, Royal Artillery] were aboard some small craft or other.

Troops who still had transport, or were able to commandeer abandoned vehicles, were spared the footslog. Despite the attempt to prevent vehicle congestion within the perimeter, Dunkirk and Malo village were packed with vehicles and countless others littered the dunes and beaches. At one in the morning, the remaining few tanks and carriers of Regimental Headquarters, 46th Division, drew up on the mud along the water's edge at Malo. The tank crews got out and spiked their guns and smashed the engines of all the vehicles. 'After which everyone waded out to sea and was sooner or later picked up by a boat'.

Twenty-four men of the 27th Field Regiment, Royal Artillery, were separated from the rest of their unit which had managed to be embarked from the breakwater. Unable to force their way on to the pier when it was crowded, the twenty-four waded out to a Thames River barge which had run aground on the beach nearby and which had been abandoned by its crew who presumably had found alternative transport home. When the barge rose with the tide, the men managed to get a sail up and headed across the Channel.

But most of the rearguard troops heading, as instructed, for the breakwater to be embarked weren't so lucky. Word had finally spread to would-be evacuees that the pier was the place to be and suddenly there was again no shortage of men jamming its approaches, anxious to be boarded and carried away. Among them was a milling multitude of French troops, belatedly aware of the breakwater embarkations. They cut into the flow of British rearguard troops for whom priority embarkation, now thwarted, had been planned.

As predawn light began to poke over the horizon, Wake-Walker, aboard a motor boat inside the harbour, gazed about, waiting for the moment when embarkation for the day would have to be suspended and men left behind, with no guarantee that it would be resumed when darkness again fell:

> Looking shoreward, the whole town and harbour were shut in by a pall of smoke overhead, which was lit up by the glare of fires in several places inland. Against the glare, the piers, harbour and town were sharply silhouetted, and on the piers and quays an endless line of helmeted men in serried ranks, sometimes moving, sometimes stationary. The funnels and masts of ships showed clear as they lay alongside or went in and out of harbour, their hulls hidden and dark and invisible.

Some men had made their way well along the pier in sight of rescue when, with light creeping across the sky, the last vessel, fully loaded, departed. Word was passed along the breakwater that it had to be

cleared at once because German planes were likely soon to come
roaring in from the distance, their machine guns blazing, their bombs
plummeting down. The men furthest along the pier, most exposed,
tried to get back to the beach as instructed. But those closer to the foot
of the pier wouldn't believe embarkation had been suspended. They
had waited too long to give ground easily. There was much jostling
and griping until the pier was finally cleared.

Informed as dawn rose that embarkation would not be resumed until
nightfall, stranded rearguard troops were marched back to the dunes to
dig in, scrounge for food and water, and hope the French troops
manning the new defence line would hold fast during the long day
ahead. They had expected no such delay and were bitter about it:

> We had been told [a Coldstream Guards colonel said] that embarkation
> would continue until such time as the BEF was evacuated or enemy
> action made it impossible. It was a poor prospect for us, with eighteen
> hours to wait through the day. We had little faith in the resistance
> which the French were likely to put up, and we had only rifles and
> Brens to fight with . . . A gunner major came to me and asked for
> orders, but apart from the necessity for dispersion, I had nothing to tell
> him. It was humiliating.

Their departure blocked, some rearguard troops were summoned from
the dunes, where they had hoped to sleep the day away, and despite
their weariness and limited fire power, were deployed as emergency
back-up for the nearby front lines. They were to cover the approaches
to the harbour in case the Germans broke through French defences.

Now that La Panne had fallen, it appeared that the Germans were
most likely to advance down the coast. The dozen remaining British
anti-tank guns were positioned to block them if they came that way – a
meagre display against the resources at the disposal of the enemy.
Seven remaining British anti-aircraft guns were deployed on the
beaches as well but they were short of ammunition. There was little
they could do against enemy aircraft when they resumed their raids at
dawn. A British army chaplain celebrated Holy Communion on the
dunes east of Dunkirk soon after sunrise but he and the men attending
were scattered by enemy aircraft swooping low. With no large ships at
sea or in the harbour during daylight hours, the *Luftwaffe* could
concentrate on the French defence line and on troops awaiting rescue.
That they did, adding to the toll of bodies on the beach.

> The final evacuation [Admiral Ramsay signalled warships still involved
> in the operation] is staged for tonight, and the Nation looks to the Navy
> to see this through. I want every ship to report as soon as possible

whether she is fit and ready to meet the call which has been made on our courage and endurance.

Drained of energy, many of the men who were called upon to reply and who had repeatedly risked death shuttling back and forth to Dunkirk would have preferred to bow out. But all ships reported either that they were 'fit and ready' or that their crews were prepared to serve in any capacity. Though not under orders or military obligation, many of the civilians who had volunteered or otherwise been drawn into the operation were equally willing to get on with the job. Indeed, some continued by choice to operate off the beaches during the day while the navy waited until nightfall. But some, like others before them, decided they had done enough and removed themselves from the operation. Armed guards were posted on some vessels to keep crewmen from abandoning ships in the harbours of south-eastern England before they could be replaced by navy personnel and to make certain that once they reached Dunkirk after dark, they did not hesitate from entering the harbour because of German shelling.

That night's evacuation procedures were more meticulously planned than at any time since the full dimensions of the evacuation came to be appreciated. The suspension of daytime sailings provided a respite in which Ramsay and Dynamo headquarters personnel could examine the situation clearly. The eleven destroyers still at Ramsay's disposal were scheduled to reach Dunkirk at half hour intervals starting at 2100 hours. The timing for the other vessels – thirteen passenger ships, two cargo carriers, fourteen minesweepers, and an assortment of other ships – was also plotted with greater thoroughness than had been possible before. Navy motor boats were to take up positions in Dunkirk harbour to guide the ships to their berths. Special ladders were constructed to speed along the embarkation of the troops. Liaison with RAF Fighter Command arranged for strong patrols over the evacuation area for the hour prior to darkness to warn the *Luftwaffe* away from the night operation. In the best tradition of the Royal Navy, Operation Dynamo was to be wrapped up before dawn with calm, meticulous efficiency.

Confusion on the numbers still to be evacuated was inevitable. It was thought there were between four thousand and six thousand British troops left, including stragglers from virtually every unit in the BEF. During the day, almost all were organized for rapid embarkation and were not expected to present much of a rescue problem if the defence line held. Assuming the Germans did not break through, the problem would be the French troops. There could be anywhere between 25,000 and 60,000 of them. Despite the careful planning, endgame calculations involved a great deal of guesswork.

The suspension of activity at the breakwater that morning gave Commander Clouston, the pier master at Dunkirk, who had been superintending the frantic evacuation from the harbour for five days, an opportunity to leave the area for a few hours. He sped by motor boat back to Dover to participate in the planning of the night's operations, as well as for some sleep, a bath, and a meal. Somewhat refreshed, he headed back to Dunkirk that afternoon to oversee the coming night's activity at the breakwater. En route, his motor boat – one that was to help guide ships to their berths in the harbour that night – was attacked and sunk by German dive bombers. Clouston and the party accompanying him were thrown into the water. A second motor boat which had been accompanying theirs turned to rescue them but Clouston, aware of the danger to any boat that stopped in those waters when enemy aircraft were in attendance, signalled it off. Instead, he and the men with him started swimming towards the ship's wreckage some distance away. His body was later spotted floating in the water. His death would have a bearing on the Dunkirk proceedings that night.

Now that restrictions on the publication of news about the Dunkirk evacuation had been eased, Britain's newspapers were full of accounts of the heroism of the men involved in the operation and of the great numbers of men brought back from France. But rumours continued to circulate in many parts of the country that the losses across the Channel had been frighteningly heavy. It couldn't be otherwise with more and more families receiving War Office regrets about men killed or wounded in France. Despite the reports of the magnificent exodus from the continent, a great many others waited in vain to hear that their kin had safely returned to the bosom of the motherland. Minister of War Eden went on the radio to boost morale and give assurances that Britain remained strong:

> The British Expeditionary Force still exists, not as a handful of fugitives, but as a body of seasoned veterans . . . [Our spirit] has been tried and tempered in the furnace. It has not been found wanting.

Though he never showed it, among those who had needed reassurance was the Prime Minister. From the moment Churchill had heard of Gort's decision to fall back to the coast, he had imagined great numbers of British troops dead and wounded in and around the 'bomb trap' at Dunkirk, and 'long, dreary processions [of captured British troops] making their way to prison camps and starvation in Germany.' He had also known how precarious his political position would have become if, as he and his advisers expected, only a small fraction of the BEF was rescued. Now, though deeply saddened by casualty levels and anxious about the naval and RAF losses in the operation, the Prime Minister, referring to the loss of most of the British Army's heavy equipment, was able to quip that though the men had been brought home, 'we lost the luggage'.

The British leader pressed relentlessly ahead with his campaign to prevent any sense of defeat or gloom from permeating both the senior councils of war, which had access to details of the serious losses sustained, and the public imagination. He told the chiefs of staff, who knew better, that 'the armed forces in Great Britain are now far stronger than they have ever been' and that German invaders would meet not 'half-trained formations, but the men whose mettle they have already tested, and from whom they have recoiled, not daring seriously to molest their departure'. Had they heard the Prime Minister's words, men whose departure from Dunkirk had been 'seriously molested' might have shaken their heads in wonder.

Meantime, the armed forces increased their vigilance along the coasts of England. In a dispatch which heightened invasion fever, an American reporter covering the war from the German side reported that correspondents had seen 'certain "specialized troops" whose nature they were pledged not to reveal'.

'MYSTERY NAZIS MASS AT CHANNEL' is the way a Chicago newspaper headlined that story, a danger with which the War Office was already trying to cope. Preparations were made for demolishing bridges on all roads in Britain going inland from the shore all the way from Kent to Scotland.

The War Office also considered organizing a campaign of guerrilla warfare against the German invader if that became necessary. All commands had been issued with instructions for making Molotov cocktails. Ironside noted in his diary that General Orde Wingate suggested the formation of the kind of organization he had established in Palestine when he was on special duty with the British administration there before the war and had formed squads of Jewish irregulars to guard a crucial oil pipeline against raids by Arab insurgents.

At Galway in Ireland, an evacuation of a different kind had taken place that day. The liner *President Roosevelt* had arrived from the United States to transport Americans who had been visiting or resident in Britain out of war's danger. The vessel normally carried 460 passengers. But for this journey, 725 passengers, some with their pet dogs, plus 375 ships' company, all wearing lifebelts, were accommodated.

Though many of these passengers were not accustomed to travelling anything but first class, the liner was so crowded that some were assigned to makeshift berths in the ship's post office and baggage compartments. To leave no doubt about the vessel's identity, large American flags had been painted on its sides. It was lit up like a Christmas tree and the Germans as well as the British had been informed of its route so that no mistakes would be made by their submarines. From Berlin came the suggestion that the British might attack the ship and then blame Germany, hoping to draw America into the war on the side of the Allies.

The publicity given this emergency evacuation assured the presence of a large crowd of onlookers as the ship set sail from Galway to carry its passengers far from the blackouts, shortages and uncertainties of the European conflict. The *Manchester Guardian* reported that, 'Very few friends [of the passengers] had been able to get to Galway to say goodbye to the Americans returning to a land where there are still lighted streets'.

As evening gave way tonight at Dunkirk, everything was ready for the final act of Operation Dynamo. A picket of men from the 5th Green Howards, who had withdrawn from the defence line but failed to be embarked the night before, formed up from the base of the breakwater along the adjoining beach. They were positioned fifty yards in from the water line for a distance of five hundred yards to keep the embarkation procession moving along quickly when the rescue ships began berthing at the pier.

It worked well. Without interruption, the troops tramped from the beach on to the access road to the breakwater, then along the pier to the vessels to which they were directed, and they clambered quickly aboard. The operation proceeded so smoothly that within a few hours, it was hard to find more men to embark. Except for the non-ambulatory wounded, those caring for them, and a number of stragglers, all British troops in the perimeter had been boarded. What had seemed beyond the realm of possibility had been accomplished. Just before midnight, Captain Tennant signalled Dynamo headquarters, 'Operation completed'. The BEF – which so many had given up as doomed – had been evacuated.

26,256 men had been embarked that day – 19,561 from the harbour, 6,695 from the beaches. That made a total of 285,305 troops ferried to England since the operation had been launched eight days earlier. It had been an extraordinary achievement. But the belief of ships' crews that Dynamo was now to be declared concluded and that they need not return again to the horrors of Dunkirk would, to their anguish, prove premature.

# Save the French

THE EVACUATION of the BEF having been completed by the previous midnight, a strange stillness had fallen over Dunkirk harbour. The oil tanks in the backdrop were still on fire and shells still fell intermittently. But it appeared as though the area – only recently clogged with men – had been vacated.

At half past midnight, a bewildered Wake-Walker reported to Dover that vessels were berthed at the breakwater but the thousands of French troops thought to be ready for embarkation were nowhere to be found. An hour later, he again signalled Dover, 'Plenty of ships. Cannot get troops.' There was no sign in the wharves of the harbour, on the breakwater or on the adjoining beach of the expected multitude of evacuees. Most troubling, there was no sign of the French rearguard troops who had manned the defence line the last two days, enabling the last of the BEF to be lifted off.

It was pointless and dangerous to keep vessels at the pier for evacuees who did not show up. The destroyer *Vanquisher* was ordered home from Dunkirk at 0230, returning to Dover with only thirty-seven evacuees, picked up from a small boat outside the harbour. The destroyer *Codrington* returned with only forty-four troops. The *Malcolm* returned with no evacuees at all. The crossing had been wasted for all the vessels, including five of Ramsay's destroyers, sent over during the early hours of June 3rd for the grand finale. Several ships waited in vain for an hour or more before heading back to England. One vessel stayed tied up in vain at the breakwater for three-and-a-half hours before finally making for home, its crew bitter at being needlessly exposed to danger.

All British troops having been evacuated and the operation seemingly concluded, General Alexander prepared to leave as well. He first boarded a motor boat in the harbour and prowled along the beach eastward for about two miles, as close inshore as the boat's shallow draft permitted while he repeatedly called in English and French over a megaphone, 'Is anyone there?' There was no reply. He returned to the harbour and toured the wrecked wharves, calling out the same question with the same result. Satisfied no one still waited for embarkation, Alexander and his aides boarded a waiting destroyer and set off for England, picking up an RAF escort when they approached the English coast as dawn broke.

But sixty thousand French soldiers were still in the perimeter, more than half of them the rearguard troops who had not yet been able to fall back on the harbour. For tactical reasons, their counterattack, to foil a German attempt to break through the new defence line, had been delayed until late the previous evening and they were still in the process of disengaging and falling back. As for the others, the absence of Commander Clouston, the pier master who had been killed on his way back from Dover the previous day, was sorely felt. Liaison between remaining British evacuation personnel and makeshift French embarkation control officers was practically non-existent, leaving thousands waiting in vain near the western rather than the eastern breakwater or in the dunes awaiting instructions to move to the harbour. The opportunity to evacuate thousands more men before sunrise was lost.

Ironically, after this missed chance, just before dawn, the harbour suddenly burst into activity once more. Men who had earlier held back in ignorance of available passage now rushed to the eastern breakwater to be embarked on an assortment of French small craft which showed up in profusion to take them away, lifting them from the west pier and the harbour wharves as well. Rearguard troops now began showing up too.

In the harbour crush, vessels got in each other's way and collided. Some ran aground in shallows of the inner sections of the harbour and had to await high water. Fearing to be left behind, men who advanced along the eastern breakwater tried to board the first vessel they came across, blocking the passage of other troops to ships tied up further along the pier. Many who could have been taken off were left behind as pre-dawn light broke through the darkness once more and the ships again hastily withdrew. The men left behind retired reluctantly to the dunes and settled in there to await either the enemy or evacuation the next night, whichever came first. Queer, quiet desolation, intermittently punctuated by the burst of shells, descended again on the harbour area.

During the morning, under Admiralty instructions to make another effort to rescue stranded French troops, Ramsay met with his chief aides at Dynamo headquarters in Dover to discuss how to proceed.

Soon after, he sent what was almost an apology to the ships under his command:

> I hoped and believed that last night would see us through, but the French who were covering the retirement of the British rearguard had to repel a strong German attack and so were unable to send their troops to the pier in time to be embarked. We cannot leave our Allies in the lurch and I must call on all officers and men detailed for further evacuation tonight to let the world see that we never let down our Ally.

Back from Dunkirk, General Alexander, who should have known as well as anyone in Britain, reported that he had no idea how many French troops were left in the bridgehead. It was therefore impossible to determine the number of ships still needed to evacuate them. The empty return of the vessels which had risked doom to make the journey the night before was infuriating, particularly as it was now possible for Dynamo headquarters personnel to review the situation and grasp how serious were the naval losses so far sustained.

Only nine of the forty destroyers which had been committed to the operation were still available to return to Dunkirk. But Churchill had personally directed that efforts continue to save as many French troops as possible. Ramsay began making arrangements for the coming night but he warned the Admiralty of problems that would arise if Dynamo was not wound up after the coming night:

> After nine days of operations of a nature unprecedented in naval warfare, which followed two weeks of intense strain, commanding officers, officers and ships' companies are at the end of their tether. I therefore view a continuance of the demands by evacuation with utmost concern as likely to strain to breaking-point the endurance of officers and men. I should fail in my duty did I not represent to Their Lordships the existence of this state of affairs in the ships under my command, and I consider it would be unfortunate, after the magnificent manner in which officers and men of the surviving ships have faced heavy loss and responded to every call made upon them, that they should be subjected to a test which I feel may be beyond the limit of endurance. If therefore evacuation has to be continued after tonight, I would emphasise in the strongest possible manner that fresh forces should be used for these operations and any consequent delay in their execution should be accepted.

Ramsay was not alone in worrying about what might happen after that night's operations. At a War Cabinet meeting, the determined resistance of the French rearguard aroused concern as well as admiration. It was recalled that Weygand had earlier wanted to defend the

Dunkirk bridgehead indefinitely instead of using it only for evacuation purposes. It was possible that the French might after all try to hold the bridgehead despite German military superiority.

The prospect did not please the British High Command. If that happened, Britain would be obliged to lend continuing support which would impose an ongoing strain on its naval and air resources. A report that only three French fighter planes had been sent airborne when more than two hundred German bombers attacked the suburbs of Paris that day, and that those three had confined themselves to patrolling above their own airfield, never challenging the German attack, did not stimulate a desire in London to commit additional British forces to the defence of Dunkirk.

Forever sounding the alarm, RAF Fighter Command chief Dowding pressed the point home by once more alerting the War Cabinet to the dangers involved in the continued commitment of his fighters to the operation. He reported that he had been forced that very day to withdraw the last three of his squadrons that had not yet taken part in Dynamo from their bases in Scotland to do their bit over Dunkirk. All his other squadrons had already lost precious planes and pilots in the operation. The previous night, it had been necessary to draw from eight different squadrons to patch together enough serviceable aircraft to constitute a strong enough Dunkirk patrol for the morning. Britain couldn't hope to fight a war with such shifting and patching. Dowding warned that if the Germans decided to launch a heavy air assault on Britain at that moment, he could not guarantee air superiority for more than forty-eight hours.

The details he provided from statistics newly gathered were indeed alarming. During the first ten days of the German offensive, 250 Hurricanes had been lost in France. That worked out to twenty-five of Britain's modern fighters each day as compared to only four replacements received each day from the aircraft factories. Justifying his earlier opposition to sending additional fighters to France, he said, 'Had this rate continued, we would have lost all our Hurricanes by the end of May.' He reported to the chiefs of staff that the number of modern fighters serviceable as of the day before, June 2nd, was only 280 Spitfires and 244 Hurricanes. But he said even those figures were, in effect, overestimates because some of his pilots, drawn from other flying duties, were still to make their first solo fighter flights.

Dowding was notorious for indulging in gloomy hyperbole in his effort to preserve Britain's home air defences but the dangers he harped upon aroused genuine jitters. The lives of many of Britain's comparatively small corps of experienced fighter pilots, who had been counted on to play a key role in the defence of Britain during the expected

German invasion, had already been claimed in the Dunkirk operation. Having lost men and planes, many of the fighter squadrons were disorganized, not yet having received aircraft replacements and having no time to assimilate newcomer pilots properly. Chief of the Air Staff Newall, who often attempted to moderate Dowding's unrelieved forebodings, warned that in view of the comparative strengths of the British and German air forces, for Britain to achieve air superiority, it would have to destroy German planes at a rate of eight to one, something that wasn't happening even if, as was the case, the inflated kill scores marked up by Fighter Command pilots were accepted as genuine. Newall pointed out that Britain's fighter defences had been organized in the build-up to the war to protect the country against bomber attacks from Germany, not to cope with enemy bombers escorted by short-range fighters flying from nearby captured airfields.

The implication of all this, compounded by the Admiralty's alarm at lost destroyers, was that Operation Dynamo had to be wound up no matter what, and soon. It was a relief to have the army back, with or without its equipment. But it would be unforgiveably reckless to continue the Dunkirk episode if it meant hopelessly crippling Britain's naval and air defences.

The operation had to be concluded that night. There could be no further extension. Churchill passed word of the wind-up to Reynaud:

> We are coming back for your men tonight. Please ensure that all facilities are used promptly. For three hours last night many ships waited idly at great risk and danger.

Weygand, for whom the Dunkirk evacuation symbolized his failure to lead the Allies back from the brink of shameful defeat, was less than impressed with this gesture. He bitterly recalled Churchill's unfulfilled promise that the British would supply the rearguard at Dunkirk till the end. It was a time for unrestrained recriminations. With the German conquest of France apparently inevitable, the French military commander charged that the British leader had played 'a double game and had abandoned France to herself'. Still harking back to imaginary might-have-beens, he insisted that Churchill had sabotaged the operation that had been ordered ten days earlier to link up the armies in the north with French forces south of the Somme. He insisted that operation would have been successful if the English, who 'cannot resist the call of the ports', had not been continually looking over their shoulders at the sea.

Such grumbling amounted to little more than a search for a scapegoat for France's monumental military bungling. With the French woefully weak in the south, had the armies of the north turned in that direction – and they might have had Belgium not capitulated, endangering the BEF's left flank – they probably would have put up a strong but brief fight before being overwhelmed by German armoured might. There would have been no Dunkirk – no rescue, no great escape, and no British army left.

Late in the day, a report came from the British liaison officer at French Naval Headquarters at Dunkirk that the number of French troops still to be embarked was thirty thousand. (Once again that figure was no more than a guess.) Among the vessels dispatched in quick succession starting that evening to lift them off were thirteen destroyers (four of them French), nine British passenger ships (the master of another refused to sail), eleven minesweepers and a flotilla of smaller British, French and Belgian craft and motor boats.

Much would depend on the Dunkirk embarkation facilities, now even more under threat from forward German artillery positions, and the speed with which men could be boarded. Some of the French troops who clogged the embarkation areas the previous night had still refused to board, fearing the sea or reluctant to leave their homeland. Others had refused to be embarked unless their entire units could board the same ship and some who had boarded tried to push their way off again when they realized there wasn't enough space for all the men in their units. French naval personnel accompanied the Royal Navy pier party sent back from Dover to help sort out such problems during the final wind-up.

Questions remained as to whether French troops still holding the line could hold fast. The Germans mounted several concerted attempts to break through during the course of the day. Though the capture of Dunkirk had been downgraded as a priority by the German command, it was obvious that its defences were about to crumble and that death or capture was the probable fate of surviving French rearguard troops. Nevertheless, they fought for every bit of land, every street, every house. In places, they fought till the last man was cut down and still a line held, further back now, in Dunkirk itself but far enough away from the harbour as the day drew to a close for the final evacuation operation to proceed as planned once darkness fell. The performance, determination, grit and soldierly skills of these French troops showed that the battle of France might have followed a totally different course had the country's senior commanders been worthy of such soldiers.

So close to final victory but warned off by the ferocity of French resistance, exhausted from battle, uncertain about the terrain, and confident of an easy triumph the following day, the Germans once more ceased pressing forward when night fell. Taking advantage of the lull, survivors of the rearguard quietly disengaged and slipped back towards the harbour for the ships sent to deliver them from death or capture.

By then, many of the vessels had arrived from England and had begun boarding. They had found the harbour 'swarming with French fishing craft and vessels of all sorts'. Some of these had tied up at the eastern breakwater. Only with difficulty were they persuaded to move off to pick up men from the west pier and the wharves and thus make room for larger vessels which couldn't berth anywhere else and which could load far more men. Wake-Walker observed the scene in amazement:

> The congestion was chaotic, ships going astern into others coming ahead. French destroyers shrieking on their sirens, small craft nipping here and there, rendering the exit most dangerous.

Bumpings and collisions abounded. Wrecks piled up in the harbour. Some skoots ran aground at the near end of the west pier and had to wait for the tide to lift them off again. Congestion ruled the breakwater as well, now with only a young British navy sub-lieutenant acting as pier master, trying to get as many French troops as possible boarded:

> Lord help us! I was grey-haired by the end of the night. First of all whenever a shell came over they all fell flat on their faces, and it took at least three minutes before they started moving again, and as the shells were arriving in salvos every two minutes they hardly moved at all. Next when they came to the first gangway at the first ship they all tried to get on board together. In consequence there was a complete block; all the other ships along the jetty were stranded with no one to go on board. If one tried to point this out to them they merely shouted that as half their regiment was on that particular ship the rest must get in too . . . In desperation I resorted to guile and force. I stationed the biggest seamen I could find near the first ships and they *threw* the French soldiers along the jetty, thus breaking up the regiments. The other method was to ask them what their regiment was and then through a megaphone to shout 'A *moi le dixieme*', and so lead them at the double up the jetty to the end ship and so fill up the whole jetty, which of course was the state of affairs at which we were aiming.

By midnight of June 3rd, with the Germans halted at nightfall barely two miles away, more than 26,746 men had been evacuated that day despite the congestion and confusion and the suspension of the operation during the daylight hours. That made a total of 312,051 since the commencement of Dynamo and the operation which had originally been expected to last forty-eight hours was going into its tenth day.

## Chapter 14 – DAY TEN OF DUNKIRK

# Close Down

NOT TILL TWO O'CLOCK in the morning on June 4th, this last day of Operation Dynamo, did the last of the rearguard make its final withdrawal from the suburbs and outskirts of Dunkirk where they had stopped the Germans at last light. There was some machine gun and rifle fire from the enemy as there had been ever since nightfall but it was sporadic and undirected, a gesture from soldiers who were as exhausted as their prey and who knew it would finally be all over come the morning. The French troops stole quietly away through the ruins of Dunkirk towards the harbour and evacuation. An alarm was raised at Dover about German torpedo boats which were reported to have left Ostend not far up the coast and which might attempt to attack the rescue ships, but the troops knew nothing of that – only that they were to be embarked and that ships were standing by to take them on board less than an hour away across town.

However, these men who had held the line so that the last of the British troops as well as thousands of their French fellow soldiers could escape were to be disappointed. As they proceeded through Dunkirk to the eastern breakwater to be lifted off, they found their way blocked by a vast multitude of men previously not taken into account. A horde of thousands of individual French soldiers who had holed up in fear in the cellars and ruins of Dunkirk and Malo for days, having learned that the Germans were about to arrive and acting through herd instinct, now emerged from their hiding places to claim priority embarkation. These were stragglers from all kinds of units, mostly non-combatant support troops who had separated from their units or been separated from them and who had earlier converged on Dunkirk for sanctuary. This vast impromptu ragtag army jammed the approaches to the breakwater, blocking the rearguard troops off from the embarkation they had made possible as effectively as a concrete wall.

They could do nothing but watch in anguish and hope that, by some miracle, this disorderly throng could be cleared away before daylight and that there would still be room enough for them aboard rescue vessels. But just before morning twilight, most were still waiting as the last of the big ships – the venerable British destroyer *Shikari* – left carrying a thousand troops.

A few smaller vessels continued to pick up small batches of evacuees from the harbour as light began to break through. But the great exodus was effectively over. Some of the men still stranded trooped back into Dunkirk city to await the arrival of the Germans. Others waited where they were.

Under orders from Paris not to be captured by the Germans, Admiral Abrial had left for England before dawn, together with Generals de la Laurencie, Fagalde and Barthelemy who, with their troops, had gone some way during the closing phase of the battle in the north to redeem the reputation of the French Army. Later that morning, Abrial conferred in Dover with Admiral Ramsay about the advisability of prolonging the operation one more night to try to rescue some of the men left behind. Abrial thought it would be a wasted effort. He said the troops still in Dunkirk were out of ammunition with which to hold back the enemy any longer and that a further attempt at evacuation would needlessly endanger the rescue ships.

In fact, shortly after dawn, both the centre of Dunkirk and the beaches east of the breakwater had come under small arms fire from the enemy:

> . . . by the time we left [said one of the last of the Royal Navy personnel to depart] the Germans had occupied most of the town . . . The town [was] a mass of flames with huge shell-ridden and gutted buildings standing out black against the flames.

All resistance having ceased, the Germans moved in quickly. They established themselves in key positions in case further action was needed to ensure their control of the city and the port. But Dunkirk was finally, unquestionably theirs. A British army ambulance driver who had been kept too busy to be evacuated and who now waited to be taken prisoner surveyed a scene of hushed devastation as morning rose and the episode drew to an end:

> It was quiet now. The ruined buildings sent up only a little smoke and in the beautiful clear morning could be seen the sunken ships all round the inner harbour, and out to sea as well, a Thames barge still floating at anchor untouched – the quays, canal sides and beaches crowded with . . . abandoned wagons – many dead upon the beach, and the greater desolation because it was obviously the end. The Navy had gone. The A.A. guns were gone. The wireless van was scuttled, and we could hope for nothing more.

At nine o'clock that morning, General Beaufrère, who had been left in command of French troops there, met with a Lieutenant-General Friedrich-Carl Kranz, commanding attacking German forces, to arrange for the surrender of the thirty thousand to forty thousand French troops (no one knew how many exactly) still in the bridgehead. The swastika flag was run up over Dunkirk town hall. Ironically, some French soldiers still lined the eastern breakwater when the Germans arrived at its foot to take them prisoner and run up a swastika banner there as well.

Ships and boats continued to arrive at English south-coast ports right through the morning, their navigation problems having been complicated by fog which also served to protect them from air attack as they negotiated the Channel passage. After unloading their passengers and being authorized by Ramsay at 10.30 that morning to disperse, they made for their home ports all over southern England for rest and repair, and for the warships to make ready to repel the expected German attack. The urgency, the pressure, the bombing and shelling, the navigation through wreckage-strewn waters pockmarked with shallows, sandbars and mines were suddenly over. For many who manned those vessels, the final return must have been, as it was for Wake-Walker, 'like waking from a dream'.

At 1423 hours that afternoon, the Admiralty in London officially announced, 'Operation Dynamo now completed.' The official War Office communiqué said, 'The outstanding success of this operation, which must rank as one of the most difficult operations of war ever undertaken, has been due to the magnificent fighting qualities of the Allied troops; to their calmness and discipline in the worst conditions; to the devotion of the Allied navies; and to the gallantry of the RAF. Although our losses have been considerable, they are small in comparison with those which a few days ago seemed inevitable.'

On that last day of Dynamo, 26,175 troops – almost all French – had been ferried to England from Dunkirk. The final total evacuated, including the 'useless mouths' lifted off in the days just before Operation Dynamo was launched, was 364,628 – 224,686 British. Within days, many of the French troops would return to France to try in vain to help stem the total conquest of their nation by Hitler's armies. But to the immense relief of Churchill, the high command in London, and the people of Britain, the British army, so nearly lost, was home.

# Finale

Had a combined staff been told to investigate the problem of evacuating 300,000 men from a harbour and beaches under the shadow of hostile shore based aircraft and in close contact with the enemy's troops, it is probable that their appreciation would have been very pessimistic. It is even possible that by all known rules the operation could have been summed up as impossible.

– Royal Navy report, June 18th, 1940

The impossible may have been accomplished. The British troops brought back from Dunkirk may have been welcomed in England as if they were heroes returning in triumph rather than an army of ragged soldiers who had found themselves in a very tight spot from which they had to be extracted. Newspapers throughout the land were rhapsodizing about the skill and daring with which the operation had been carried out. But the fact remained that Britain had just suffered a major defeat, acknowledged by Churchill in his refusal to authorize the minting of a Dunkirk medal for the evacuees.

Right up to the minute of landing in England [said a soldier], the general feeling was that we were in disgrace, that it was a shameful thing that we'd been kicked out of France like that. It was certainly a marvellous operation put on to evacuate us, but we had no idea that people would be pleased about seeing us back. We felt that we were an army in defeat and people would look pretty glum about it. Instead of which they were on the train stations with their chocolates and oranges and all kinds of greetings. We felt in a way that we really didn't deserve it.

In fact, not a few Britons wondered what the cheering was all about. More than 68,000 men of the British Expeditionary Force had been killed, captured, wounded or were missing in action, including at least two thousand killed or wounded by enemy action during the course of Operation Dynamo. The families of casualties already knew that they were dead or wounded or hadn't heard of their safe return and feared the worst.

RAF Fighter Command had lost 106 fighter aircraft and eighty fighter pilots during the operation and was urgently tallying up its resources for the expected enemy aerial assault on the homeland. RAF Bomber Command had lost seventy-seven of its aircraft. Of 693 British ships which had taken part in the operation, 226 had been sunk, including six destroyers. Nineteen other destroyers had been put out of action. Seventeen of 168 ships of the other Allies had also been sunk. The bulk of the British Army's heavy equipment – including virtually all its tanks and anti-tank guns and heavy artillery, as well as 64,000 vehicles, almost all of the army's machine guns, and half a million tons of stores and ammunition – had been left behind in France.

The experience of the BEF had been catastrophic. There were many who maintained that despite everything that had happened, the performance of both officers and men under pressure had been above reproach, considering the circumstances. But there were others for whom the simple, unpalatable fact was that the British Army had been driven into the sea and that it was too easy to hold the French exclusively to blame. Inevitably, there was some second-guessing about what should have been done and who should be held responsible. The irrepressible General Montgomery – who was convinced that Gort was a total incompetent – insisted on a private interview with Chief of Staff General Dill to tell him that certain officers were not fit to command. Dill subsequently felt obliged to put a stop to the backbiting in a message to all divisional commanders:

> I learn there is a certain amount of rather loose criticism going on among commanders of the BEF regarding the manner in which their seniors, their equals and their juniors conducted the recent operations in France and Belgium. Such criticism is calculated to shake the confidence of the Army in its leaders of all ranks, and I need not emphasise the dangers, particularly at a time like the present. I look to you to put a stop to all this. Any failings of commanders or staff officers should be submitted confidentially through the proper channels but on no account must they be discussed unofficially.

It would be a long time before some of the men who had gone through the horror of Dunkirk would recover their emotional balance. Many had seen their comrades killed and had almost been killed themselves. Many could not easily shake free of the recollection of the terror at being dive-bombed or strafed or floundering in the water after rescue vessels had been blasted from under them. Some were subject to terrifying nightmares for a long time afterwards. Some who, during the retreat and on the beaches, had behaved in ways they preferred to forget at the expense of their comrades or the men who served under them had trouble coming to terms with themselves. They had seen the face of war and had been confounded, frightened and humiliated by it. Many withdrew within themselves for weeks and months after their homecoming, seeming dazed and saying little. Pretentious newspaper claims that all the returned soldiers wanted now was 'another crack at Jerry' were the fabrications of people who had no idea of what the men had gone through.

Despite all of this, army morale was on the whole much better than might have been expected. The nation was in danger and a sense of urgency and commitment in preparing to repel the enemy prevailed. Inevitably, many feared for the future. But though deeply worried by what might lie in store, the people of Britain and their leaders, buoyed up by the rescue of their army, were generally confident that whatever happened, all would work out well in the end. This would be called the Dunkirk Spirit, the belief in ultimate triumph regardless of the odds and no matter how forbidding the long, bleak corridor that had to be traversed. Most important for practical purposes, RAF Fighter Command, believing its own vastly inflated kill claims, had emerged from the operation convinced that, despite its losses, it was more than a match for the German air force against which it would soon have to defend the skies over Britain.

Nevertheless, in cold, practical terms, the outlook for the country generally was not at all promising. France was about to be forced to its knees and the British knew they were about to stand alone against the might of Nazi Germany whose triumphant, better equipped forces sat perched a mere twenty miles away across the Channel. The *Luftwaffe* had already taken possession of airfields a few minutes' flying time from the English coast. For all its confidence in the final outcome, Britain anxiously awaited a rain of death from its skies and ruthless marauders at its shores.

It was left to Churchill, who would have been destroyed politically if Operation Dynamo had been a fiasco, to offer a public summing up of the situation when the House of Commons assembled a few hours after the conclusion of the operation. He confessed that it had seemed to him that the 'whole root and core and brain of the British Army . . . [had been] about to perish upon the field or to be led into an ignominious and starving captivity'. But he would not let his people delude themselves into believing that in having to be rescued from annihilation, the BEF had achieved a victory. 'Wars,' he declared, 'are not won by evacuations.' Nor did he permit the deliverance of the British Army to detract from public awareness of the great danger which still confronted the country.

However, he did invoke the remarkable achievement of Operation Dynamo to shore up public confidence in final victory in the war no matter what difficulties lay ahead. In one of the most memorable public speeches of modern times, he proclaimed unwavering defiance of Nazi Germany:

> Even though large tracts of Europe and many old and famous States have fallen or may fall into the grip of the Gestapo and all the odious apparatus of Nazi rule, we shall not flag or fail. We shall go on to the end. We shall fight in France, we shall fight on the seas and oceans, we shall fight with growing confidence and growing strength in the air, we shall defend our island, whatever the cost may be. We shall fight on the beaches, we shall fight on the landing grounds, we shall fight in the fields and in the streets, we shall fight in the hills; we shall never surrender, and even if, which I do not for a moment believe, this island or a large part of it were subjugated and starving, then our Empire beyond the seas, armed and guarded by the British Fleet, would carry on the struggle, until, in God's good time, the new world, with all its power and might, steps forth to the rescue and the liberation of the old.

In the weeks that followed, Churchill was able to employ his extraordinary personal qualities to prune away remaining doubts in Parliament, the Foreign Office and the War Office about his ability to lead Britain in its moment of supreme peril. The most articulate exponent of the Dunkirk Spirit, the Prime Minister was soon a hero even to men who had scorned his abilities a few weeks before. Like the weary, hungry Tommies who had peered anxiously out to sea from the Dunkirk beaches and who had scooted along the eastern breakwater to be embarked, the man who would lead Britain back from the edge of defeat had been rescued by Operation Dynamo.

# Postscript

A S THE LAST OF Operation Dynamo's rescue vessels reached port in England, the German army command proclaimed that the triumph of its forces in northern France and Belgium would 'go down in military history as the greatest battle of annihilation of all time'. Hitler could boast that his armies had scored a tremendous victory. In less than a month, the British had been driven out of Europe and France was staggering towards capitulation. But though he did not know it, and though further notable victories lay ahead for him, the German leader had more reason to be downcast than elated. The escape of the British Expeditionary Force from Dunkirk was the first step towards the defeat of his armies, the collapse of his Nazi empire, and his own suicide five years later. Dunkirk was the beginning of the end of the Third Reich.

Ifs and buts are uncomfortable factors in any equation. But from what had gone before and from what was to follow, it is not unreasonable to conjure up the elements of an alternative scenario, a what-might-have-been if Hitler had not stopped his panzers on the Canal Line for three days, if Gort had not made his decision to withdraw to the coast, if the weather in the English Channel had been as blustery as it usually is, or if the Royal Navy and Royal Air Force had not made the great escape possible.

Before Hitler learned that the BEF had been extracted from the Dunkirk trap and that Britain still had an army, he confidently told one of his senior generals that he expected the British to come to a 'sensible peace arrangement' so that he could turn his attention to conquering the Soviet Union. Even afterwards, when France was forced to capitulate, the German dictator bombarded Britain with a spate of armistice proposals through neutral intermediaries. If Operation Dynamo had been a fiasco rather than the masterstroke of improvision it turned out to be, Britain, the bulk of its army in captivity, would have had to give very serious consideration to whatever peace terms Hitler was prepared to offer.

Churchill's uncompromising determination not even to examine whether an honourable settlement could be negotiated with triumphant Nazi Germany had already exasperated Lord Halifax. Other senior figures in London also wondered whether acceptable terms could be found that would spare Britain the death and devastation Hitler's air force promised to deliver. In their search for a way to extract Britain from the war, they would have been joined by countless others of their countrymen and countrywomen worried about the fate of a quarter of a million British young men who would have been held hostage by the Germans.

Having been chosen Prime Minister to lead the British to victory, Churchill would instead have led them to the most ruinous rout in their history within weeks of taking office. His position would have been untenable. With prominent figures critical of his leadership, it is likely he would have had to step down. If victory in the war appeared unattainable and devastation imminent, popular pressure for peace on whatever 'honourable' terms could be extracted from Hitler would have been well-nigh impossible for any British government to resist.

If Britain were removed from the war at that stage, the situation would have been fundamentally altered as well for the Soviet Union and the United States. For the Soviet Union, the consequences would have been grim indeed. The Battle of Britain, in which the Germans tried but failed to seize mastery of the skies over Britain, would not have taken place. During that historic battle, which commenced six weeks after the conclusion of Operation Dynamo, the *Luftwaffe* lost 1,882 aircraft as well as great numbers of its most experienced pilots and bomber crews. Had they not been lost, Hitler would have had an air force more than half again as large as the one at his disposal when his *blitzkrieg* against the Soviet Union was launched the following June.

In addition, he would have been able to dispatch up to forty more divisions of troops against Russia, ones which he would not have needed to deploy on his Atlantic Wall, elsewhere in Western Europe, and in combat against the British in the desert sands of Western Egypt and Libya. Even without these additional divisions and aircraft, the German Army took some three million Soviet prisoners of war during the first four months of its invasion of Russia. Within the first five months, it occupied territory inhabited by forty per cent of the entire Soviet population. Before winter set in, the Germans had cracked Moscow's outer defences and the Soviet government had felt obliged to begin abandoning the city.

It is not difficult to imagine even greater Soviet reverses if the German armed forces had not had to contend with the consequences of the escape of the British Army from Dunkirk. They might have launched their invasion of Russia early in May of 1941 instead of late in June and covered much more ground before the weather turned. Moscow might have fallen. Leningrad too. And the historic winter battle of Stalingrad, which foretold the doom of Nazi Germany, might well have had a different conclusion.

During the first winter of the German invasion of the Soviet Union, the United States began shipping desperately needed war equipment to the Russians to help them bring the German advance to a halt and then go on the offensive. But if Dunkirk had been a fiasco and if Britain had been forced out of the war as a result, it is likely the United States would have stuck to its earlier determination not to be drawn into the European conflict. According to Secretary of State Cordell Hull, 'Had we had any doubt of Britain's determination to keep on fighting, we would not have taken the steps we did to get material aid to her.' And if not to Britain, certainly not to Communist Russia. This is not to suggest that the Soviet Union, the largest nation on earth, would necessarily have been crushed. But a different outcome to the war, and to the character of postwar Russia, might indeed have resulted.

The fall of France three weeks after the BEF had been rescued came as a great shock to Americans. But the determination of Britain to hold out against Nazi Germany, the blossoming of the Dunkirk Spirit, aroused admiration, sympathy and growing support across the United States. The day after the conclusion of Operation Dynamo, the *Washington Evening Star* reflected government and popular feeling in America in asserting, 'It is a matter of inestimable importance to our own security that we should instantly remove all restrictions on the rendering of realistic, material aid to the Allies.' A few days later, Secretary of the Treasury Morgenthau confided to an official, 'We are doing everything we can, within and without the law,' to get the flow of arms to the Allies going. After that, direct American involvement in the war, essential for blocking Nazi domination of the Western world, became inevitable.

All things considered, the escape from Dunkirk was one of those rare events when, in a matter of only a few days, accident and design conspired to check and ultimately turn the tide of history.

# Notes

*Abbreviations*

FDR – Franklin Delano Roosevelt Library, Hyde Park, New York
IWM – Imperial War Museum
NA – National Archives, Washington DC
NAM – National Army Museum
NHB – Navy Historical Branch
NMM – National Martime Museum
PRO – Public Record Office, Kew

The ranks by which the Dunkirk veterans cited below are identified are those they held at the time of the Dunkirk evacuation.

*Chapter One:* Dunkirk

4. *I should count it a privilege* . . . Cadogan, p. 327

*Chapter Two:* . . . Prelude

7. *Like frightened householders* . . . Malcolm Muggeride, *The Thirties*, 1940, p.291
8. *Every resource of material The Times,* . . . 20 March 1936
8. *Aircraft do not decide* . . . Chapman, p.22
8. *no belief whatever* . . . Feiling, p.403
8. *He would be a rash man* . . . CAB 23/90, PRO
9. *Heaven knows* . . . Hearden, p.156
10. *William Dodd, the American ambassador* . . . Arnold Offner, *American Appeasement,* 1969, p.104
10. *Germany does not have* . . . Hearden, p.160
10. *What an avalanche* . . . Langer, p.470
10. *Like little boys* . . . Bullitt, p.287
11. *to arouse the Germans* . . . Churchill, Vol. 1, p.330
12. *even begin to know* . . . Ironside, p.83
12. *had no confidence* . . . Bryant, p.41
16. *that such a catastrophe* . . . Gilbert, Vol. 6, p.47
16. *judging from his record* . . . Colville *Diaries,* p. 29

*Chapter Three:* Onslaught

20. *So there's to be* . . . Bartlett, p.47

20. *The battle which begins today* . . . Horne, p.198
20. *Everything wonderful* . . . *The Rommel Papers*, B.H. Liddell Hart, editor, 1953, p.7
20. *reports on the whole* . . . Halder, p.3
21. *speedily become more or less* . . . Birkenhead, p.269
22. *It was only the realization* . . . Cowling, p.383
22. *I cannot yet think* . . . David Duff, *George and Elizabeth*, 1983, p.174
22. *I hope it is not* . . . W.H. Thompson, *I Was Churchill's Shadow*, 1951, p.37
22. *The Tories don't trust* . . . Gilbert, Vol. 6, p.327
22. *described him as 'useless'* . . . Cadogan, p.277
22. *has not got the stability* . . . Ironside, p.248
22. *We had known of Churchill* . . . Sir Ian Jacob, *Atlantic Monthly*, March 1965.
23. *the mere thought of Churchill* . . . John Colville in *Action This Day*, John Wheeler-Bennett, editor, 1968, p.48
23. *the country had fallen* . . . Ibid
23. *You ask,* . . . he told Parliament: *Hansard*, 13 May 1940
24. *Quite intolerable* . . . Birkenhead, p.457
24. *There seems to be* . . . Gilbert, Vol. 6, p.327
24. *The battle is joined* . . . Horne, p.191
24. *We shall see* . . . Baudouin, p.27
25. *It is not often* . . . Angus Calder, *The People's War*, 1969, p.85
26. *the German hordes* . . . Gilbert, Vol. 6, p.306
26. *So far so good* . . . Pownall, p.309
26. *welcomed by cheering, waving* . . . Interview with Private Cyril Thompson, Suffolk Regiment, May 1988
26. *Are they letting us* . . . Baudouin, p.28
26. *An offensive on the scale* . . . *Daily Mail*, 11th May 1940
27. *no defence works* . . . Goutard, p.110
27. *A long battle* . . . Ironside, p.302
27. *This time at least* . . . *The Times*, 11th May 1940
29. *trouble getting into his car* . . . Andre Maurois, *Why France Fell*, 1941, p.89
29. *Several of its most senior officers* . . . Goutard, p.104
29. *Bouillon is a summer resort* . . . Horne, p.194
30. *avoid bombing* . . . Ibid, p.196
30. *main thing is our and French troops* . . . Cadogan, p.282
31. *to get accurate information* . . . Baudouin, p.28
31. *Almost the whole* . . . Cooper, *German Air Force*, p.115
32. *The gunners stopped firing* . . . Goutard, p.133
32. *If I am obliged* . . . Shirer, *Third Republic*, p. 625

33. *means victory or defeat* . . . Goutard, p.138
33. *The atmosphere was that* . . . Bond, p. 102
34. *Almost every evening* . . . Bullitt, p.423
35. *There was no intelligence* . . . Interview with Flight Lieutenant Frederick Rosier, December 1984
35. *One aircraft!* . . . Interview with Flight Lieutenant Sir Archibald Hope, January 1985
36. *ten times more than Britain* . . . BBC Broadcast, 11th May 1940, BBC Archives Centre
36. *we cannot continue* . . . Richards, p.119
36. *these calls . . .will continue* . . . Ironside, p.308
36. *bled white and in no condition* . . . Richards, p.123
37. *to defend by every means* . . . *New York Times*, 11th May 1940
37. *an orgy of destruction* . . . Cordell Hull, *The Memoirs of Cordell Hull*, Vol. 1, 1948, p.775
37. *The voice and force* . . . PREM 3/468, PRO
38. *vigorously contested* . . . *New York Times*, 13th May 1940
38. *if things kept up* . . . Lash, p.123
38. *There are no real leaders* . . . Harold L. Ickes, *The Secret Diaries of Harold L. Ickes*, Vol. 3, 1954, p.146
38. *holding the bag* . . . *Foreign Relations of the United States, 1940*, Vol. 1, 1959, p.222
39. *Joe always has been an appeaser* . . . Henry Morgenthau Jr., *Presidential Diaries*. Microfiche, Card 4. FDR
40. *unless . . . things got* . . . Lash, p.128
40. *The question of whether* . . . Ibid.


*Chapter Four*: Rampage

42. *The German advance* . . . Horne p. 298
42. *When the destiny of France* . . . Ibid, p.278
42. *No information* . . . Chapman, p. 152
43. *I spent more than an hour* . . . Bloch, p.28
43. *No one really wanted* . . . Goutard, p.181
43. *were quite frankly* . . . Major O. A. Archdale, War Notes, IWM
45. *Taxis hooted* . . . Clare Booth, *European Spring*, 1941, p. 270
45. *The German army has pierced* . . . Paul Reynaud, *In the Thick of the Fight*, 1955, p.310
46. *We are beaten* . . . Churchill, Vol. 2, p.38
46. *seen a good deal* . . . Ibid, 39
46. *What you tell me* . . . Pertinax (pseudonym), *The Gravediggers of France*, 1944, p. 74
46. *unless God grants* . . . Shirer, *Third Republic*, p.659

46. *in an indescribable disorder* . . . Spears, Vol. 1, p. 146
47. *If this goes on* . . . Baudouin, p. 30
47. *obvious that the situation* . . . Gilbert, Vol. 6, p. 349
48. *Where is the strategic reserve* . . . Churchill, Vol. 2, p. 42
48. *The hard point* . . . Baudouin, p. 32
48. *We had a right to know* . . . Churchill, Vol. 2, p. 43
48. *into a warlike mood* . . . Colville, *Man of Valour*, p. 197
50. *drained away* . . . Francis Mason, *Battle Over Britain*, 1969, p. 115
51. *It was no uncommon occurrence* . . . CAB 65/13, PRO
51. *water level so low* . . . Pertinax, op. cit., p. 76
52. *Belgian civilians who had welcomed their arrival* . . . Interview with Lance-Corporal Albert White, Royal Signals, October 1987
52. *wrong turning* . . . Nicolson and Forbes, p. 22
52. *it became one retreat after another* . . . Interview with Sergeant Richard Merritt, Royal Artillery, January 1988
52. *withdrawal party prepare* . . . Captain A. M. Bell MacDonald, War Journal, IWM
52. *We weren't given* . . . Merritt interview
52. *We haven't slept* . . . letter home from Sapper A. J. Hooker, IWM
52. *Germans have broken through* . . . Bell MacDonald, op. cit.
52. *in no mood to halt* . . . W. G. Blaxland, Journal, IWM
52. *endless mining towns* . . . Bell MacDonald, op. cit.
53. *subjected to the attentions of Stuka* . . . Merritt interview, interview with Corporal Harold Robinson, Royal West Kents, May 1988, and others
53. *It seemed all hell* . . . L. H. Vollans, Journal, IWM
53. *the wretched refugees* . . . White interview and others
54. *The Führer is terribly nervous* . . . Halder, p. 17
54. *Frightened by his own temerity* . . . Guderian, p. 109
55. *My country has been beaten* . . . Shirer, *Third Republic*, p. 677
55. *I am shattered with fatigue* . . . Archdale, op. cit
55. *be at liberty to appeal* . . . Ellis, p. 11
56. *singularly stupid and unhelpful* . . . Pownall, p. 323
56. *bomb trap* . . . CAB 65/13, PRO
57. *The 'unlikely' possibility* . . . ADM 199/792, PRO
58. *A scandalous – i.e. Winstonian* . . . Pownall, p. 323
59. *in a state of complete depression* . . . Ironside, p. 321
59. *Situation desperate* . . . Ibid, p. 328
59. *Worst of all* . . . Summer Welles, *The Time for Decision*, 1944, p. 119
60. *'absolutely reliable' informant* . . . *Foreign Relations of the United States*, op. cit, p. 224

60. *A stiff return message* . . . President's Secretary's File, Safe Box 5, FDR

60. *I think it may possibly be* . . . Bullitt, p. 427

60. *The British ambassador in Washington* . . . Lash, p. 135

61. *If members of this administration: Roosevelt-Churchill Correspondence, 20th May 1940, FDR*

62. *not only that our codes* . . . Lash, p. 137

63. *scamper unceremoniously back* . . . Interview with Guardsman Thomas Griffiths, Welsh Guards, January 1988

63. *Guderian's newly committed* . . . Guderian, p. 114

64. *The only complaint* . . . Baudouin, p. 39

65. *at the earliest moment* . . . Ellis, p. 111

65. *Can nobody prevent him* . . . Pownall, p. 333

65. *criticism . . . that the BEF* . . . Colville, *Man of Valour*, p;. 215

65. *Clearly at home* . . . Pownall, p. 340

66. *tell the government* . . . John Cairns, Great Britain and the Fall of France, *Journal of Modern History*, December 1955

66. *We were making stands* . . . Interview with Gunner John Gunn, Royal Artillery, October 1988

66. *put on half rations* . . . Interview with Guardsman Thomas Noyce, Grenadier Guards, December 1987

66. *living off the land* . . . Interview with Second-Lieutenant John Carpenter, Royal Army Service Corps, February 1988.

66. *a sort of licensed pillage* . . . Bell MacDonald, op. cit.

67. *gathered the impression* . . . Bryant, p. 119

67. *Blanchard was overheard*: Bloch, p. 110

67. *Blanchard incapable of command* . . . Colville, *Man of Valour*, p. 214

67. *Marshall Pétain also suggested* . . . Spears, Vol. 1, p. 230

68. *overcome by the defection* . . . Baudouin, p. 45

68. *'criminal' to have sent* . . . Ibid, p. 46

68. *incredible mistakes* . . . BBC broadcast, 21 May 1940, BBC Archives Centre

68. *always made for harbours* . . . Horne, p. 478

68. *In the voice of a seasick passenger* . . . Spears, Vol. 1, p. 189

69. *any relatively advantageous offer* . . . Baudouin, p. 53

69. *It was his contention* . . . Ibid, p. 54

69. *We knew nothing* . . . Blaxland, p. 184

69. *I must know at earliest* . . . Gilbert, Vol. 6, p. 394

69. *Gort seems – inexplicably* . . . Cadogan, p. 289

70. *large white balloon-like objects* . . . CAB 80/11, PRO

70. *there appeared to be* . . . CAB 120/439, PRO

71. *might be faced with a situation* . . . CAB 65/13, PRO

71. *His Majesty's Government are confident* . . . Gilbert, Vol. 6, p. 395
72. *Nothing but a miracle* . . . Bryant, p. 117
72. *On many occasions* . . . WO 197/119, PRO
72. *a British liaison officer* . . . Blaxland, p. 250
73. *the ring around the British* . . . Masefield, p. 90
73. *looking rather bewildered* . . . Archdale, op. cit.
74. *The defection of the English* . . . Baudouin, p. 56
76. *Panzer Group Commander von Kleist* . . . Hans-Adolf Jacobson and Juergen Rohwer, *Decisive Battles of World War II – the German View*, 1965, p. 54
77. *The principal thing now* . . . Ellis, p. 150
77. *would give an unconditional assurance* . . . Walter Warlimont, *Inside Hitler's Headquarters*, 1964, p. 98
77. *occupy the territory* . . . Jacobson and Rohwer, op. cit., p. 56
77. *divergence of views* . . . Halder, p. 35
78. *It was forbidden to cross* . . . Guderian, p. 117
78. *which has no enemy before it* . . . Halder, p. 35
78. *Are we going to build* . . . Goutard, p. 230
78. *ordered to withdraw them* . . . Liddell Hart, p. 139

*Chapter Five:* Day one of Dunkirk

82. *for our soldiers in dire peril* . . . *The Times*, 17th May 1940
82. *she had shouted 'Peace'* . . . *New York Herald Tribune*, 17th May 1940
83. *I have information* . . . PREM 3/204
83. *. . . in the meantime* . . . Ibid
83. *I must not conceal from you* . . . Ibid
83. *I never thought I'd lead* . . . Richard Collier, *1940 – The World in Flames*, 1979, p. 16
84. *This bridgehead* . . . Divine, p. 83
84. *examine possibilities for reembarkation* . . . Ellis, p. 174
84. *Darlan's reflexive response* . . . Goutard, p. 238
84. *suddenly realized . . . that* . . . Spears, Vol. 1, p. 192
84. *It's every man for himself* . . . Interview with Gunner Victor Slaughter, Field Artillery, May 1988
85. *as though we were an army* . . . Gun Buster, p. 173
85. *. . . the Germans may try* . . . Ironside, p. 335
85. *so that you can take* . . . Harold Nicolson, *Diaries and Letters: 1930–1964*, Stanley Olson, editor, 1980, p. 186
85. *will seem trifling* . . . Anthony Weymouth, *Plague Year*, 1942, p. 87

85. *within a few weeks* . . . *Washington Post*, 26th May 1940
85. *great secret weapon* . . . Ibid
85. *I believe that the British* . . . Microcopy, M982/740.0011/3274/8/ 10, FDR
85. *Churchill prepared to plead* . . . CAB 80/11, PRO
86. *Reynaud said that he feared* . . . Gilbert, Vol. 6, p. 403
87. *We must take care* . . . Cosgrave, p. 213
87. *we would not* . . . Gilbert, Vol. 6, p. 404
87. *possible to get out* . . . CAB 65/13, PRO
88. *Postulate the destruction* . . . Gilbert, Vol. 6, p. 404
88. *too rambling and romantic* . . . Ibid
88. *If we could get* . . . Collier, op. cit., p. 68
88. *The only one who understands* . . . Baudouin, p. 58
88. *Prime Minister has had* . . . Ellis, p. 165
89. *forbids evacuation* . . . Ellis, p. 165
89. *for the sake of* . . . Ibid
89. *Whether we ever get to the sea* . . . Pownall, p. 342
90. *we shall be lucky* . . . Bryant, p. 134
90. *Our armoured and mechanized forces* . . . Halder, p. 37
91. *Operation Dynamo is to commence* . . . T.S.D. 64/48, NHB. 170. *It is imperative* . . . Ibid
91. *He thought the BEF* . . . Ironside, p. 234
91. *two vessels every four hours* . . . ADM 792/199
93. *'In war', Morrison told people* . . . The *Listener*, 30th May 1940
93. *whether the Allied forces* . . . MID 2016, 1297/107, NA
93. codenamed *Rainbow* . . . Conn and Fairchild, p. 34
94. *protective occupation* . . . WPD 4157–7, NA
94. *. . . if the bad boys win* . . . Letter from Charles H. Baker Jr. to President Roosevelt, 16th May 1940, FDR
94. *. . . if [the British colony of] Bermuda* . . . Ibid President's Official File, 335/Box 2. FDR
95. *control of several commercial airlines* . . . *Daily Mail*, 1st June 1940
95. *initiate conversations* . . . WPD 4115–14, NA
95. *The only sure way* . . . Ibid, 4115–15
95. *You're going to need it* . . . New York Times, 4th June 1940
95. *6,000 Nazis* . . . Watson, p. 95
96. codenamed *Pot-of-Gold* . . . Ibid
96. *Tonight over the once peaceful* . . . 26th May 1940. *Public and Private Addresses of Franklin Delano Roosevelt*, 1940 Volume, FDR
96. *a charade meant to scare the American people* . . . *New York Times*, 28th May 1940

97. *The US Army had* . . . Watson, p. 305

*Chapter Six:* Day Two – Outlook Grim

100. *extremely difficult* . . . ADM 199/792, PRO
100. *the only authority* . . . Ibid
100. *Early that morning* . . . D. W. Hughes, *History of Tough Brothers of Teddington*, IWM
101. *There they lay* . . . Ibid
101. *personal appeal* . . . Ellis, p. 198
101. *Situation demands hard hitting* . . . Ibid
102. *quite clear that sole task* . . . Divine, p. 96
102. *Until French ships materialize* . . . ADM 199/792, PRO
102. *I have been sent by Lord Gort* . . . Goddard, p.251
103. *Massacre at Paradis* . . . Blaxland, p. 286
103. *At every position* . . . Ellis, p. 191
104. *BRITISH SOLDIERS* . . . Barker, p. 145
104. *We sat down on chairs* . . . Howard and Sparrow, p. 49
104. *Large ships are being made fast* . . . Jacobson and Rohwer, p. 65
105. *The [withdrawal] plan* . . . Supplement to *The London Gazette*, 17th October 1941.
105. *It is no good* . . . Pownall, p. 344
105. *ensure the protection* . . . *RAF Narrative*, p. 323
107. *We were jumped* . . . Interview with Pilot Officer Peter Brown, April 1984.
107. *The flight and combat tactics*: Interview with Flight Lieutenant Robert Stanford-Tuck, December 1984
107. *Criticism of the RAF* . . . Merritt Interview and others
108. *Communist coup* . . . Baudouin, p. 59
108. *Britain's refusal to fight* . . . Spears, Vol. 1, p. 235
108. *This is awful* . . . John Reith, *The Reith Diaries*, Charles Stuart, editor, 1975, p. 254
109. *most of the cards* . . . Gilbert, Vol. 6, p. 408
109. *there are signs* . . . Colville *Diaries*, p. 140
109. *Suppose, the Foreign Secretary said* . . . CAB 65/13, PRO
110. *evil must be met by force* . . . *The Times*, 28th February 1940
110. *long and rather confused* . . . Birkenhead, p. 458
110. *To Cadogan, he declared* . . . Cadogan, 291
110. *If the Germans made Britain* . . . *Foreign Relations of the United States*, op. cit. p. 233
110. *Those were the days* . . . Welles, op. cit., p. 149
111. *practically no help* . . . Gilbert, Vol. 6, p. 410
111. *Bermuda rather than Canada* . . . Colville *Diaries*, p. 141

111. *to pick up bits* . . . Gilbert, Vol. 6, p. 413
112. *blood, toil, tears and sweat* . . . *Hansard*, 13th May 1940
113. *several men [there]* . . . Rhodes, p. 215
114. *Please send every available craft* . . . The Evacuation of the Allied Armies from Dunkirk and Neighbouring Beaches, Supplement to *The London Gazette*, 15th July 1947
114. *Dunkirk is in enemy hands* . . . T.S.D. 64/48. NHB
114. *with utmost despatch* . . . Ibid
115. *The galleys [of the destroyer* Gossamer] . . . James Dow, 'Dunkirk 1940 – An Eye-Witness Account', *Journal of the Royal Naval Medical Service*, Spring 1978
116. *[The king] wishes* . . . Ellis, p. 198
117. *seems to have vanished* . . . Gilbert Vol. 6, p. 414
117. *No one in this country* . . . *New York Herald Tribune*, 27th May 1940
117. *Now Duff Cooper urged in Cabinet* . . . CAB 65/7, PRO
117. *The situation is past belief* . . . Chalmers, p. 73

Chapter Seven: Day Three – The Long Retreat

119. *You can rummage through* . . . Hanson Baldwin, *The Crucial Years*, 1976, p. 119
119. *They must now stand by us* . . . Spears, Vol. 1, p. 253
119. *might sting the French* . . . CAB 65/7, PRO
119. *The move back* . . . Howard and Sparrow, p. 37
119. *because the middle of the road* . . . *Account of Movements and Actions Fought by 1st Battalion Welsh Guards in France and Flanders from 17th May to 1st June 1940*. NAM
120. *These officers soon discovered* . . . Interviews with Commander Stanley Nettle, July 1988 and Petty Officer John Agate, August 1988
121. *Then, and not until then* . . . E. Hamilton-Piercy, diary, NMM
122. *I . . . begged General Blanchard* . . . Ellis, p. 209
123. *Massacre at Wormhout* . . . Leslie Aitken, *Massacre on the Road to Dunkirk*, 1977
123. *From every house* . . . Gun Buster, p. 183
124. *like thousands of sticks* . . . Divine, p. 145
124. *The beach was an extraordinary sight* . . . Hadley, p. 137
125. *followed the crowd* . . . Interview with Lance-Bombardier Richard Maycock, Royal Artillery, May 1988
125. *We all had one idea* . . . Rhodes, p. 225.
125. *odds and sods* . . . Maycock interview
125. *You don't belong to us* . . . Ibid

125. *It would start off as a queue* . . . Slaughter interview
126. *where they felt safer* . . . Carpenter interview
126. *the sand muffled the bomb explosions* . . . Interview with Guardsman Thomas Noyce, Grenadier Guards, December 1987, and White interview.
126. *I saw a man suddenly* . . . Rhodes, p. 228
126. *Tired, wet and hungry* . . . Sergeant W.C. Brodie, diary, IWM
128. *in urgent need of repair* . . . Ellis, p. 208
128. *A tank attack* . . . Ibid
128. *Sir Roger Keyes returned that day* . . . CAB 65/7 PRO
128. *I expect to make a statement* . . . Hansard, 28th May 1940
129. *We must not ignore the fact* . . . CAB 65/13, PRO
129. *We should find* . . . Ibid
129. *nations which went down* . . . Ibid
129. *It should be done, the former prime minister said* . . . Ibid
130. *Quite a number* . . . Churchill, Vol. 2, p. 88
130. *supreme control* . . . Keesing Contemporary Archives 1937–1940, 27th May 1940
130. *Fighter Command flew 321 sorties* . . . RAF Narrative
131. *Our men can find no words* . . . BBC broadcast, 31st May 1940, BBC Archives Centre
131. *For all the good* . . . Interview with Flight Lieutenant Alan Deere, April 1984
131. *I and the Forces* . . . Chalmers, p. 97
131. *Rightly or wrongly* . . . Richards, p. 132
131. *The sky is a big place* . . . ADM 199/788, PRO
132. *It was no good* . . . Interview with Pilot Officer Steve Stephen, June 1984
132. *fighter-defences were almost* . . . CAB 65/7, PRO
132. *a curious old thing* . . . Ironside, p. 346
132. *There can be no doubt* . . . CAB 120/247, PRO
133. *The BEF commander asked London* . . . CAB 65/13, PRO
133. *We have every confidence* . . . Ibid
133. *It will be necessary* . . . Daily Sketch, 29th May 1940
133. *The British Expeditionary Force* . . . New York Herald Tribune, 29th May 1940
134. *Poor chap* . . . Pownall, p. 352

*Chapter Eight:* Day Four – Journey Through Hell

135. *Personnel vessels* . . . Supplement to The London Gazette, 15th July 1947
136. *exercising navigational caution* . . . ADM 199/792, PRO

137. *On arrival alongside* . . . T.S.D. 64/48, NHB
137. *in an endeavour to take charge* . . . Ibid
137. *Some soldiers did row back* . . . Interview with Gunner Patrick Hennessy, Royal Artillery, May 1988
138. *often brandishing a weapon* . . . Agate interview
138. *I took my revolver* . . . Nettle interview
138. *At three in the morning* . . . Bartlett, p. 120
139. *As one man* . . . Brodie, op. cit.
140. *dispense with full cover* . . . ADM 199/792, PRO
141. *On our way to the coast* . . . Interview with Sapper Leslie Ginsberg, Royal Engineers, September 1988
141. *There was an awful lot of transport* . . . Gunn interview
141. *We ended up* . . . Ibid
142. *A fresh traffic block* . . . Barlone, p. 56
142. *A party of about twenty French troops* . . . Brodie, op. cit.
143. *a big fuss* . . . Pownall, p. 353
143. *to hold on to Dunkirk* . . . Ibid
143. *every Frenchman embarked* . . . ADM 199/792, PRO
143. *While it is eminently desirable* . . . Ibid
144. *We wish French troops* . . . CAB 65/7, PRO
144. *a rabble . . . panicking* . . . Gilbert, Vol. 6, p. 428
144. *absurd state of affairs* . . . Baudouin, p. 63
144. *the British government should be informed* . . . Ibid, p. 62
145. *less than completely forthcoming* . . . Cosgrave, p. 223
145. *should be able to obtain* . . . CAB 66/8, PRO
145. *omniverous strain of grasshopper* . . . *New York Times*, 29th May 1940
146. *We do not consider* . . . CAB 80/12, PRO
146. *In these dark days* . . . PREM 4/68/9, PRO
147. *dill was worried* . . . CAB 65/13, PRO
147. *relinquish the struggle* . . . Ibid
147. *Churchill disagreed* . . . Ibid
147. *If you are cut from* . . . Ellis, p. 218
147. *Every road scoring the landscape* . . . Gun Buster, p. 184
148. *Weariness came down* . . . Howard and Sparrow, p. 47
148. *We continued towards Malo-les-Bains* . . . Gun Buster, p. 242
149. *[It hung] like Death's hovering wing* . . . Ibid, p. 214
149. *In the basements of the houses* . . . P. G. Ackrell, Journal, IWM
149. *One soldier stumbled across* . . . White interview
150. *I can still see* . . . Bell MacDonald, op. cit.
151. *sea-going ships and vessels* . . . ADM 199/792, PRO
151. *Just as it would have been* . . . Les Shorrock, Diary, IWM
151. *more 'suitable motor boats'* . . . T.S.D. 64/48, NHB

152. *had been affected by the events* . . . ADM 199/792, PRO
153. *As soon as we have reorganized* . . . CAB 65/7, PRO

*Chapter Nine:* Day Five – Armada in Miniature

154. *Ships out there were sinking* . . . Agate interview
154. *not immediately engaged* . . . BBC broadcast, BBC Archives Centre
154. *It was a dirty, tired army* . . . *Sheerness Times and Guardian*, 7th June 1940
155. *Saturated with sea water* . . . *East Kent Times*, 5th June 1940
155. *dog-tired, wounded and unkempt* . . . *Washington Post*, 31st May 1940
155. *shattered remnants of the BEF* . . . Ibid, 30th May, 1940
155. *The news is bad* . . . *Manchester Guardian*, 30th May 1940
155. *Invasion of England* . . . *Washington Post*, 31st May 1940
156. *Admiral of the Fleet Sir Dudley Pound* . . . Gilbert, Vol. 6, p. 434
156. *had the right to do* . . . CAB 65/7, PRO
157. *Any organization for forming groups* . . . ADM 199/788, PRO
158. *get enough men together* . . . Hennessy interview
159. *A destroyer going full out* . . . ADM 199/788, PRO
160. *the water was like a mill pond* . . . Maycock interview
160. *God had work for the British* . . . Interview with Ordinary Seaman Stanley Allen, May 1988
160. *The snag was* . . . Divine p. 134
161. *a man stark naked:* Lieutenant R. N. Irving, Journal, MS 67/050, NMM
161. *at the port of Ramsgate alone:* ADM 199/792, PRO
161. *engineer troops, among the comparatively few* . . . Ginsberg interview
161. *Fifteen or more lorries* . . . Sergeant H. J. Cornwall, Journal, IWM
162. *in the very best spirits* . . . MS 67/050, NMM
162. *He was to consider* . . . Ibid
163. *every Frenchman embarked* . . . Pownall, p. 356
163. *for the good of the common cause* . . . Gilbert, Vol. 6, p. 431
163. *congested mass of disorganized Frenchmen* . . . CAB 65/7, PRO
164. *if the German armoured divisions* . . . Sir Ian Jacob, op. cit.
164. *To the fullest possible extent* . . . CAB 65/13, PRO
164. *The War Office in London* . . . Blaxland, p. 329
164. *last 'reasonable' date* . . . ADM 199/792
165. *Continue to defend* . . . CAB 65/7, PRO

166. *he broke down and wept* . . . Nicolson, *Alexander*, p. 104
166. *A report by Sir Charles Teggart* . . . Fisk, p. 121
167. *the Germans have concerted* . . . PREM 3/130, PRO
168. *until [Ireland] abandons her attitude* . . . CAB 66/8, PRO
168. *have the greater part* . . . CAB 80/12, PRO
168. *under the conditions specially favourable* . . . Ibid
169. *ineptitude of the navy* . . . ADM 19/792, PRO
169. *countless thousands of the enemy* . . . Halder, p. 43
169. *effects of the blunders* . . . Ibid
169. *no one is interested in Dunkirk* . . . Ellis, p. 390
169. *fighting back very stubbornly* . . . Ibid, p. 225

Chapter Ten: Day Six – The People are Told

171. *A newspaper cartoon* . . . *Daily Mirror*, 31st May 1940
172. *a nasty surf* . . . T.S.D. 64/48, NHB
172. *My crew and myself* . . . Lieutenant Irving, op. cit.
172. *Majority of boats* . . . ADM 199/792, PRO
172. *Dunkirk our only hope* . . . Ibid
173. *Long columns of men* . . . Sapper A.J. Hooker, Journal, IWM
173. *We have been continuously* . . . T.S.D. 68/48, NHB
173. *Half way along the mole* . . . Signalman L.H. Vollans, Journal, IWM
173. *Wake-Walker sent messages* . . . ADM 199/792, PRO
173. *Why the jetty was not blown* . . . Letter from Sub-Lieutenant Roger Wake published in *King's Royal Rifle Corps Chronicle*, 1941, NAM
173. *Gort reported from La Panne* . . . CAB 65/7, PRO
174. *Gort wanted to know* . . . CAB 65/7, PRO
174. *Reynaud urgently renewed* . . . Spears, Vol. 1, p. 292
174. *King George felt inclined* . . . *The Second World War Diary of Hugh Dalton*, Ben Pimlott, editor, 1986, p. 31
175. *as fresh as a daisy* . . . Spears, Vol. 1, p. 293
175. *But how many French* . . . Ibid, p. 295
175. *We are companions* . . . Ibid
175. *arm in arm* . . . Baudouin, p. 69
175. *I will not* . . . Spears, Vol. 1, p. 308
176. *His emotions were leading him* . . . Ibid, p. 309
176. *England did not fear* . . . Gilbert, Vol. 6, p. 444
176. *if one of the two comrades* . . . Baudouin, p. 73
176. *England has already coolly assumed* . . . Ibid
177. *realized in his heart* . . . Spears, Vol. 1, p. 319

178. *Behind the dunes* . . . Interview with Surgeon-Lieutenant William Kershaw, July 1988
178. *no troops on the shore* . . . ADM 199/792, PRO
179. *Our motor yacht* . . . Agate interview
179. *A horrible stench of blood* . . . Gun Buster, p. 254
180. *The Kurfuerstendamm jammed* . . . Shirer, *Berlin Diary*, p. 308
180. *It was always impossible for me* . . . ADM 199/792, PRO
180. *to imperil the safety* . . . CAB 44/69, PRO
180. *no further organized evacuation* . . . Ibid
181. *His idea* . . . William Morgan, 'With Alexander to Dunkirk', *Army Quarterly*, April 1972
181. *Abrial threatened to use his authority* . . . Blaxland, p. 331
181. *'General,' he scolded* . . . John Cairn, op. cit.
181. *did not take into account* . . . CAB 44/62, PRO
182. *as rapidly as possible* . . . Ibid
183. *The streets of La Panne* . . . *Diary of the 2nd Battalion, The Bedfordshire and Hertfordshire Regiment in France, May to the Early Part of June 1940*, p. 23, NAM
183. *'Off the streets'* . . . Private F.R. Farley, Middlesex Regiment, Memoir
184. *cannibals or murderers* . . . M982 740.0011/3416, NA

*Chapter Eleven:* Day Seven – Death from the Skies

185. *stricken with a form* . . . ADM 199/788, PRO
185. *We were standing* . . . Kershaw interview
186. *jocular, robust men* . . . Smith, p. 52
186. *The minesweeper Hussar* . . . Ibid
186. *mass hysterical epilepsy* . . . Ibid
186. *We were just about* . . . Kershaw interview
187. *It was evident that my crew* . . . ADM 199/788, PRO
187. *The effect of the consequent plunging* . . . Commander H. Lightoller, Memoir, MS 67/050, NMM
187. *force them back to their duty* . . . ADM 199/792, PRO
187. *We were running this RAF launch* . . . Agate interview
188. *Spotting a tug making for Dover* . . . ADM 199/792, PRO
188. *Navy personnel on the shore* . . . Ibid
189. *To my right and left* . . . Farley Memoir, op. cit.
189. *0243 – Minesweeper Gossamer* . . . T.S.D. 64/48 NHB
189. *A-Company, Green Howards* . . . Gun Buster, p. 243
190. *I saw what appeared to be* . . . R. B. Brett, Memoir, MS 67/050, NMM

190. *have a go* . . . Interview with Private F. R. Farley, Middlesex Regiment, August 1988
190. *A solid block of troops* . . . CAB 44/62, PRO
191. *The litter on the beach* . . . Nicolson and Forbes, p. 41
191. *The troops on the shore* . . . K.C. McGriffie, Memoir, MS 67/050, NMM
192. *Get out of here* . . . Smith, p. 59
192. *she turned turtle* . . . ADM 199/792, PRO
193. *Gort doubted if many French troops:* CAB 65/13, PRO
194. *already considerably below* . . . CAB 80/12, PRO
194. *The War Cabinet was told:* Ibid
195. *The critical point of the evacuation* . . . PREM 3/175, PRO
195. *to decide for himself* . . . Ibid
195. *the abysmal collapse* . . . Spears, Vol. 2, p. 7
196. *An officer of the 5th Borderers:* Lord, *p.*232
197. *hold on as long as possible* . . . CAB 44/69, PRO
197. *It was almost like a motorway* . . . Ginsberg interview
198. *In these circumstances* . . . ADM 199/792, PRO
198. *There have been trapped armies* . . . *New York Herald Tribune,* 31st May, 1940
199. *So long as the English tongue survives* . . . *New York Times,* 1st June 1940

*Chapter Twelve:* Day Eight – Thwarted Hopes

200. *A ballot was taken:* Divine, p. 205
201. *We entered the town* . . . MID 2016–1297/118, Park 1, NA
201. *That the British* . . . Ibid
202. *Equally unsuccessfully* . . . Divine, p. 209
202. *A still close dark night* . . . CAB 44/62, PRO
203. *After which everyone* . . . Ibid
203. *Twenty-four men* . . . Ibid
203. *Looking shoreward* . . . ADM 199/792, PRO
204. *The men furthest along the pier* . . . CAB 44/62, PRO
204. *We had been told* . . . Quilter, p. 34
204. *The final evacuation* . . . T.S.D. 64/48, NHB
205. *fit and ready* . . . Ibid
205. *Armed guards were posted* . . . Ibid
206. *The British Expeditionary Force* . . . *The Listener,* 6th June 1940
206. *bomb trap* . . . CAB 65/13, PRO
206. *long, dreary processions* . . . Hugh Dalton, *The Fateful Years,* 1957, p. 341

207. *we lost the luggage* . . . Ibid
207. *the armed forces* . . . Gilbert, Vol. 6, p. 452
207. *certain 'specialized troops'* . . . *Chicago Herald American*, 4th June 1940
207. *MYSTERY NAZIS MASS AT CHANNEL* . . . Ibid
207. *Preparations were made* . . . CAB 66/8, PRO
207. *Ironside noted in his diary* . . . Ironside, p. 348
208. *Very few friends* . . . *Manchester Guardian*, 5th June 1940
208. *A picket of men* . . . CAB 44/62, PRO
208. *Operation completed* . . . T.S.D. 64/48, NHB

*Chapter Thirteen:* Day Nine – Save the French

209. *At half past midnight* . . . Supplement to *The London Gazette*, 17 July 1947
209. *Plenty of ships* . . . Ibid
209. *The destroyer Vanquisher* . . . Ibid
210. *Is anyone there?* . . . Nicolson, *Alexander, p. 113*
211. *I hoped and believed* . . . T.S.D. 64/48, NHB
211. *After nine days* . . . Ibid
212. *The prospect did not please* . . . CAB 65/7, PRO
212. *Forever sounding the alarm* . . . CAB 65/13, PRO
212. *Had this rate continued* . . . Ibid
213. *rate of eight to one* . . . Ibid
213. *We are coming back* . . . PREM 3/175, PRO
213. *a double game* . . . Baudouin, p. 76
213. *cannot resist the call of the ports* . . . Ibid
214. *Late in the day* . . . Divine, p. 219
215. *swarming with French fishing craft* . . . T.S.D. 64/48, NHB
215. *The congestion was chaotic* . . . Ibid
215. *Lord help us!* . . . Wake, op. cit.

*Chapter Fourteen:* Day Ten – Close Down

216. *An alarm was raised*: ADM 199/792, PRO
217. *Later that morning* . . . PREM 3.175, PRO
217. *. . . by the time we left* . . . Wake, op. cit.
217. *It was quiet now* . . . Private W.B.A. Gaze, Journal, IWM
218. *Like waking from a dream* . . . ADM 199/792, PRO
218. *Operation Dynamo now completed* . . . T.D.S. 64/48, NHB

*Chapter Fifteen:* Finale

219. *Had a combined staff* . . . ADM 199/792, PRO

219. *Right up to the minute* . . . Gunn interview
220. *The irrepressible General Montgomery* . . . Montgomery papers, IWM
220. *I learn there is* . . . Ibid
221. *whole root and core* . . . Hansard, 4th June 1940
222. *Even though large tracts* . . . Ibid

*Chapter Sixteen*: Postscript

223. *go down in military history* . . . Cooper, *German Army*, p. 236
225. *Had we had any doubt* . . . Hull, op. cit., p. 775
225. *It is a matter of inestimable importance* . . . *Washington Evening Star*, 5th June 1940
225. *We are doing everything* . . . Hearden, p. 155

# Bibliography

*Account of Movements and Actions Fought by 1st Battalion Welsh Guards in France and Flanders from 17th May to 1st June 1940. B Echelon Diary.* Welsh Guards Archives, Guards Museum, London

Barker, Arthur, J., *Dunkirk: The Great Escape* (Dent, 1977)

Barlone, D., *A French Officer's Diary*, (CUP, 1942)

Bartlett, Basil, *My First War*, (Chatto & Windus, 1940)

Baudouin, Paul, *The Private Diaries of Paul Baudouin*, (Eyre & Spottiswoode, 1948)

Birkenhead, Earl of, *The Life of Lord Halifax* (Hamish Hamilton, 1965)

Blaxland, Gregory, *Destination Dunkirk*, (William Kimber, 1973)

Bloch, Marc, *Strange Defeat* (Oxford University Press, 1949)

Bond, Brian, *France and Belgium: 1939–1940* (Davis Poynter, 1975)

Bryant, Arthur, *The Turn of the Tide* (Collins, 1957)

Bullitt, Orville, editor, *For the President, Personal and Secret – Correspondence between Franklin D. Roosevelt and William C. Bullitt*, (Houghton Mifflin, 1972)

Butler, Ewan and Bradford, J. Selby, *Keep the Memory Green* (Hutchinson, 1950)

Cadogan, Alexander, *The Diaries of Sir Alexander Cadogan: 1938–1945*, David Dilks, editor (Cassell, 1971)

Carroll, Joseph T., *Ireland in the War Years*, (David & Charles, 1975)

Chalmers, W.S., *Full Cycle, The Biography of Admiral Sir Bertram Home Ramsay* (Hodder & Stoughton, 1959)

Chapman, Guy, *Why France Collapsed* (Cassell, 1968)

Churchill, Winston S., *The Second World War*, Volumes 1 and 2 (Cassell, 1948 and 1949)

Collier, Richard, *The Sands of Dunkirk* (Collins, 1961)

Colville, John, *The Fringes of Power, Downing Street Diaries 1939–1955* (Hodder & Stoughton, 1985)

Colville, John, *Man of Valour: The Life of Field Marshal The Viscount Gort* (Collins, 1972)

Conn, Stetson and Fairchild, Byron, *The United States Army in World War II – The Western Hemisphere, the Framework of Hemisphere Defense*, (Office of the Chief of Military History, Department of the Army, 1960)

Cooper, Matthew, *The German Air Force* (Jane's, 1981)

Cooper, Matthew, *The German Army* (Macdonald and Jane's, 1978)

Cosgrave, Patrick, *Churchill at War* (Collins, 1974)

Cowling, Maurice, *The Impact of Hitler* (Cambridge University Press, 1975)

Divine, David, *The Nine Days of Dunkirk* (Faber & Faber, 1959)

Duggan, John P, *Neutral Ireland and the Third Reich* (Barnes & Noble, 1985)

Eden, Anthony, *The Eden Memoirs – The Reckoning* (Cassell, 1965)

Ellis, L.F., *The War in France and Flanders 1939–1940*, (HMSO, 1953)

*Evacuation from Dunkirk of the British Expeditionary Force and French Troops*, (Tactical and Staff Duties Division: Historical Section, Naval Staff, Admiralty, 1947)

Feiling, Keith, *The Life of Neville Chamberlain* (Macmillan, 1946)

Fisk, Robert, *In Time of War* (André Deutsch, 1983)

Gilbert, Martin, *Winston S. Churchill*, Volumes 5 and 6 (Heinemann, 1976 and 1983)

Goddard, Victor, *Skies to Dunkirk* (Kimber, 1982)

Goutard, A., *The Battle of France* (Muller, 1958)

Guderian, Heinz, *Panzer Leader* (Hulton, 1952)

Gun Buster (pseudonym), *Return Via Dunkirk* (Hodder & Stoughton, 1940)

Hadley, Peter, *Third Class to Dunkirk* (Hollis & Carter, 1944)

Halder, Franz, *The Halder Diaries*, Volume 4 (*The Infantry Journal*, 1950)

Harman, Nicholas, *Dunkirk – The Necessary Myth* (Hodder & Stoughton, 1980)

Hearden, Patrick, *Roosevelt Confronts Hitler* (Northern Illinois University Press, 1987)

Hoehling, A.A., *America's Road to War: 1939–1941* (Abelard-Schuman, 1970)

Horne, Alistair, *To Lose a Battle* (Macmillan, 1969)

Howard, Michael and Sparrow, John, *The Coldstream Guards* (Oxford University Press, 1951)

Ironside, Edmund, *The Ironside Diaries*, Roderick Macleod and Denis Kelly, editors (Constable, 1962)

Langer, William L. and Gleason, S. Everett, *The Challenge to Isolation* (Royal Institute of International Affairs, 1952)

Lash, Joseph, *Roosevelt and Churchill* (André Deutsch, 1976)

Lees-Milne, James, *Harold Nicolson – A Biography*, Volume 2 (Chatto & Windus, 1981)

Liddell Hart, B.H., *The Other Side of the Hill* (Cassell, 1948)

Lord, Walter, *The Miracle of Dunkirk* (Allen Lane, 1982)

Masefield, John, *The Twenty-Five Days* (Heinemann, 1972)

Nettle, S.A., *Dunkirk – Old Men Remember* (March Press, 1988)

Nicolson, Nigel, *The Life of Field Marshall Earl Alexander of Tunis* (Weidenfeld & Nicolson, 1973)

Nicolson, Nigel and Forbes, Patrick, *The Grenadier Guards in the War of 1939–1945* (Gale & P., 1949)

Pownall, Henry, *Chief of Staff – The Diaries of Lieutenant-General Sir Henry Pownall*, Brian Bond, editor (Leo Cooper, 1972)

Quilter, D.C., *No Dishonourable Name – The 2nd and 3rd Battalion Coldstream Guards* (Clowes, 1972)

*RAF Narrative, The Campaign in France and the Low Countries* (Air Historical Branch, Air Ministry, undated)

Richards, Denis, *Royal Air Force 1939–1945*, Volume I (HMSO, 1953)

Rhodes, Anthony, *Sword of Bone* (Buchan & Enright, 1986)

Shirer, William L., *The Collapse of The Third Republic* (Heinemann, 1970)

Shirer, William L., *The Rise and Fall of the Third Reich* (Secker & Warburg, 1960)

Smith, Peter, *Hold the Narrow Sea* (Moorland, 1984)

Spears, Edward, *Assignment to Catastrophe*, Volumes 1 and 2 (Heinemann, 1940)

Taylor, Telford, *The March of Conquest* (E. Hulton, 1959)

Turnbull, Patrick, *Dunkirk – Anatomy of Disaster* (Batsford, 1978)

Vince, Charles, *Storm on the Waters* (Hodder & Stoughton, 1946)

Watson, Mark Skinner, *United States Army in World War II – Chief of Staff: Prewar Plans and Preparations* (Department of the Army, 1950)

Westphal, Siegried, *The German Army in the West* (Cassell, 1951)

Williams, John, *The Ides of May* (Constable, 1968)

# Acknowledgments

Thanks are due to many people whose assistance was of great value in the writing of this book. They include the late Harold Robinson who, as general secretary of the Dunkirk Veterans Association, offered much practical and helpful advice. Also of great help were the staffs of the following: the Documents and Printed Books Divisions of the Imperial War Museum, the Colindale Newspaper Library, the British Library, the London Library, the Documents Section of the National Maritime Museum at Greenwich, the Public Record Office at Kew, the excellent Special Collection at the West Hill Public Library in Wandsworth, the Reading Room of the National Army Museum, the Military Reference section of the National Archives in Washington D.C, and the Franklin Delano Roosevelt Library at Hyde Park, New York. My thanks too to Eric Munday of the Air Historical Branch of the Ministry of Defence, Paul Melton of the Royal Navy Historical Branch, and K.W. Scott of English Heritage for showing me the remains of Operation Dynamo headquarters in the cliffs of Dover.

Particular thanks to the survivors of Dunkirk I was privileged to meet – including those I accompanied on the Dunkirk Veterans Association pilgrimage to Dunkirk in May 1988 – many of whom permitted me to probe their memories and who, in some cases, lent or showed me personal diaries, letters, photographs and other unpublished materials. They include in particular John Agate, Reverend Leslie Aitken, Stanley Allen, General John Carpenter, Sid Dodd, James Else, F.R. Farley, Harry Genders, Leslie Ginsburg, Tom Griffiths, John Gunn, Patrick Hennessy, Arthur Hopkins, Professor William Kershaw, Richard Maycock, Major Richard Merritt, Commander Stanley Nettle, Tom Noyce, Ernest Richards, Victor Slaughter, Frank Tabrar, Reverend Cyril Thompson, Albert White, Major Bernard Whiting, General Ashton Wade, and Bill Warwick.

I am much obliged to Lieutenant Colonel Michael Burkham, Royal Welch Fusiliers, who was good enough to read the manuscript of this book and offer wise and useful advice though all remaining errors are, of course, my own. My thanks as always most of all to my wife, Barbara, for all sorts of things.

NG

# Index

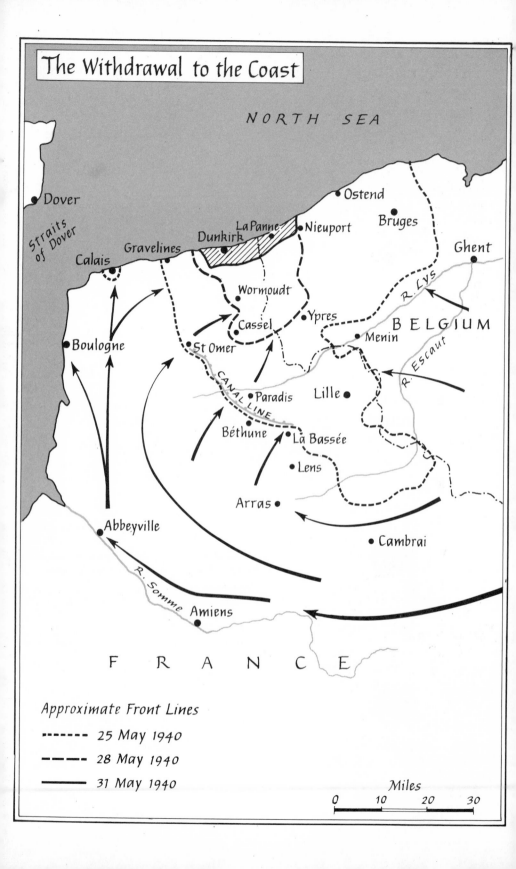

# The Withdrawal to the Coast

NORTH SEA

Dover

Ostend

Bruges

Ghent

Straits of Dover

Calais

Gravelines

Dunkirk

La Panne

Nieuport

R. Lys

BELGIUM

Boulogne

St Omer

Wormoudt

Cassel

Ypres

Menin

CANAL LINE

Paradis

Lille

R. Escaut

Béthune

La Bassée

Abbeyville

Lens

Arras

Cambrai

R. Somme

Amiens

FRANCE

Approximate Front Lines

------- 25 May 1940

— — — 28 May 1940

——— 31 May 1940

Miles

0    10    20    30